JACK M. WATSON
*Dean, College-Conservatory of Music
of the University of Cincinnati*
ADVISORY EDITOR TO DODD, MEAD & COMPANY

UNDERSTANDING AND
ENJOYING MUSIC

D0965015

UNDERSTANDING AND ENJOYING MUSIC

John D. White

Kent State University

DODD, MEAD & COMPANY

New York   Toronto   1968

ACKNOWLEDGMENTS

Boosey and Hawkes, Inc.: for excerpts from *Rite of Spring* and *Symphony of Psalms* by Igor Stravinsky, *String Quartet No. Six* by Bela Bartok, and *Appalachian Spring* by Aaron Copland.

Wilhelm Hansen: for excerpts from *Symphony No. Seven* by Jan Sibelius.

Howard Hanson and Carl Fischer Company: for excerpts from *Symphony No. Two "Romantic"* by Howard Hanson.

W. W. Norton and Company: for the excerpt from *Vivaldi* by Marc Pincherle, translated by Christopher Hatch.

Oxford University Press: for the excerpt from *Essays in Musical Analysis, Volume IV* by Donald Francis Tovey.

G. P. Putnam's Sons: for excerpts from *Kobbé's Complete Opera Book*, Edited and Revised by the Earl of Harewood.

G. Schirmer, Inc.: for excerpts from and the composer's description of the *Third Symphony* by Roy Harris.

B. Schott's Soehne, and Associated Music Publishers: for excerpts from *Mathis der Maler* by Paul Hindemith.

M. J. Steuer: for the excerpt from the *Autobiography* of Stravinsky.

EDITOR'S INTRODUCTION

In writing this book, Dr. White has aimed squarely at a single target, the development of musical understanding. In so doing, he has, of course, made certain assumptions. He has assumed that music itself has such intrinsic motivational power that sugar-coating and other forms of extrinsic motivation are unnecessary. He has assumed that college and university students who are not music majors have the intelligence, the seriousness of purpose, and the potentiality (for musical development) to study music literature at a conceptual and technical level. He has assumed that a positive relationship exists between musical understanding and the enjoyment of music. All three assumptions, in my judgment, are valid.

The overall organization of the book is well suited to serve the author's purpose. Knowledge of the elements of music is essential bedrock for any degree of insight into the literature of music. Dr. White conveys an impressive amount of information in Part I of this book, which he calls "Perspectives," with no loss of simplicity, clarity, or logic.

Beginning analytical treatment of specific compositions with the late baroque makes good sense to me; so does moving, chronologically, from this period through the periods of classicism and romanticism. From this material students gain ample information and experience for insight into the stylistic characteristics of a sample of compositions by major composers of the periods and into the evolution of eighteenth and nineteenth century music—the music they hear most frequently and with which they are most familiar. With this background, students have perspective for listening to and learning about music of the sixteenth and seventeenth and then of the twentieth century, which concludes the text.

Dr. White's handling of technical matters is a real achievement. He never oversimplifies, nor does he overwhelm the reader with undefined technical terms. Step by step, he carefully clarifies the meaning of concepts and techniques. Often, he begins with a very simple definition; later (sometimes in the same chapter, other times in another one), he elaborates and illustrates, frequently with analogy; still later, he may differentiate the concept or term from one with which it might be confused. A remarkable illustration of this pattern is his treatment of the concepts of variation and development.

The many distinctive features of this text all contribute to its overriding purpose, the development of musical understanding.

That Dr. White is a composer (with successful publications and performances by leading American symphony orchestras to his credit) is suggested in his perceptive treatment of elements of musical composition. That he is a conductor and professional cellist is demonstrated in the insight he gives into the "insides" of a symphony orchestra and other matters involving musical performance. That he is a theorist, who has specialized in teaching courses in form and analysis, can be seen in his precise definitions of terms, his detailed attention to form, and his careful treatment of style. That he has had a wealth of teaching experience can be seen on every page of the text.

JACK M. WATSON

CONTENTS

FOREWORD

Understanding and Enjoying Music grew out of the belief that the live sound of music itself should furnish the basis for introductory courses in music literature (or music appreciation). Granting this premise there are still many ways to teach the subject and this book is designed to be adaptable to a variety of teaching approaches. While the book does offer an organization for the course, it is quite possible, even desirable, for the teacher to depart from this plan according to his own inclinations. The five chapters of Part One ("Perspective") furnish the student with general background sufficient for him to begin a chronological approach to music. On the other hand, if the instructor favors a non-chronological approach, the basic concepts and terminology acquired from Part One make it possible to begin almost anywhere—with seventeenth century music or with the music of today, as the teacher may see fit.

In writing *Understanding and Enjoying Music* my aim has been to present the more accessible aspects of the structure of music, music history, performance practices, and musical esthetics in such a way as to furnish the student with a useful body of knowledge divested of unnecessary peripheral information. The emphasis is upon the music itself, for biographical material cannot, except in a few instances, shed much light upon a composer's work. But cultural history and the history of musical thought are also of importance and I hope that, where I have not been able to be comprehensive enough in these areas, I have at least piqued the student's imagination sufficiently for him to investigate further on his own.

Several of my colleagues at the University of Michigan and at Kent State University have furnished their counsel and assistance in the preparation of this volume. In particular I would like to mention Dr. Martin Nurmi, Graduate Dean at Kent, and his wife Ruth Nurmi for their interest and encouragement, and for Dr. Nurmi's reading and criticism of certain parts of the book. The advice of Dr. Albert Cohen of the University of Michigan was useful during the early stages of the book; and

Professors Robert and Margaret Palmieri of Kent also contributed their help.

In the final stages, Dr. Donald Erb of the Cleveland Institute of Music and Dr. Eugene Selhorst of the Eastman School of Music were most helpful; and, in his capacity as advisory editor, Dean Jack Watson of the College-Conservatory of Music, University of Cincinnati, furnished valuable counsel. Acknowledgment must also go to secretaries Helen Krikos and Carol Healy, who were most helpful. Finally, I wish to thank my wife Majorie for her constant encouragement and inspiration as well as for her assistance in reading proofs.

JOHN D. WHITE

PART ONE

PERSPECTIVE

CHRONOLOGICAL CHART OF
THE MAIN PERIODS IN MUSIC HISTORY

THE MIDDLE AGES   850 to 1450

Gregorian chant—beginning of vocal polyphony—church music —instrumental music

ARS NOVA SUBPERIOD   1300 to 1450

Secular currents in music—instrumental music—solo vocal music

THE RENAISSANCE   1450 to 1600

Beginnings of triadic harmony—highly developed vocal poly-phony—masses, madrigals, and motets—beginning of idiomatic instrumental music

THE BAROQUE PERIOD   1600 to 1750

Basso continuo—fugue—binary form—development of opera, oratorio, and cantata—highly developed instrumental styles in concerto grosso, trio sonata, and solo sonata—development of the violin family and the orchestra—keyboard music

PRECLASSICAL AND ROCOCO SUBPERIODS   1725 to 1750

Beginning development of classical forms—the classical orchestra

THE CLASSICAL PERIOD   1750 to 1820

Classical symphony and concerto forms— sonata, rondo, variation, and minuet forms—development of the string quartet—opera—piano music

THE ROMANTIC PERIOD   1820 to 1900

Expansion and breakdown of classical forms—programmatic music—nationalism—the art song—cyclical form—new piano styles—expansion of the orchestra and coloristic orchestration—new theories for opera—harmonic innovation

IMPRESSIONISTIC SUBPERIOD   1885 to 1910

Harmonic innovation—evocative instrumental writing—musical counterparts of Symbolist poetry

THE MODERN PERIOD   1900 to the present

Neoclassicism—primitivism—expressionism—breakdown of to-nality—twelve tone technique—polytonality—rhythmic innova-tion—freedom of form—new musical media

ONE

THE LISTENER'S ART

There are many ways to listen. Musical enjoyment and understanding are limited only by the response of the listener, by the extent of his own experience, knowledge, and imagination. Some listeners are charmed by the sound of the individual instruments in a symphony orchestra. Others thrill to the sheer brilliance and scope of the sound. Some are captured by the emotion and drama evoked by the music of an opera and still others become involved with the intellectual aspects of music. For many people there is great pleasure in physical reaction to music such as dancing, clapping, beating time, or other motions. There is no single correct way to listen, but the listener who most fully understands music is the one who listens most carefully, the one who experiences the physical, as well as the emotional, dramatic, and intellectual aspects of music.

Hearing recorded music as background to other activities is not careful listening. In fact, it tends to inhibit our perception of music. Only when we listen to a performance with our minds as well as our ears can we begin to understand it.

Every piece of music should be approached on its own terms, and in order to understand today's highly varied concert fare, a listener should have a knowledge of many different kinds of music. One cannot, for instance, listen to a Mozart concerto in the same manner as a Wagnerian opera; their meanings are quite different and they should be approached differently. Sometimes even the experienced listener may encounter a piece of music which is not readily understandable to him on first hearing. Such works frequently reveal themselves gradually so that each subsequent hearing becomes a revelation. A late quartet of Beethoven, for example, probably requires several hearings and perhaps some study of the score before it begins to be understood. Listeners who do not read music may be enlightened by conversations with people well acquainted with music, for musi-

3

cians, amateurs and professionals, as well as a vast group of intelligent listeners, find talking about music to be a most rewarding pastime.

Some understanding of the elements of music and a knowledge of its history and literature can be helpful in orienting one's mind to specific compositions, for all music is in some way related to the music of preceding periods. There is no music so new and original that it has nothing in common with the past. The fact that some of the great works of Beethoven, and in our century some of the works of Stravinsky or Schoenberg, have not been generally well received or understood on first hearing is an indication that the composer is a step or two ahead of his audience. This has been true of some of the greatest composers from the time of Beethoven, Mozart, and even earlier. But while exploring new forms and breaking new paths, these composers have always drawn upon a vast cultural and musical heritage, and some knowledge of this heritage is valuable in understanding the music of any period.

Ultimately, however, the best means to acquiring musical knowledge and perception is listening to the music itself, preferably in live performance. Let us imagine ourselves attending a symphony orchestra concert. We arrive at the concert hall a few minutes early and, as we take our seats, the members of the orchestra begin to take their places on the stage. The most numerous instruments are those of the string section. These include violins, violas, cellos, and string basses or bass viols (also called double basses). The strings are the foundation of the symphony orchestra and are prominently placed near the front of the stage. At the rear of the stage is the brass section, in this case, two trumpets and two French horns. Directly in front of the brass is the woodwind section, two each of flutes, oboes, clarinets, and bassoons.

At one side, near the rear of the stage, are three or four kettledrums (timpani) which require a great deal of preconcert attention from the timpanist who hovers over each of them in turn with his ear close to the head of the drum, carefully tuning each one by means of a pedal and turn screws placed around the top of the drum. Close to the timpanist but clearly separated from him are the percussion instruments, many of which do not have a definite pitch and therefore do not require tuning. These instruments of indeterminate or indefinite pitch include the snare drum, triangle, cymbals, gong, bass drum, and many others. We also see some of the percussion instruments which do have a clearly discernible pitch, such as the xylophone, bells, and celesta.

A completely assembled symphony orchestra a few minutes before performance emits a sound that defies description. This cacophony of tuning strings and other potentially musical sounds produces a most remarkable effect and for many concertgoers the warming-up process is an important and necessary prelude to the concert itself.

Now a man carrying a violin walks to the center of the stage, faces the orchestra, and raps on a music stand for attention. The random tuning and warming up subside and the newcomer, the concertmaster of the orchestra, asks the first oboist to play an A for the orchestra to tune by. Its clearly focused tone and relatively inflexible pitch make the oboe well suited for this traditional duty. After the orchestra has tuned, the concertmaster takes his seat just to the left of the conductor's podium and at the outside front of the violin section. He is the representative of the orchestra players and, presumably, the finest violinist in the orchestra. In a moment the conductor arrives, acknowledges the applause of the audience, takes his place on the podium, and the concert begins.

The first work on the program is Mendelssohn's *Hebrides Overture* and with the first sounds in the low strings we hear the tune which is the primary building block of the entire piece. This tune is really nothing more than a fragment of six tones which continues to be repeated in changing forms throughout the composition. Musicians refer to such a melodic fragment as a motive, and a very beautiful and evocative motive it is. A glance at the program notes reveals that the work is also called *Fingal's Cave Overture* and that this six-note motive was, in fact, conceived by the composer on the occasion of a visit to Fingal's Cave in the Hebrides Islands. The term overture began as the title of the initial movement of a suite or multimovement work in the seventeenth century. In the eighteenth century the term referred almost exclusively to the orchestral prelude of an opera. In the early part of the nineteenth century Ludwig van Beethoven (1770–1827) composed several overtures for plays which soon came to be performed separately as concert overtures. From this came the nineteenth century practice of composing single orchestral pieces, unassociated with larger works, and calling them overtures. Many of these, from their dramatic origin, were programmatic in content; that is, they told a story in music. Today concert overtures as well as overtures taken from opera are frequently used as opening works on symphony orchestra concerts.

The *Hebrides Overture,* composed in 1830, is one of the earliest examples of the concert overture and, in addition to being somewhat program-

Figure 1.

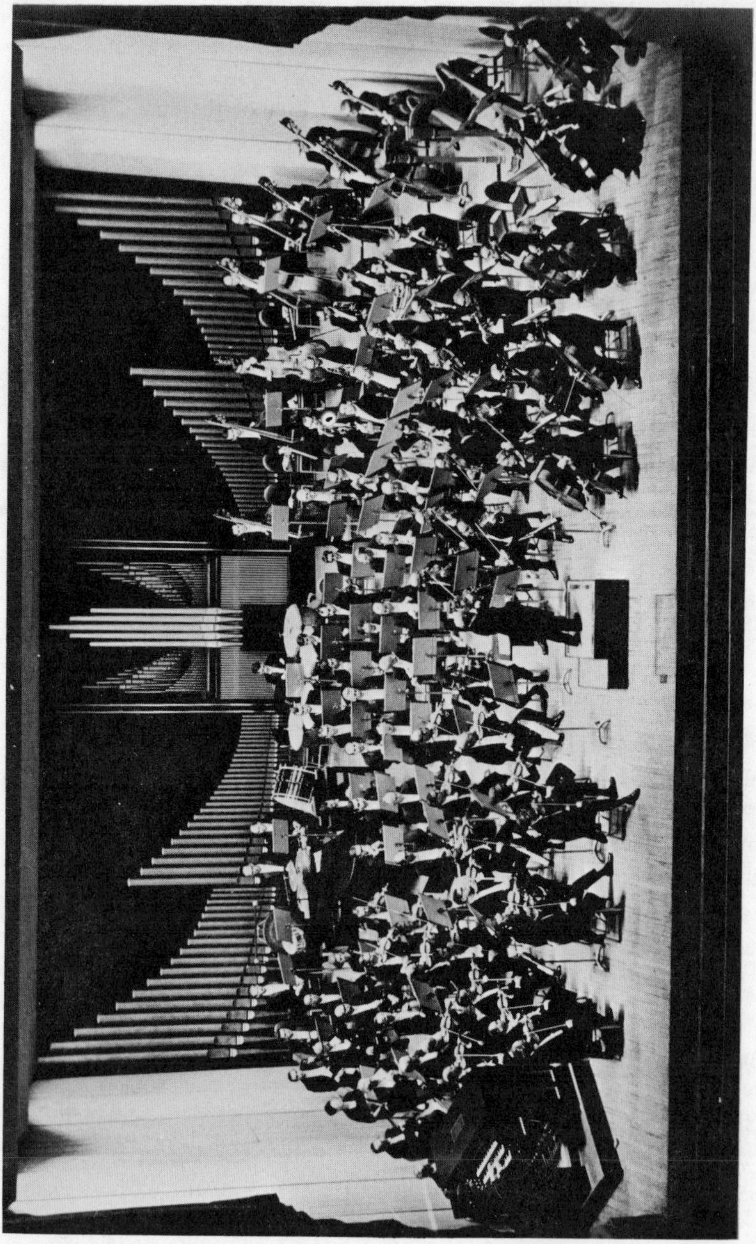

Courtesy The Philadelphia Orchestra

Performance photograph of the Philadelphia Orchestra, Eugene Ormandy conducting matic, demonstrates another aspect of romanticism, the interest in subjects in nature. The romantic period in music is generally dated 1820–1900 (see chart) but it is important to remember that there is never an abrupt switch from the practices of one period to those of another. Such changes come gradually. For example, Felix Mendelssohn (1809–1847), chronologically a romantic composer, has many characteristics of the preceding era which is called the classical period (1750–1820). One of these characteristics is apparent in the manner in which the six tones heard at the very beginning of the *Hebrides Overture* have been worked and developed so that the entire piece seems to be a fabric woven out of this motive. To do this the composer uses skills called developmental techniques which will be discussed later.

The six-note motive is not the only thematic material that we hear in the overture. Another theme, singing and lyrical in quality, is played by the cellos shortly after the beginning and again near the end of the piece by the clarinets. This theme plays an important part in the overall form of the overture. The general shape or form of this piece is called sonata form and this lyrical theme is the second subject of the form.

The *Hebrides Overture* was written during the romantic period and as we listen to it we may begin to understand some of the aspects of romanticism in music. First among these is the orchestration. Orchestration is the technique of combining the many instruments of the orchestra— what instruments are used at what time, what they play, and how loudly they play it. We shall see later that orchestration of the romantic period is quite different from that of the classical period. The manner in which the strings rustle through the texture, the way in which the French horns are used, the fact that the clarinets are used so expressively, and many other characteristic devices of romantic orchestration are apparent in the overture.

The symmetry and beauty of form characteristic of the classical period are still present in Mendelssohn's music but in addition there is a more personal element in this music—in this case, the artist conveying *his* idea of a subject in nature. As the overture draws softly to a close one musicologist's description of the piece comes to mind.

From the moment when Mendelssohn, while actually standing in Fingal's Cave, jotted down, in crotchets and quavers,[1] the first

---

[1] "Crotchets and quavers" are British terms for notational symbols, specifically, quarter notes and eighth notes.

bar, to the moment when he wrote the last *pizzicato* notes below
the mysteriously sustained trumpets and the flute with its last
fleeting allusion to the second subject, the composer was surely
occupied chiefly with the unconscious digesting of his impressions of Hebridean scenery, the roar of the waves rolling into the
cavern, the cries of the seabirds, and perhaps more than anything
else, the radiant and telescopic clearness of the air when the mist
is completely dissolved or not yet formed.[2]

As the last sound of the overture dies away there is a moment of hush
before the audience breaks the spell with applause. The conductor turns
and bows, signals the orchestra to stand in acknowledgment, shakes the
hand of the concertmaster, and leaves the stage.

The next work on the program is Beethoven's Fifth Symphony, a
composition in four movements. Movement is the term used to describe the
several separate sections of an extended instrumental composition, each
movement being a self-contained but not necessarily wholly independent
section. The movements of a large work are usually separated by a short
pause of unspecified length. It is conventional for the audience to refrain
from applauding between movements, though this rule is occasionally
broken at the end of the first movement of a concerto for solo instrument
and orchestra when the audience may choose to applaud a particularly
brilliant performance by the soloist.

The Fifth Symphony calls for several instruments not used in the
Mendelssohn overture and as soon as the applause dies out the players of
the additional instruments appear. Among these are the lowest and the
highest pitched instruments of the orchestra—the contrabassoon, looming
like an artillery piece next to the two ordinary-sized bassoons, and the
piccolo, tiny relative of the flute. Also, three trombonists join the brass
section at the back of the orchestra. There are a few more moments of
tuning and then the conductor reappears, acknowledges the applause of
the audience, and stands for a moment poised in preparation for the attack.
The baton falls and the famous four-note motive begins its repetitions and
transformations that will not end until the last measures of the final movement.

Theorists and musicologists talk about music in terms of harmony and
counterpoint but technical terminology will always fall short of the mark.
It cannot, by itself, begin to describe the beauty, coherence, and expression

[2] Donald Francis Tovey, *Essays in Musical Analysis,* Vol. IV, New York, Oxford
University Press, 1954, pp. 91–92.

with which a succession of sounds has been endowed by a great artist, as in this piece of music. This can be done only by relating technical matters to the real experience of music, and it is to this end that men have for centuries thought and written about music, finding a constant source of delight and wonder in its many-faceted qualities.

The listener is captured immediately by the powerful dramatic appeal of this symphony. Whatever this appeal is—a struggle against malign providence, the torment and release from moral and mental torture, or a stern grapple with thoughts of suicide—the symphony is a musical utterance that transcends the conventional forms discernible in it. It is also admirable on a purely formal level because of the amazing compactness and unity within its massive structure. The four-note motive, which has been described as "Fate knocking at the door," is used throughout in various forms but in the first movement is developed in a manner similar to the treatment of the six-note motive of the *Hebrides Overture*. As we shall see, this technique of thematic development, inherited from Joseph Haydn (1732–1809), is a hallmark of most of Beethoven's music.

The first movement comes to a crashing close and the orchestra relaxes momentarily. The length of the pause between movements is at the discretion of the conductor and is varied on the basis of the character and duration of the movements and the length of the total work. In this case it is a relatively long pause, perhaps close to thirty seconds. Since the first movement was quite long and very intense, this gives the listener a moment to prepare for the slow movement which follows.

The second movement begins with a melody played by the violas and cellos which sounds deceptively simple on first hearing. As the movement progresses, however, we become aware of the careful construction of this melody for, in addition to its intrinsic beauty, it has properties of malleability which permit it to be varied without sacrificing its identity or its expressive qualities. This is quite different from the motivic development observed in the first movement. A short motive, because of its incompleteness, requires thematic development while a melody of this length usually cannot be developed as a whole but must be varied in a different way. There are four statements of the theme in this movement and, although certain short motives from the theme (and a form of the four-note motive from the first movement) are developed in the sections between these statements, the statements themselves preserve the theme in its original length and general contour. Each statement of the theme sounds different because of the use of techniques of variation. (Variation technique will be discussed further in Chapter Four.) The second statement or variation, still played by the violas and cellos, smooths out the original rhythm of the theme by adding a few notes and by making all of them equal in length. In the third statement the cellos and violas play about twice as many notes to ornament or embellish the theme. Because these notes are played twice as fast, the length of the theme is not increased. This variation is repeated by the violins and then tossed back to the cellos. The final complete statement comes near the end of the movement after the intensity has been built up by more development. It is a big statement with all the violins and most of the woodwinds playing the theme, and its effect is heightened by the fact that it is now back in its original form, though played by a larger number of instruments. Returning at the end to something that was heard near the beginning is one of the basic principles of musical form. It satisfies the ear and gives a feeling of circular perfection, a kind of consummation of form that can also be found in the other arts.

The third movement is a scherzo and we shall learn later how this form evolved from the minuet, the traditional third movement of the classical symphony. As we listen to the somber yet intense opening in the cellos, we have the feeling that great power is being held in reserve and when we arrive at the trio or middle section of the movement our expectations are fulfilled. The cellos and basses suddenly burst forth with a volley of running notes bubbling with a mixture of strength and gaiety that is irresistible. This material passes through the rest of the string section like contagious laughter and returns to the somber material of the first section. Then, with a gradual accumulation of volume, a transition leads directly into the triumphal opening of the finale without the conventional pause between movements. The piccolo, contrabassoon, and trombones now serve their purpose, for, by saving them until the final movement, Beethoven was able to unleash the maximum volume at the crucial moment as the final movement swings into full force. Vital and intense as the preceding movements were, this carries us still further with its rhythmic energy and forceful sonority. The driving pulse of the music seems bent on bringing the conflicting elements of the composition to their final resolution. Suddenly, when it seems that the intensity can build no more, the scene shifts in a startling way and all that we hear is the sound of the violins repeating the same detached tone, gradually softening, and then presenting the four-note motive as it appeared in the third movement. This release of tension is just long enough to prepare for the return of the forceful material found at the beginning of the fourth movement and from here to the end we are carried along by the surging and accelerating pulse of the rhythm. The coda or closing section hurls the final chord at us again and again as the symphony concludes triumphantly.

During the ensuing intermission we learn from our program notes that the next and concluding composition on the program is actually the combined work of two composers separated by a generation. The work, entitled *Pictures at an Exhibition,* was originally a set of piano pieces by the Russian composer, Modeste Moussorgsky (1839–1881). The French impressionist composer, Maurice Ravel (1875–1937), later orchestrated it and it is best known in this version.

The history of this composition began in the year 1874 when an exhibition of the work of the Russian painter and architect, Victor Hartmann, was held in Moscow. The artist, an intimate friend of Moussorgsky, had died the year before. He had been a prominent member of a group of young Russian artists who were striving for the establishment of a purely Russian art, free of all foreign influence. *Pictures at an Exhibition* is Moussorgsky's description of certain pictures from his friend's exhibition and, as such, is a distinguished example of nineteenth century program music.

After intermission we find that two harps have been placed to our extreme right in front of the basses and cellos and, as the players arrive, we see several more instruments that were not present during the first half. The brass section has been enlarged to include the standard complement of four French horns and the trumpets have been increased to three. In addition, a large upright bass tuba takes its place next to the three trombones.

In the woodwind section the piccolo and two flutes and the bassoons and contrabassoon are still present, but the oboes are increased to three. Also, two additional instruments are next to the clarinets. One is an alto saxophone; the other is an instrument made partly of wood, shaped like a saxophone, called the bass clarinet.

The percussion section comes to life as three players take their places behind the fascinating array of noisemakers. Only the strings remain the same with the usual basses, cellos, violas, and two sections of violins. This large symphony orchestra, considerably expanded from that of the first half of the program, represents the general size and type of orchestra used by symphonic composers of the late nineteenth and early twentieth centuries. Later we shall discuss some of the reasons for their use of so large an orchestra.

Now the concertmaster appears and the sound of warming up subsides. He requests the A from the oboe, tunes his instrument, and takes his seat. In a few moments the conductor appears and we are soon transported into the colorful, exotic, and, at times, shadowed world of *Pictures at an Exhibition.*

Ravel's orchestration is, for the most part, a faithful reproduction of the piano version, more vividly colored, and more clearly delineated. The piano writing in the original may not be particularly well suited to the instrument yet the imaginative listener may prefer the piano version because its understatement and spareness of texture encourage free interpretation. But for many listeners Moussorgsky's profound imagination and powers of expression are best revealed through the medium of the symphony orchestra. It required a master orchestrator to bring to life the hints and sketchy shapes hidden in the piano version and reveal it as the composer may have conceived it in his own imagination. As we listen we become aware that Ravel, who undertook the task in 1929, fully succeeded, for it is not only the work of a skilled craftsman but the interpretation of a great artist.

The "Promenade," first movement of the composition, depicts the composer amid a crowd of visitors, looking around for the most attractive exhibits. The theme, in the style of a Russian folk tune, begins with one trumpet but soon enlists the entire brass section in full and stately sonority. The rest of the instruments soon follow and the short "Promenade" ends with all of the instruments playing. The *tutti* (meaning *all* or nearly all of the instruments) ending is followed by Moussorgsky's interpretation of the first picture, "Gnomus." Here we see the virtuoso orchestra really come to life as the percussionists unearth, among other things, such unique instruments as the whip (a wooden apparatus producing a sound like the crack of a whip) and the rattle. The harp and xylophone are also used and with the swiftly shifting colors we begin to see why Ravel is considered one of the great masters of orchestration. The depiction of a grotesquely limping dwarf is followed by "The Old Castle" with the two movements separated by a variation on the "Promenade."

The saxophone is used as a solo instrument in "The Old Castle" and, somehow, in the context of Ravel's orchestration, its typical jazz character disappears. In this environment it sounds more like an ancient reed instrument than an exponent of popular music. Its lyrical quality prevails throughout as the movement proceeds serenely to its end. Before "Tuileries" begins we hear another variation on the "Promenade."

"Tuileries," with its capriciously chattering woodwinds depicting children playing in the famous Paris gardens, is over before we know it and we proceed directly to "Bydlo," picturing a lumbering Polish ox wagon with huge wheels. To evoke an image of the motion of such a vehicle Moussorgsky used thick chords in the bass register which move steadily along to the very end of the piece. The opening melody above this accompaniment figure is given, in Ravel's orchestration, to a most unlikely solo instrument, the bass tuba. We are amazed to discover that the tuba can, in fact, be quite expressive and the combination of instruments is exactly the right one for this movement. After the tuba solo the middle section continues the steady rhythm, but uses the entire orchestra in a tremendous crescendo or gradual increase in volume. At the height of the crescendo the entire orchestra plays the original tuba melody followed by a gradual softening or diminuendo. The tuba once more plays the melody and the movement ends softly.

The next movement, preceded by one more "Promenade," is entitled "Ballet of the Chickens in Their Shells." It is a fast, light movement staying mostly in the high register of the orchestra.

The sixth movement, "Samuel Goldenburg and Schmuyle," opens with a unison passage in the strings and woodwinds. That is, all of the instruments play the same melody simultaneously, each in its own register. This depicts Goldenburg while the chattering trumpets that follow represent Schmuyle. The return of the unison passage at the end of the movement rounds out the form and gives the impression of dialogue between the two figures in the picture.

In the succeeding three movements—"Limoges: The Market Place," "Catacombs" (paired with "Cum Mortuis in Lingua Morta"), and "The Hut of Baba-Yaga"—the percussion and harps are used a great deal to add new color to the texture. These instruments are used very successfully in combination with the other sections of the orchestra. In fact, we hear them more as an addition of new color to other instruments than for their own separate timbres.

"The Hut of Baba-Yaga" is one of the longest movements of the composition and, to sustain continuity, there is no pause before the final movement, "The Great Gate of Kiev." This movement begins majestically with full brass chords and, as other instruments are added, sustains this mood to the end. For the total work to end convincingly, however, it was necessary to have some release from the intensity of sound already built up. Shortly after the beginning of the final movement, a passage of soft chords in the low woodwinds serves this purpose, creating a feeling of momentary calm. This is followed by a brilliant orchestral flourish and then the soft chords once more return, this time (by the addition of instruments) building a crescendo that ultimately utilizes the maximum resources of Ravel's orchestra. The brilliant ending is impressive from the standpoint of sight as well as sound, for Ravel calls for bells, gongs, and other noisemakers in addition to the two harps to augment the color and volume of the final orchestral sonorities.

As the audience applauds, the conductor requests the orchestra to stand, shakes hands with the concertmaster and a few other key players, takes his curtain calls, and the concert is over.

Although we have learned much from this concert, there were many points which were only touched upon or mentioned in an oversimplified manner. Most of these things can be discussed in detail only after we have acquired a working vocabulary of musical terminology and a greater knowledge of both the theoretical and practical aspects of music.

Let us touch, for a moment, on the basic elements of music which will be discussed in greater detail in succeeding chapters. The basic elements of music are (1) rhythm, (2) melody, (3) harmony, and (4) tone color. These are the materials with which the composer works, but all of the elements are not necessarily present in every kind of music. For example, a piece of music which uses an unaccompanied solo voice lacks the element of harmony. Of the four, rhythm is the only one that has a life of its own, and none of the elements can exist without it. It is possible for a rhythmic pattern to be clearly defined on a drum which has no definite pitch but the element of melody enters only when definite pitches are assigned to a rhythmic pattern. Harmony is utilized when two or more different pitches are sounded simultaneously and the element of tone color or timbre enters only when parts are assigned to specific instruments or voices. A fifth element, somewhat less fundamental than the others, is dynamics or loudness. It is of great expressive value in combination with the four basic elements.

These materials have been used in many different ways during various periods of music history. The earliest music probably existed purely as rhythm produced by primitive percussion instruments such as pieces of wood or stone. Vocal music of some kind was perhaps almost as early, probably sung by a single voice with no thought of another voice harmonizing with it. Music consisting of a single voice line is called monody. Most folk songs fall into this category.

Monodic, or monophonic, music, in spite of its apparent simplicity, can be endowed with great beauty, as in Gregorian chant and other forms of plainsong and chant. Chants of various kinds have continued to be used in churches and synagogues for thousands of years and are of the most profound musical value.

The element of harmony was used in primitive cultures but did not become a part of our Western heritage until about a thousand years ago. Since then it has been a part of every composer's art and is an indispensable element of today's concert repertoire (with some exceptions among the works of certain contemporary composers).

Tone color is heard whenever a tone is produced, but its conscious use as an expressive element is relatively new. As recently as the sixteenth century composers did not usually specify the instrument or instruments that were to play the various parts of the music. Gradually composers began to select and specify instruments to play certain things because of their timbres. Today orchestration is one of the most important features of a composer's technique. Dynamic markings in music, indicating relative degrees of loudness, are also part of the art of orchestration and were first used in the late sixteenth century.

Music is one of the temporal arts. That is, its performance takes place within a given period of time. It is important to remember that the composer has weighed and proportioned his materials within a framework of specific duration. One should listen to a piece of music as a whole, for the full emotional and intellectual meaning of a composition is realized only by hearing it in its entirety, and its form or shape is apparent only in this way. We may enjoy various parts of the work more than others but the full effect of something that takes place near the end is dependent upon everything that happened earlier. A clear example of this is found in the spacious proportions of Beethoven's Fifth Symphony. For almost half a minute at the end of the final movement (the last 29 bars) nothing is heard but a single sonority, the same chord repeated over and over again by the entire orchestra. If one were to hear only the fourth movement of the symphony this final section would seem excessive, but in terms of the work as a whole the ending is perfectly proportioned and anything less would be insufficient.

Music is a performing art. It requires a "middle man" to bring it to its final realization in performance. A fine performer may illuminate, amplify, or even alter the composer's concept by the way in which he interprets the work, while a thoughtless or technically incompetent performer may completely lose the point. One of the great attractions of live concerts is the unpredictability of a performance. A fine artist may outdo himself on a certain evening and convey an inspiration of meaning that the work did not formerly possess. Occasions of this sort may be rare, but are well worth waiting for.

This aspect of action and unpredictability is one of the great pleasures in attending concerts. A recording is unable to capture the excitement and drama of a live performance. In some instances recorded performances are so perfect as to be a bit too immaculate and lacking in the stuff of human emotion. Recordings are a fine means of becoming acquainted with a great deal of music that we might otherwise never hear, but if we are particularly fond of a certain piece of music we will want to hear it performed in different ways and not always in the stereotype of the recorded performance that we happen to own. To see and hear a symphony orchestra in concert, inspired by a great piece of music and conveying its meaning and emotion to the audience, is an experience that cannot be recreated by mechanical means.

LISTENING SUGGESTIONS

Hebrides Overture	Felix Mendelssohn
Symphony No. 5	Ludwig van Beethoven
Pictures at an Exhibition	Moussorgsky-Ravel

Gregorian Chant: The Proper and the Ordinary of the Mass for Easter Sunday.

SUGGESTED ASSIGNMENTS

1. List the areas of knowledge that are of value to the listener in understanding music.
2. Outline a plan for understanding a piece of music that is new to you. When attending concerts try to put the plan to work.
3. Appraise your present knowledge and ability as a music listener determining the areas in which you will be able to improve.
4. Listen to the pieces listed above and attempt in your mind to separate the four elements of music, noting how each is used in combination with the others.

TWO

THREE ELEMENTS OF MUSIC:
RHYTHM, MELODY, AND HARMONY

RHYTHM

The organization of a group of musical sounds according to the time interval between them, according to accents, and according to their duration is called rhythm. It is at once the most important and the most complex element in music. Rhythm is commonly associated with meter, which is the measurement of the flow of music by the use of regularly recurring accents. In a waltz we feel three basic impulses or beats, of which the first is the heaviest: *one,* two, three—*one,* two, three. Each of these groups of three is a measure and is indicated visibly in musical notation by the use of vertical lines called bar lines.

Figure 2.

When there are three basic beats within a measure as in Figure 2, the meter is described as a triple meter. When there are two or four as in a march, it is called duple meter.

Figure 3.

The pulse of the measure is often felt even when it happens that there is no sound on some of the beats. Frequently the actual rhythm of the music does not correspond to the rhythm of the beat, as shown by the melody in Figure 4.

17

Figure 4.

The vertical lines below the melody in Figure 4 show when the sound is initiated in each tone of the melody in relation to the rhythm of the beat indicated by the numerals. It would be very monotonous if a piece of music did nothing but follow the rhythm of the beat. Nevertheless, the steady presence of the pulse of the beat serves an important purpose, for it gives the composer a framework upon which to build the rhythm of the music, as well as aiding the performer, who can use it as a guide in playing the more complex rhythms. The speed or frequency of the beat of a piece of music is called its tempo. The tempo is indicated at the beginning of the piece and anywhere else in the course of the music where it is to be changed. These tempo indications are traditionally written in the Italian language although some composers have preferred to use their native tongue for tempo markings.

Sometimes an accent occurs in the rhythm of a melodic line which seems to conflict or be at odds with the rhythm of the beat or with the rhythm of another melodic line. This is a cross rhythm and, when it occurs between two or more instruments or voices, results in an interesting counterpoint of one voice against another (as in Figure 5). Counterpoint can be defined as the combining of two or more independent parts or voice lines to create a musical effect. The melodic or pitch element is of great importance, for counterpoint does not usually exist without melodic character in the voice lines.

In writing counterpoint the composer must consider the interrelationships of the pitches and rhythms of the voice lines. Since there is more than one pitch sounding at a given point, harmony is an indispensable element of counterpoint. It is, of course, possible in certain kinds of music to have several melodic lines (voice parts) sounding the same rhythm at the same time but on different pitches. This results in a series of vertical chords in which the voices have very little rhythmic independence. Music of this sort is said to be written in a homophonic texture. Probably the most familiar type of homophony is that seen in harmonizations of hymn tunes or chorales in which all of the voices sound the same words and rhythms simultaneously in a four-part texture of soprano, alto, tenor, and bass. The opposite of homophonic is polyphonic, referring to a texture in which the several voices have considerable rhythmic independence. Polyphonic is a close synonym of contrapuntal.

Figure 5 is an example of cross rhythm (omitting the pitch notation) taken from *The Art of Fugue* by J. S. Bach (*Contrapunctus 15,* measures 5–7).

Figure 5.

On another level, and in longer time intervals, rhythm exists as form in music, that is, as organization within a specific duration. The motive, which is the smallest formal unit in music, is frequently nothing more than a fragment, a group of tones possessing a great deal of rhythmic or melodic character. It may consist of as few as three or as many as five or six tones organized in such a way as to be clearly discernible in its recurrences throughout a piece of music. An entire movement might be built almost completely out of a single three-note motive as, for example, in the first movement of the third *Brandenburg Concerto* by J. S. Bach (Figure 6). This very characteristic Bach motive consists of three equally spaced tones, of which the third is accented. Although the movement contains other material, this motive is the primary building block and is clearly discernible throughout.

Figure 6.

In the motive from Beethoven's Fifth Symphony (Figure 7), the fourth tone is distinguished by being longer and on a lower pitch than the other three. In both the Bach and Beethoven examples the motive can be clearly identified throughout the piece.

Figure 7.

Motives may be used to build another small formal unit called the phrase. The phrase is a short musical thought, more complete than a motive, and it ends in a cadence. A cadence is a stopping place in music corresponding to the end of a sentence in speech. The word "cadence" comes from the Latin word, *cadere,* to fall, and has slightly different meanings in the various periods of music history. Phrases are used to construct larger units and forms in music although some kinds of music are almost continuous in texture, with few cadences, with the result that the phrase feeling may be very obscure—even nonexistent. Fugal writing is of the latter type, consisting of a continuous contrapuntal texture of several voices or instruments.

Rhythm—a primary aspect of form in music—cannot be separated from the other elements. Melody, for example, cannot exist as an abstract arrangement of pitches without rhythmic organization. The pitches by themselves are meaningless as music until they are placed within a metrical framework or given more or less specific durations.

MELODY

The "tune" or melody often seems to be the most important part of the music. It seems somehow to emerge as the surface of the music, the most apparent and perhaps the most easily recalled portion of the musical texture. Frequently when we leave the concert hall there are several melodies running through our heads which we are tempted to hum or whistle. A melody that can be easily recalled often exists as a complete entity—separate from the musical texture of which it is a part. Such a melody has an existence of its own. It may even have its own meaning quite separate from the total composition, and for this reason it is sometimes remembered and enjoyed more than the complete piece of music from which it is taken.

A great many composers are gifted in writing this kind of tune, but it is not the only kind of melody; and for this reason it is necessary that we broaden our concept of melody to include thematic elements which contribute to the organic structure and unity of a composition. Organic unity is a term used to describe a structure in which all parts are essential to the whole and in which none of the parts can exist separately. There are certain kinds of melody, such as motives or fragments, which are important for their potential in a musical composition—important to the structure as a whole. These melodies are frequently very unsatisfying by themselves but are important for what they become or what they do later on in a composition. Often they are nothing more than short, terse motives (as in Beethoven's Fifth) while the other "complete" type of melody is usually in a more singing style, longer, and with a satisfying overall shape or contour.

This complete, singable type of melody does not usually lend itself well to development. Consequently, pieces by some very gifted melodists are often short, repetitive, or lacking in unity. Examples of this may be found in the music of (among many others) the nineteenth century Russian composer, Alexander Borodin, who had a great flair for writing charming and expressive melodies. So appealing are some of his melodies that today they are quite famous in various arrangements other than the original compositions and have even been used as the basis for a Broadway musical. Although the compositions from which these tunes were taken are still performed today, they are not nearly as well known as the melodies themselves. Since Borodin's melodies can be successfully removed from their context, it follows that structural unity was not an important aspect of his art. In listening to Borodin's music—for example, the "Nocturne" from *String Quartet No. 2*—it will be apparent that the esthetic effect is not dependent upon the total movement but primarily upon the evocative qualities of a single appealing melody. The melody would be almost as meaningful if it were heard by itself rather than within the movement.

A portion of a Beethoven symphony performed out of context could not possibly approach the meaning and significance of the total work. Beethoven's melodic material is frequently in the form of short terse motives, motives which are used as building blocks for the large composition, but which are not particularly beautiful in themselves. The primary motives of the first movements of both the First and Second Symphonies are good examples of this (see Figure 8). These motives are important for what they contribute to the overall effect rather than for their intrinsic beauty. An

Figure 8.

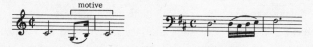

examination of these pieces will reveal that these motives are extremely important elements of the movements. It is because of the use of a single motive in various guises throughout a complete movement that we seldom find a Beethoven melody that retains its meaning and beauty independently of the total work. The melodies or motives are not intended to stand by themselves, but to serve the movement as a whole. This is one of the reasons why a Beethoven movement is likely to be much more significant and meaningful than, for example, the Borodin movement mentioned earlier. There are, of course, lengthy melodic passages in Beethoven's music, such as the opening melody of the slow movement of the Fifth Symphony (Figure 9). But even here the motivic construction is apparent in the use of the dotted rhythm indicated by the bracket. Beethoven's sketchbooks re-

Figure 9.

veal the painstaking care with which the composer constructed this melody to serve the movement as a whole rather than as a moment of melodic grace.

It should be remembered that organic unity in art is not an end in itself but a means to an end. A mathematical equation is perhaps the highest form of organic unity, yet it does not have esthetic value except perhaps in the mind of the mathematician. It remains for the composer to infuse a work of art with something that speaks from within its highly wrought framework. This "thing" is the spark of musical genius, evoking in the listener complex feelings that are inadequately described as the esthetic experience.

Melody can generally be defined as an organized succession of musical tones. Melodies differ greatly in their character and emotional effect, the primary factors determining this effect being (1) mode, (2) rhythm, and (3) general shape or contour. Mode can be loosely defined as the raw material of pitches which the composer uses for a specific melody. For our purposes it is convenient to think of modes as scales. The familiar diatonic scale (Figure 10) found in many traditional melodies is only one of many various modes and scales usable as the basis for a melody.

To discuss scales it is necessary that we understand the concept of the half step in terms of today's tuning system. Any two adjacent keys on the piano are a half step apart. The octave (distance on the piano from one letter name to the nearest note of the same letter name, up or down) in tempered tuning is divided into twelve equal half steps.[1] (The half step is also called the minor second.) Let us also establish the definition of an interval as being the distance between two tones, each interval being a

[1] Tempered tuning or "equal temperament" is the type of keyboard tuning in universal use since the eighteenth century. In tempered tuning the octave is divided into twelve equal half steps.

combination of a certain number of half steps spanned by the two tones. A whole step (also called major second) spans two half steps. Figure 10 shows the arrangement of half steps and whole steps in the diatonic scale. Other intervals can be extracted from this scale, such as the major third (1 to 3), minor third (3 to 5), perfect fifth (1 to 5), and so on. Interval

Figure 10.

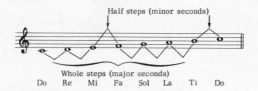

Half steps (minor seconds)

Whole steps (major seconds)
Do   Re   Mi   Fa   Sol   La   Ti   Do

names (without the adjectives perfect, minor, major, etc.) can be determined in musical notation by counting the lines and spaces included by the two notes (see Figure 11). Each interval may be varied by the use

Figure 11.

second   third   sixth

of sharps, flats, or naturals—symbols which alter the note one half step up or down. *Accidental* is the collective term for any sharp, flat, or natural sign. Major, minor, perfect, and diminished intervals can all be found in the diatonic scale and any of them may be altered by the use of accidentals. For example, E to G, a minor third, may be changed to a major third by sharping the G or flatting the E. Thus each interval has at least two forms, depending upon the accidental used.

The position of the two kinds of seconds or steps in relation to each other determines the character of the diatonic scale. A half step is found between the third and fourth scale degrees (E to F) and between the seventh and eighth scale degrees (B to C). All of the other intervals between adjacent tones in the diatonic scale are whole steps. (The term stepwise is used to describe passages in which the melodic motion is in seconds. Intervals larger than a second are called leaps or skips.)

A scale quite common in folk music is the pentatonic scale, which uses five tones of the diatonic scale to set up a new pattern of intervals. In terms of the diatonic scale (Figure 10) the pattern of the pentatonic scale would

be D, E, G, A, B. Note that the scale contains the interval of a third between E and G. The particular character and quality of this scale, as in any
scale, comes from its arrangement of intervals. The folk tune in Figure 12
is built out of the pentatonic scale. Note that the tone G is the most frequently used tone and the other tones seem to gravitate toward it. It is also
the resting point of the phrase in that it ends on G. Every scale or mode

Figure 12.

American Folk Tune

has one tone that functions as a focal point for a melody written in the
mode. This is called the tonal center and is very important in musical
composition.

In Gregorian chant the final (last tone in a Gregorian chant melody)
may be loosely referred to as the tonal center. The finals of the various
church modes can be seen by referring to the diatonic scale in Figure 10.
Each of the modes spans an octave (C to C, D up to the next D, and so
on). The Dorian mode uses D as its final, the Phrygian uses E, the Lydian,
F, and the Mixolydian, G. A chant written in a specific mode usually begins
and ends on the final of that mode. The character and effect of the different
modes depend upon the changed position of the half steps among the
various modes. The Phrygian mode, for example, has a half step between
its first and second degrees and between its fifth and sixth degrees, a
pattern that is unique to the Phrygian mode. Each mode has its own unique
pattern which gives it a particular quality distinct from the other modes.
The famous Gregorian chant given below is in the Mixolydian mode.

Figure 13.

Hymn, *Veni Creator Spiritus*

1. Ve - ni Cre - a - tor__ Spi - ri - tus,   Men - tes tu - o - rum_ vi - si - ta: Im - ple__

su - per - na__ gra - ti - a Quae__ tu cre - a - sti____ pec - to - ra.   A - men__

The system of modes used for Gregorian chant was used as the basis of most musical composition in Western civilization from about A.D. 500 to A.D. 1600. The Aeolian mode (using A as its final) and the Ionian (using C as its final) complete the list of modes in common use during this period. The Ionian mode, since it begins on C, sounds exactly like the diatonic scale and may be considered its ancestor. Musicians often speak of this scale as the major scale or major mode. The Aeolian mode shown in Figure 14 is the ancestor of our modern minor scale or minor mode which came into common use around 1600. There are several forms of the minor scale created by raising the sixth and seventh scale degrees by means of accidentals.

Figure 14.

Further study along these lines would require a discussion of music theory beyond the scope of this book. Suffice it to say that there are a number of other scales used today and by composers of past generations —the whole-tone scale, gypsy scales, Oriental scales, scales of primitive cultures, and so on. Many scales use intervals which cannot be played on modern keyboard instruments. Today's composers draw heavily upon these vast resources of scales and modes.

Rhythm is a primary organizing factor in the construction of melodies, for no succession of tones can exist without some kind of rhythmic pattern. Certain tones of a melody can be lengthened or accented for emphasis while others can be rhythmically deemphasized. Frequently, a rhythmic motive may persist throughout a melody in varying pitch patterns. By the use of certain rhythms at certain places, a feeling of motion or thrust, of increased progress in time, can be created in the musical phrase. Relating the rhythmic element to the contour or general shape of the melody is one of the most important aspects of the composer's craft.

The contour of the melody or phrase is determined by the selection of the pitches. A melody moving predominantly in small intervals such as seconds or thirds would have a smoother contour than one employing many leaps. Few melodies are completely stepwise, however, because of the extreme blandness of this kind of motion. A few leaps create greater interest and perhaps emphasize important high or low points in the phrase.

A melodic phrase usually has at least one clearly discernible high point with a feeling of intensity built up to this point and of relaxation following it. Often there is a comparable low point. These focal points are usually delineated or emphasized in some way by the rhythmic element.

The instrument or voice performing the melody is another factor in determining its contour. If the melody is to be sung rather than played by an instrument, the range of the melody will have to be determined by the range of the specific voice. Most singers have, at best, a working range of two octaves, and the center of this range is usually more usable than either extreme. Certain kinds of melodies or melodic devices will work better on one instrument or voice than on another. Stepwise motion with a few moderate skips is preferable for the human voice, while wide skips are quite possible on certain instruments. The oboe is particularly effective on sustained tones while the trumpet is well adapted to fast, repeated notes. Such idiomatic peculiarities must be taken into consideration in melodic writing and for that reason the skillful composer thinks of his melodies in terms of the instruments or voices that are going to perform them. The terms "voice," "voice line," or "voice part" are used quite indiscriminately by musicians to mean a single melodic line within a texture of several voices or instruments regardless of whether it is executed by an instrument (or instruments) or by human voices.

Small forms can exist purely as melody without the element of harmony. However, the tonal center—even for an unaccompanied melody—is a vital aspect of musical form. The folk tune in Figure 15 has a very simple and logical tonal organization. It is in the key of C major, meaning that it is based on a diatonic scale beginning on C. Section A is very strongly in the key of C but contains a secondary tonal center made apparent by the frequent repetitions of the tone G, a fifth above the primary center of C. This relationship of the fifth above or the fourth below (which amounts to the same thing since they have the same letter name) is frequently found in traditional music and is an important aspect of form. The tone a fifth above the first tone of the diatonic scale (that is, the fifth scale degree) is called the dominant and may be indicated by Roman numeral V. The first tone of the scale is called the tonic and is indicated by Roman numeral I. Each of the other scale degrees has a similar name and may be indicated by the corresponding Roman numeral. In traditional harmony the tonic and dominant are very important because together they define the tonality of a piece of music.

The tonal center of C is established in the melody in Figure 15. This is

Figure 15.

The Vicar of Bray (England)

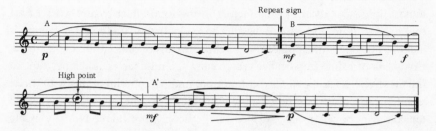

most clearly apparent in that the section ends on C, although there are other factors that contribute to this feeling. Section A is repeated by means of the repeat sign, strengthening the feeling of C as the tonal center and of G as the secondary tonal center. The B section begins and ends on G, the dominant, and seems somehow to be organized around this tone. Although the motivic material and flow of the melody in the B section is similar to that of the A sections, the shift in tonality makes B seem fresh and new. A suspensive or unfinished feeling is created at the end of B by not returning to the tonic but stopping on the dominant—setting the stage for the final repetition of A. A¹ (the final repetition) is made more interesting by virtue of its contrast to B. The feeling of "rightness" or logic that we feel upon our arrival at A¹ is caused by two things. First, A¹ represents a return from the dominant to the tonic, a progression which is very strong and logical to the ear. Second, it gives a feeling of circular perfection or completeness because the melody now ends with the same thematic material with which it began.

The contour of a melody is also important to its form. Note that this melody has the total range of a ninth, from the C below the staff (middle C) to the D on the fourth line. Its first tone is at the midpoint of this range and most of the melody lies in the middle. The high point is found several measures past the middle of the melody. The highest pitch in a melody is frequently the point of greatest emotional intensity (that is, the climactic point). The location of the high point is very important to the overall emotional and esthetic effect of the melody. The most "expected" or logical location of a high point has been demonstrated in this melody, but frequently a melody can be made more interesting by locating the high point at an unusual place or by using a low point in place of the high point.

To the composer the degree of tension and relaxation at different points in a melody is very important because it has a great deal to do with the emotional and esthetic qualities of the melody. The ebb and flow of tension and relaxation, the relative degrees of thrust and repose, the inertia of the musical phrase—all are prime factors in the total effect of any work of art that exists within a specific time duration. Control of these motor factors is achieved through manipulation of all the elements of music but, among these, rhythm is of prime importance. Increasing the number of notes per unit of time will give a feeling of forward motion, and by combining this with a rise in pitch the phrase can be given a tremendous feeling of thrust. Increased tension can be achieved by increasing the rhythmical complexity while points of rest or repose are the result of relative inactivity in the rhythm of the melody. Even periods of silence can have great significance, particularly when they create a feeling of tense expectancy for the passage that follows. A high point in a melody will often, but not always, come at the point of greatest tension or emotional intensity. Large or unusual leaps may also add to the tension, as will the use of extremes in the dynamic level.

The simple melody in Figure 15, because it is very usual and traditional in form, demonstrates some of the principles that have guided composers for centuries. If we give its form a name, as music theorists and musicologists are inclined to do, it would be called a double period. This means that it is in two sections with each of the sections being made up of two phrases. Section one is A and its repeat, while section two consists of B and A^1. Within each section there is a feeling of question and answer between the two phrases and because of this the first phrase of each section may be called the antecedent and the second, the consequent. Periods and double periods are frequently used in the construction of larger forms.

The term double period is one of a number of musical terms which indicate a specific kind of preconceived formal unit based on rhythmic and harmonic considerations. It is important to remember that usually these forms have been observed *after the fact* by musicologists rather than first being "invented" and then put to use by composers. After a form has evolved, it may be used by later composers as a sort of matrix upon which to build their musical ideas. Forms should never be thought of as stereotypes, for composers bend and alter them to suit their own needs and it is through this process that new forms evolve.

HARMONY

Think, for the moment, of music in dimensional terms. Melody is the linear or horizontal aspect of the texture; harmony adds the dimension of depth and density and can be thought of as the vertical aspect. This analogy works very well up to a point, although there is an overlapping between melody and harmony that is particularly apparent in defining the terms polyphonic and contrapuntal. We are using these terms interchangeably to mean two or more voices sounding different pitches and with independent rhythms but written so that together they will have a musically pleasing sound. The manner in which two contrapuntal voices are written is controlled by the way they will sound together. The voice parts in sixteenth century polyphonic choral music weave a beautiful harmonic texture but, in doing so, each part still maintains a melodic or horizontal beauty of its own. The beauty in the resulting contrapuntal-harmonic texture comes from a combination of many factors. In addition to the melodic aspect there is the harmonic interest created by the combination of two or more pitches. There is further attractiveness in the counterpoint of the rhythms of the voices as well as a kind of counterpoint of words. The listener may attune his ears to any of these levels or he may hear several of them simultaneously for their combined effect. By practicing listening skills, it will be possible to distinguish several things simultaneously, or to flit from one aspect of the texture to another, singling out that which has the most appeal at a given moment. Harmony overlaps with the other elements of music in such a way that it is difficult to think of by itself.

In order to understand more about harmony, let us examine a kind of music with a very strong and readily apparent vertical organization, the chorale. Because the horizontal dimension and polyphonic aspects of the chorale do not call too much attention to themselves, it is easier for us to concentrate on the harmony. Chorales are usually written in four voices, all of the voices in similar rhythms. Because the voices coincide rhythmically, chorales are classified as homophonic music. The chorale in Figure 16 is by J. S. Bach (1685–1750) who, in addition to a vast output of the finest vocal and instrumental music, composed nearly four hundred chorale harmonizations, most of which were incidental to larger works called cantatas.

This chorale is in the key of G major which means that, with the diatonic scale as a basis for its harmonic structure, its tonal center is G. The key of G is indicated by the sharp (#) found at the left of each line of

Figure 16.

Was Gott tut, das ist wohlgetan

music. Note that each of these sharps is on the line F which means that, since the chorale is in the key of G, all F's are to be raised one half step by means of the sharp. The use of F sharp instead of F natural produces the proper arrangement of half steps and whole steps for a diatonic scale beginning on G. Other patterns of sharps or flats ($\flat$) are used to indicate other diatonic key centers. The pattern of sharps or flats found at the left of each line of music is called the key signature and produces the proper arrangement of whole steps and half steps for a diatonic scale built in the major key indicated by the key signature.

Each key signature may also indicate a key center in the minor mode which is always a minor third lower than the major key center indicated by the same signature. The major and minor keys indicated by any given key signature are said to be "relative" to each other. Thus, C is the relative major of A minor and A is the relative minor of C major. The same relationship exists between G major and E minor, F major and D minor, and so on for all of the major and minor keys. Musicians determine which mode—major or minor—the key signature indicates in a specific piece by examining the music itself. (For further information on keys and key signatures see Appendix I.)

Chords called triads are built out of the major and minor scales. In traditional harmony a triad is a group of three tones, each separated from the next by the interval of a third. These tones are sounded simultaneously to form a chord. The tonic triad (I) is a chord built up from the first scale degree or tonic note of the key. The dominant triad (V) is a triad built on the fifth scale degree. These two triads are the most frequently used triads in traditional harmonization, and together they define the key or tonality of a piece of music. (Many theorists include IV, the triad built on the fourth scale degree, with V and I to form the "primary triads." IV is called the subdominant.) In the key of G major the tonic triad is G B D and the dominant triad is D F# A. The term "dominant seventh" indicates a dominant triad in which the projection of intervals of the third has been extended to include a fourth tone above the other three. This tone is called the seventh of the chord. The harmonic function of the dominant seventh is identical to that of the dominant triad except that it has a greater feeling of unrest—more urgently requiring the resolution to the tonic.

The phrase endings in the chorale in Figure 16 are indicated by *fermata* signs (⌒) indicating a pause. Notice that the first phrase is built almost entirely out of tonic and dominant sonorities; that is, each vertical structure (with the exception of the fifth chord) is I or V. Since the chorale is written in a four-voice texture, and since a triad has only three tones, it is possible for any one of the tones of a triad to be doubled—the same tone is used in two of the voices, frequently an octave apart. This also makes it possible, instead of doubling a tone, to use a tone other than the three tones of the triad (such as the seventh of a dominant seventh) to create a more interesting and complex harmonic structure.

When three of the voices outline the triad and the fourth voice sounds another tone, we have introduced the element of dissonance into the harmony. Such a tone is not a member of the triad and is therefore called a nonharmonic tone. There are two examples of such tones in the first phrase of the chorale. One is on the fifth chord of the phrase and the other is on the seventh. In this case they add not only harmonic, but also rhythmic interest. Bach was capable of writing very powerful dissonances of tremendous musical and emotional impact, although in this instance the amount of dissonance is relatively small and of the sort that one would expect to find in most music by composers of this period. A *relatively* small amount of dissonance produces a feeling of consonance in music so that this chorale could be described as being relatively consonant.

These two terms must be treated carefully, for that which is dissonant in music of a certain time may be considered quite consonant in another period of music history. A point of relative harmonic relaxation is consonant while a point of relatively greater tension (in terms of the specific piece of music) is dissonant. In the music of such twentieth century composers as Bartók, Berg, or Stravinsky, a portion of music may seem quite dissonant by itself, yet, in terms of the piece, the composer, and his time, it may actually have a consonant effect. This, of course, is one of the frequent pitfalls for the listener who has not heard a great deal of contemporary music. Ideally, the listener's ears should adjust to the kind of music that he hears, so that when he is listening to a new composition, even if it seems filled with strange and unusual effects, it can be made more meaningful by being placed in the proper frame of reference.

Beethoven, Chopin, Wagner, and many other composers were criticized by their contemporaries at one time or another for writing music which was, in their time, considered by many to be unusually dissonant. When we hear the same music today, it no longer seems strange to us because we have become familiar with the kind of harmonies that these composers were using. We have learned to think of Beethoven's dissonance relatively —in terms of Beethoven's own harmonic style. Innovators are sometimes not fully understood by their contemporaries. This is not meant to suggest that the composer who uses established harmonic practices is any less great than the innovator, or that the innovator is great simply by virtue of his having anticipated future developments. Many fine composers of the past were innovators, but one of the outstanding exceptions to this is J. S. Bach, who was considered quite traditional by his contemporaries and even a little old fashioned in his later years. Though very likely the greatest composer of all time, he was not particularly an innovator. Conversely, there are composers such as Franz Liszt, known for innovations, but whose music, in retrospect, may be somewhat less than great.

Returning to the chorale in Figure 16, note that the first and second phrases remain in the tonic key of G major. The cadence at the end of each of these phrases is a standard cadential formula of the baroque period (1600–1750) and of traditional harmony even up to this century. It is the progression of the dominant triad (V) to the tonic triad (I) and is called the authentic cadence. The progression of V to I and its relation to musical form was certainly the most important single harmonic concept from 1600 to 1900 and still exerts a powerful influence upon musical composition.

Phrases three, four, and five of the chorale (after the repeat sign) are in the keys of the dominant, subdominant, and dominant, respectively. The final phrase of the chorale is once more in the tonic. As in the folk tune discussed earlier, there is a middle section in the chorale (phrases three, four, and five) which utilizes the device of key contrast and which emphasizes the final return to the tonic by remaining, for the most part, in the dominant. This short composition has remained predominantly in the tonic; in a sense, it has not been out of the key of G at all because the keys of the dominant (D) and subdominant (C) are very closely related to the tonic (G). In works of greater length and in compositions by later composers, the key contrast is made greater by the use of more distantly related keys. Composers from the early baroque to the present gradually expanded this concept of tonality. Works of the early seventeenth century remained predominantly in the tonic but even here the need for key contrast began to be felt.

The process of moving from one key to another is called modulation. From about 1600 on, composers gradually became more and more free in their use of modulation so that during the baroque and classical periods frequent excursions were made into the keys of the dominant, subdominant, and relative major or minor. During the nineteenth century, modulations to more distantly related keys became quite common. Up to about 1900, however, there was almost always a final return to the tonic or home tonality no matter how far the composer may have strayed harmonically during the course of the piece.

In the twentieth century, radically new harmonic practices began to emerge. Many composers felt that they could maintain a tonal center without returning to it at the end of the piece while others attempted to completely discard the traditional concept of a tonal center. New ways of building vertical sonorities began to develop, such as using two or more key centers simultaneously (polytonality), building chords out of fourths, fifths, and seconds instead of thirds (quartal harmony), and using the technique of composition known as the twelve-tone system. These and other twentieth century harmonic practices will be discussed later.

Falling into the realm of both harmony and counterpoint is a technique called imitation. The simplest kind of imitation is the round: one voice begins a melody and before it is completed a second voice begins the same melody on the same beginning note, then a third is added, and so it continues, "round and round" in a pleasant, harmonious texture of several voices. The harmony in a round is controlled by keeping all the voices in the same key and by keeping the melody at all times within the framework of a single sonority so that the melody will harmonize against itself at any given point. A more complex kind of imitation allows the imitating voices to be altered according to set rules or to begin on different tonal levels than the first voice. This permits greater key contrast and can result in a longer and more significant composition. This technique, called canon or canonic imitation, attained a high degree of perfection during the Renaissance and, in the seventeenth century, evolved into the most highly developed kind of imitative composition, the fugue.

The fugue can be partly defined as a highly organized imitative composition based primarily upon one thematic idea called the subject. A fugal subject is usually no more than a few measures long (too long, however, to be called a motive) and is composed very carefully so that most of the material for the entire composition can be extracted from it. (Imitative pieces of the Renaissance often use a number of subjects, each treated imitatively.) J. S. Bach, universally acknowledged as the greatest master of the fugue, composed fugues and a few other contrapuntal works in a volume entitled *The Art of Fugue*. The volume is based, for the most part, on the fugal subject shown in Figure 17. It is a concise and yet malleable subject, well adapted to the many fugal devices used in the work.

Figure 17.

Figure 18 presents a diagram of a typical structure at the beginning of a four-voice fugue. This section, in which each of the voices enters with a statement of the subject, is called the exposition. The conventional key pattern of the entries in the exposition consists of an alternation between the tonic and dominant keys.

Figure 18.

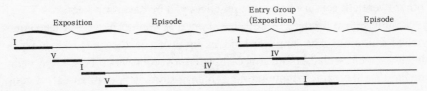

Sample diagram of the beginning of a four-voice fugue. Each level represents a voice. Heavy lines indicate subject statements.

The formal plan of the material following the exposition may vary greatly from one fugue to another. In a sense, the fugue is not a form at all, but a texture in which the preestablished patterns and practices do not suffice to determine the shape of the composition as a whole. Among the many fugues of Bach many different forms or formal plans are apparent, some of which bear resemblance to preexisting forms, but many of which are valid only for a particular fugue.

Certain aspects of fugal procedure are more or less common to all fugues: (1) A fugue is based primarily upon one short thematic idea called the subject. (The counterpoint used against the subject in the exposition may also become an important thematic element.) (2) The number of voices (two or more) remains constant throughout the work, all of them first being presented in the exposition, though for variety of texture all the voices need not be present at all times. (3) Techniques called fugal devices, which develop or treat the exposition material in various ways, are used in the section following the exposition and may continue to the end of the fugue. (4) In addition to incidental entries of the subject which may occur throughout the fugue, a final statement or final exposition of the subject in the home tonality is found near the end.

Occasionally, in the middle section of a fugue, a group of two or more subject entries may occur, passed from voice to voice in a manner similar to the initial exposition. Such sections are sometimes called interior expositions or entry groups and frequently, to achieve contrast, are in a key other than the home tonality. Sections of a fugue in which no subject entries are found (or which may contain isolated subject entries that are very developmental in character) are called episodes, and it is in these sections that the composer demonstrates great contrapuntal skill and musical imagination.

The form of a fugue is determined by (1) the pattern or arrangement of material (expositions, episodes, etc.) following the initial exposition, (2) the key centers of the various sections, and (3) the manner in which the fugal devices are used.

These fugal devices include inversion or mirroring (turning the subject upside down so that every descending interval becomes an ascending interval and vice-versa), retrogression (playing the subject backward so that the last note of the subject becomes the first, the next to the last becomes the second, and so on), diminution (shortening all the notes of a subject in proportion), augmentation (lengthening all the notes of a subject in proportion), and several others. Fugal techniques and devices are often used as resources in compositions which are not called fugues but which utilize these techniques for developmental purposes.

The link between harmony and rhythm is very strong. Conventional practices during the sixteenth century, for example, indicate that certain dissonances were preferable when used at certain points in the rhythmic structure. Such conventions appear throughout the history of music. Certain musical styles made use of a fast harmonic rhythm, meaning that the chord changes (changes of harmony) occur at a relatively fast pace. An example of fast harmonic rhythm is found in the chorale in Figure 16 in which a chord change occurs on nearly every beat. A slow harmonic rhythm occurs when each separate sonority is sounded for a relatively long period of time. A slow harmonic rhythm is found at the beginning of Mendelssohn's *Italian Symphony* where, in spite of the fast tempo and lively rhythm, the chords change at a relatively slow pace.

LISTENING SUGGESTIONS

String Quartet No. 2	Borodin
"Veni Creator Spiritus"	Latin Hymn
Symphony No. 1	Beethoven
Symphony No. 2	Beethoven
Motet: "Tristis est Anima Mea"	Di Lasso
String Quartet No. 6	Bartók
Contrapunctus 1 from *The Art of Fugue*	J. S. Bach
Italian Symphony	Mendelssohn

SUGGESTED ASSIGNMENT

1. Define the following terms. When necessary use supplementary reference material recommended by the instructor.

rhythm	contour	key signature
melody	diatonic	triad
harmony	tempered tuning	scale degree
meter	half step	primary triads
bar lines	whole step	doubling
measure	interval	dominant seventh
triple meter	accidentals	dissonance
duple meter	pentatonic	consonance
beat	tonal center	nonharmonic tones
tempo	church modes	resolution
cross rhythm	range	modulation
counterpoint	voice part	secondary key center
homophonic	key	imitation
polyphonic	tonic	fugue
texture	dominant	entry
motive	subdominant	fugal exposition

phrase
cadence
organic unity
mode
scale

antecedent
consequent
double period
relative major and mi-
    nor

fugal episode
fugal devices
harmonic rhythm

THREE

TONE COLOR,
THE FOURTH ELEMENT,
AND MUSICAL INSTRUMENTS

Tone color, or timbre, refers to the characteristic quality of sound in a specific instrument or voice. If an oboe and a violin sound the same pitch at the same dynamic level we are able to distinguish between the two because of their differences in tone quality. Every tone is made up of a fundamental tone and a composite of lesser tones above the fundamental. These lesser tones are interchangeably called overtones, harmonics, or partials. The mathematical ratio of the frequency of each of these tones to the fundamental tone remains constant regardless of the pitch of the fundamental. For example, the frequency of the first overtone above a fundamental will always be twice the frequency of the fundamental. A similarly constant ratio exists for each of the overtones. The harmonic or overtone series is illustrated in Figure 19.

Figure 19.

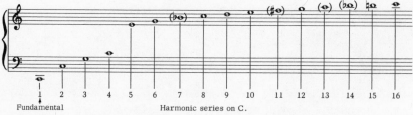

Fundamental   Harmonic series on C.

Some physicists theorize that timbre or tone quality is determined by the variation in intensity of these overtones in relation to each other. According to this theory, the clarinet has its characteristic tone because the odd-

38

numbered partials in a clarinet tone have greater intensity than the even-numbered. Similarly, the tone quality of the flute (if this theory is accepted) is the result of its strong fundamental and relatively weaker partials. (When using the term "partials" the fundamental tone is called the first partial. The first overtone is the same as the second partial.)

Performers have a certain amount of control over tone quality. An oboist may use a certain kind of reed for a particular piece of music and a violinist may draw his bow in a certain part of the string, closer or further from the bridge, for the purpose of varying tone quality. For the composer, variation in tone quality is achieved primarily by assigning various parts of the music to different instruments. In the hands of master orchestrators like Ravel, Rimsky-Korsakov, or Stravinsky, this can be one of the most expressive elements at the composer's command.

Human voices vary greatly in timbre. First, there is the obvious difference between a male and a female voice singing the same pitch. But even among voices of the same range there are pronounced differences in quality. For this reason we have such terms as lyric tenor, heroic tenor, basso buffo, and basso profundo. Normally, voices are divided into four general categories: soprano, alto, tenor, and bass. These are the four voice parts in a mixed chorus. Further subdivisions are necessary when the music calls for it, such as separate parts for first and second soprano. The indescribable quality of a beautiful singing voice cannot be equaled by an instrument, for the voice is the most perfect of all instruments—the instrument to which other melodic instruments aspire. Since it is the oldest of instruments, it is natural that it has wielded a strong influence on the course of music history.

The first instrumental melodies could have been nothing more than an imitation of vocal music. The fact that instruments existed in very ancient times is proven by specimens of instruments which have been unearthed and by the presence of instruments in pictures and sculpture of early civilizations. Notated music for instrumental ensembles has been known since the late thirteenth century. Music of that time and even up to the end of the sixteenth century was strongly influenced by vocal music. One of the aims of composers during the Renaissance (1450–1600) was to write music beautifully adapted to the human voice. This led toward predominantly stepwise vocal lines and frequent sustained tones, characteristics which were also found in the instrumental music of the period.

Instrumental pieces called *ricercari* and *canzoni* were originally nothing more than literal transcriptions of vocal ensemble music of the sixteenth century. That is, the vocal parts were simply played by instruments rather than sung by voices. The instruments used were groups of viols (stringed instruments similar to the violin family), recorders (ancestors of the modern flute), and occasionally early keyboard instruments such as the harpsichord. Since the vocal music was written for voices of different registers such as soprano, alto, tenor, and bass, it was quite natural that the instruments be built in varying sizes so that they would be capable of duplicating the various vocal registers. Both viols and recorders were built in families spanning the entire range of human voices from bass to soprano. An ensemble of instruments of the same type, all viols or all recorders, was called a "whole consort." If instruments from different families were used together in the same piece of music the ensemble was called a "broken consort."

Composers gradually began to compose music specifically for instruments rather than using vocal transcriptions. Some of the first music of this kind was composed at St. Mark's Cathedral in Venice at the end of the sixteenth century. This was an important step in the development of idiomatic writing for instruments. Composers began to take into consideration the individual tone characteristics and relative capabilities of the various instruments. With the development of the instruments of the violin family in Italy around 1600, a whole new area was opened up for the instrumental composer. Toward the end of the seventeenth century a group of Italian violinist-composers began to exert a profound influence upon composition for stringed instruments. Composers of this group, such as Corelli and Vivaldi, developed a violin technique which, with some changes, is still used today. The music of these composers is among the very finest ever written for stringed instruments.

The development of the orchestra began during the baroque period in the opera houses of seventeenth century Italy. Orchestra music of this period is distinct from the earlier consort music because larger combinations of instruments were used (winds and strings), and because each of the string parts was played by a group of players. That is, a section of violins played a single line in unison, a section of violas played another part, and so forth.

Another, and very important member of the opera orchestra was the continuo group. Continuo is the name given to the accompaniment group used in almost all music of the baroque period. It developed first in opera, and consisted of a keyboard instrument and a bass instrument. The keyboard player in the continuo group, frequently a harpsichordist, read his part by means of a system of musical shorthand called figured bass. The bass player played the bass line, both players reading from music such as that shown in Figure 20. Frequently, in accompanying a solo voice, the continuo would be the only part of the orchestra that would play. The bass

Figure 20.

Monteverdi, *Orfeo*, Act II

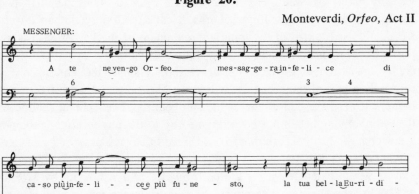

line might be played by any one of several bass instruments such as cello, bassoon, or bass viol.

The continuo was present in almost all ensemble music of the period and was very important in the development of the trio sonata, the dominating chamber music medium of the baroque period. The trio sonata consisted of two solo instruments, frequently violins, accompanied by continuo (often harpsichord and cello). The string quartet (two violins, viola, and cello) evolved from the trio sonata around 1745 with the addition of the viola and the elimination of the keyboard instrument. The string quartet has remained the most important chamber music medium from the late eighteenth century to the present.

In the baroque period, orchestras were used in sacred choral works called oratorios and cantatas, in concertos, and in opera. The instrumentation and number of players in these orchestras varied according to the requirements of a particular composition. The orchestra might contain as few as ten instruments or as many as thirty or more, and the continuo was always present. It was not until about 1740 that a permanent instrumentation for the symphony orchestra was established. This development took place primarily in the orchestras at Mannheim and Vienna. The strings consisted of a section of first violins, a section of second violins, a section of violas, a section of cellos, and a section of bass viols. The woodwind section also became more or less permanent, including one or two each of flutes, oboes, and bassoons. By the end of the eighteenth century, two clarinets were invariably used, as well. The rather small brass section included two trumpets and two or four French horns. Two kettledrums (timpani) were frequently used, tuned to the tonic and dominant of the key of each composition. This instrumentation was followed more or less strictly by composers throughout the classical period. Though the continuo was originally a part of the orchestra, it began to be more and more frequently omitted toward the end of the eighteenth century. This general outline of the symphony orchestra has been retained up to the present time, although a few changes have occurred, such as the addition of extra wind and percussion players and the use of larger string sections. Thirty to thirty-five players would be sufficient for the performance of a symphony by Mozart or Haydn, whereas many late nineteenth century works, such as the Strauss tone poems, require orchestras of over a hundred players.

The standard instrumentation of the modern symphony orchestra is given in the following pages. It must be remembered that this instrumentation will vary according to the needs and desires of the composer.

THE STRING SECTION

In all of the stringed instruments (see Figure 21) the tone is produced by drawing the bow across the string. Illogical as it may seem, instruments constructed with strings but not producing their tone by means of a bow, such as the harp or piano, are not conventionally called stringed instruments. The largest stringed instrument is the bass viol, only true descendant of the viol family in the string section. The other instruments are members of the violin family which evolved from earlier instruments around 1600. The instruments of the violin family are the most perfectly constructed instruments of the entire orchestra. The art of making them reached such perfection during the eighteenth century that instruments made at that time are still in use and are, in fact, the finest instruments in existence. The best products of these early Italian violin makers such as those by Stradivarius or Amati have recently brought prices in excess of $100,000. Since that time there have been many fine violin makers, but none to equal the excellence of the eighteenth century masters.

The violin is the smallest instrument of the violin family. As in all violin-

Figure 21.

Violin   Viola

Cello   Double bass

type instruments, the interval between adjacent strings (tuned E, A, D, G) is a perfect fifth. The lowest notes of the violin, roughly in the range of the alto voice, are very rich and full in melodic passages, while the high register is silvery in quality. Fast, brilliant passages can be executed with great agility on the violin and chords are also possible to a limited degree. These virtuoso attributes coupled with its beautiful singing quality make it one of the finest solo instruments. The vibrato on the stringed instruments is similar in sound to that of the human voice. It is produced by moving the left hand (which fingers the strings) in a fairly rapid back and forth motion, very slightly altering the pitch of the tone in such a way as to produce the characteristically vibrant string tone. The violin has a range extending from the middle of the register of the tenor voice up to well beyond the highest reaches of the soprano voice.[1]

There are two sections of violins in a modern orchestra. In music written before the middle of the nineteenth century, the first violin part was usually more interesting and more demanding than the second violin part. In late

[1] Exact ranges of all orchestral instruments are given in Appendix II.

nineteenth century music this was not always the case, and since that time the second violin part has often been as difficult as the first.

The viola is slightly larger than the violin and is tuned a fifth lower. It can be thought of as the alto voice of the string section. Its upper register is not as brilliant as that of the violin while its middle and low registers have a unique quality, rich and throaty, that is very expressive. Because of its size, it presents technical problems not found on the violin though it is played in basically the same position. Although it may not be as distinguished a solo instrument as the violin and cello, several brilliant violists have gained impressive reputations on the instrument.

The cello (full name, violoncello) is the bass instrument of the string quartet but not of the orchestra. A composer may occasionally use it as the bass instrument in the orchestra, but the real bass is most often furnished by the bass viols. In orchestral music up to the end of the eighteenth century the bass line was usually doubled by the cellos and the bass viols in octaves. As cellists became more skillful and developed the technical possibilities of the instrument, it began to be used in new ways, other than simply as a bass instrument. As a solo instrument it is capable of singing beautifully in all parts of its range, which extends from the lowest tones of the bass voice up to the very highest extremes of the soprano voice. Its richly expressive quality is often described as being very much like the human voice. The cello is played from a sitting position, held between the knees, and with the endpin of the instrument resting on the floor. As a solo instrument it is on a par with the violin—a virtuoso instrument in spite of its size.

The four strings of the bass viol or double bass are tuned in fourths and its range is roughly an octave below that of the cello. Its upper register is not nearly as usable as that of the cello and it is seldom used as a solo instrument. Rapid virtuoso passage work is not often found in music for the double bass, but when necessary the skillful bassist can rise to the challenge as, for example, in the scherzo of Beethoven's Fifth Symphony. The basses are usually arranged around the back of the orchestra and are played from a semistanding position, the player being supported by a stool.

The size of the string section in a modern symphony orchestra may vary, but a typical professional orchestra would probably have at least eighteen first violins, eighteen second violins, sixteen violas, twelve cellos, and eight string basses. All of the string players are seated, with two players reading from one stand of music. When it is necessary for the members to divide (separate into two or more different parts within the section), the player seated on the outside will take the upper part and the inside player will take the lower. Further subdivisions may be arranged according to the needs of a particular composition.

The outside player at the first stand of the first violin section is the concertmaster. His is a position of great prestige in the orchestral hierarchy. He is the soloist for any incidental violin solos in the music and it is his responsibility to represent the orchestra in dealings with the conductor or with the management. As stated in Chapter One, he is responsible for tuning the orchestra at the beginning of a concert by requesting an A from the first oboe. The first player in each of the string sections is called the principal of his section and has certain responsibilities such as deciding how a passage should be bowed and other decisions which may assist the conductor. Well over half the orchestra is made up of strings and for this reason the string section can be thought of as the foundation of the orchestra. A great deal of music has been written for the string section alone. A wide range of coloristic and expressive effects are made possible by playing the stringed instruments in different ways. Among these are several methods of varying the quality of tone such as *pizzicato* (plucking the string), *con sordino* (with a mute), *sul ponticello* (drawing the bow close to the bridge), and many others.

THE WOODWIND SECTION

All of the instruments of the woodwind (see Figure 22) and brass sections are solo instruments in the sense that each has its own part which is not doubled by other players. It is only in the strings that a large number of instruments of the same kind play the same part. Normally there are at least two each of flutes, oboes, clarinets, and bassoons. Each has its own separate part (flute I, flute II, oboe I, oboe II, etc.). The first flute has a more difficult and soloistic part than the second flute, the first oboe part is more demanding than the second, and so on throughout the rest of the woodwind section. This is the general rule although there are times when it is necessary for the composer to assign difficult or brilliant parts to the second player as well as to the first. In addition to the instruments mentioned above, there frequently are parts for piccolo, English horn, bass clarinet, the high E flat clarinet, and the contrabassoon. The number of wind players in a specific performance is determined by what the composer has called for in the score. For example, the woodwind instrumentation of Mozart's *Symphony No. 41* (*Jupiter*) calls for one flute, two oboes, and two bassoons; while the woodwinds used in Stravinsky's *Symphony in Three Movements* are piccolo, two flutes, two oboes, two clarinets, bass clarinet, two bassoons, and contrabassoon. The number and variety of instruments is determined by the composer's requirements for a specific composition. Only the string section remains relatively constant in five parts.

Figure 22.

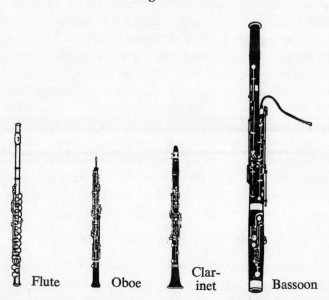

Flute   Oboe   Clar-   Bassoon
                     inet

The instruments of the flute family include the flute, piccolo, and the alto flute (rarely used in the symphony orchestra). All of them are whistle-type instruments—the tone is produced by blowing across the open hole in the mouthpiece to set the air column in vibration. The flute plays roughly in the range of the soprano voice although its highest note is about an octave beyond the capabilities of most sopranos. Its upper register is brilliant to the point of shrillness in its highest tones. The lower register does not have a big sound but can be very expressive in soft passages. Its agility in difficult scale and arpeggio passages is phenomenal, a feature which composers have often used to great advantage. The piccolo (in other languages called the small flute) has a range roughly an octave higher than that of the flute. Fingered the same as the flute, it is usually played by the third or fourth flutist of the orchestra. It can be very shrill in its highest register and is often heard punctuating loud passages at the very top of the orchestra. Its agility is almost on a par with the flute. The alto flute, as its name implies, is a larger and lower instrument than the flute and has a rich throaty quality. It is rarely used in the symphony orchestra although twentieth century composers have occasionally experimented with it. Today it is quite frequently used in jazz (also in television and movie music).

In the oboe family the tone is produced by forcing air between the two parts of a double reed. The double reed instruments are the oboe, English horn, bassoon, and contrabassoon. The oboe has approximately the same range as the soprano voice, though it is not able to play as high as the flute. The English horn (which is neither a horn nor English) is the alto of the woodwind section. The bassoon covers the tenor and bass registers, while the contrabassoon is a bass instrument with a range extending down to the lowest tones of the piano. The characteristic double reed tone is penetrating and poignant. The oboe and English horn sound particularly well on sustained tones and lyrical passages. The double reeds are not noted for their agility but in the hands of expert players can negotiate rapid passages remarkably well. The bassoon and contrabassoon are invaluable as bass instruments in the symphony orchestra.

The clarinets are single reed instruments. The reed is set in vibration by forcing air between the mouthpiece and the reed. The smallest of the clarinet instruments is the high E flat clarinet whose range is similar to that of the flute. Its sound is not as mellow as the ordinary clarinet and is sometimes used to strengthen the orchestral sound in high passages. The ordinary clarinet is a much more versatile instrument. Throughout its range it has a full mellow tone (somewhat weaker in the middle register) and it is well adapted to melodic playing. It is also very agile, easily executing wide leaps, scale passages, and arpeggios. Its range extends from the low register of the tenor voice up to the very top of the soprano voice. There are two kinds of these so-called ordinary clarinets, both having about the same range, and almost identical in appearance. They are called the A clarinet and B flat clarinet because of their difference in *transposition*. (See Appendix III for an explanation of transposition.) The composer will select one or the other of these instruments primarily on the basis of the key in which the music is written. The choice is also determined by what sounds best on which clarinet and sometimes it is necessary for the composer to indicate a switch from one clarinet to the other during the course of the piece, or even to have one player use the A clarinet simultaneously with another using the B flat instrument. The largest

member of the clarinet family, the bass clarinet, is a transposing instrument
in B flat with a range similar to that of the bassoon. All of the members of
the clarinet family are transposing instruments, which enables the player
to use similar fingerings on all four instruments.

The saxophones, ranging in size from soprano to bass, are also single
reed instruments. They are all transposing instruments and their technique
is similar to that of the clarinet. They are not normally found in the
symphony orchestra but occasionally are used for special effects as in
Ravel's orchestration of *Pictures at an Exhibition*.

THE BRASS SECTION

All of the brass instruments (see Figure 23) are lip reed instruments,
which means that the sound is produced by using the lips as a reed, vibrat-
ing within or against a metal mouthpiece. Valves were not used on the
brass instruments until about the middle of the nineteenth century and for
this reason horn and trumpet parts written before this time use primarily
the tones of the overtone series (Figure 19). We can understand the significance of this in terms of the military bugle, the only valveless brass instrument in common use today. Partials three through eight are the only
tones easily playable on the bugle and this accounts for the fact that bugle
calls are limited to these four or five members of the overtone series outlin-
ing the notes of a triad. The range of the valveless French horn (now obsolete) included higher partials than those used by the bugle. Although it
could play only a limited number of tones, stepwise passages were possible
because the higher partials in the overtone series are closer together. Partials seven through sixteen, in fact, are completely stepwise. The pitch of
the playable partials could be altered slightly by placing the hand in the bell
of the instrument or by changing the pressure of the lips without switching
to an adjacent partial (lipping the tone), thus increasing the number of
playable tones on the valveless horn.

The fundamental pitch of the overtone series in which a brass instrument
can play is determined by the length and diameter of the tubing, but in
modern instruments the length of the tubing can be rapidly and conveniently changed by means of valves. Prior to the use of valves this was
possible only by the use of a removable section of tubing called a crook
which could be replaced by another of different length. The player read all
of his music in the key of C, using the overtones of a C fundamental, and,
when required to play in another key, would insert the proper crook for

Figure 23.

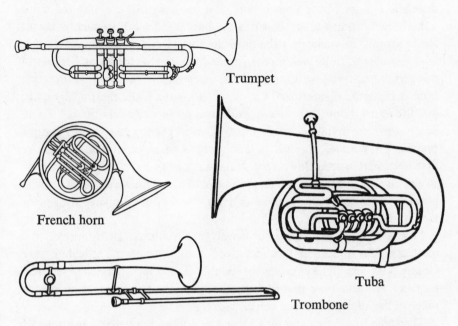

Trumpet

French horn

Tuba

Trombone

that key though still reading the notes as they were written with C as the fundamental. This provided a workable though somewhat cumbersome means of transposition and left us today with a literature of brass music from earlier periods using many different transpositions. The convention of using transpositions for the brass instruments still persists, though today these have been narrowed down, for the most part, to the transposition of F for the French horn and B flat for the trumpet. Brass players must develop great skill in transposition in order to read the music of earlier periods.

Because of the limitations of the valveless instruments, brass music of earlier periods has certain idiomatic characteristics that distinguish it from music written after the invention of valves. These characteristics include fanfarelike passages as well as frequent repeated notes and sustained tones. With the ability of modern brass instruments to play all the notes of the musical scale (within their respective range limitations) much more is possible, but the traditions carried down from earlier periods still persist, and continue to exert an influence on music written for brass instruments.

There are usually four French horns in a symphony orchestra although some late nineteenth century scores call for eight or more. The most characteristic register of the French horn is in the range of the alto and tenor voice. The horn can reach down to the bass register but its tone is not as strong in this area and thus the horn does not serve particularly well as a bass instrument. In its best register it can be heroic or tender and is one of the most eloquent instruments of the orchestra. Traditionally, the first hornist plays the highest part, the second a low part, the third a high part, and the fourth hornist, the lowest part. The players cultivate the register in which they are required to do most of their playing, the fourth hornist practicing low tones, the first practicing high passages, and so forth. The first horn part is frequently very demanding, both technically and expressively, and for this reason the first hornist will usually have an assistant who plays the less important parts so that the first hornist can save his lip for the difficult solo passages.

Most symphonic scores call for two to four trumpets. The trumpet is the most agile instrument of the brass section and is able to articulate very cleanly and rapidly by means of double and triple tonguing.[2] Lyrical passages are also very beautiful on the trumpet. The trumpet spans the range of the alto and soprano voice.

The three trombones and tuba form a quartet of low-pitched instruments for the brass section. The trombone and tuba were practically never used in symphonic music of the eighteenth century but are found almost invariably in scores from the nineteenth century to the present. The first and second trombones are tenor trombones whose best range is similar to that of the tenor voice. The third trombone, called the bass trombone, is a slightly larger instrument, producing a more substantial sound in the bass register. The trombone first began to be used in the fifteenth century and, unlike most instruments, its essential structure has not changed up to the present. Because it has always been possible to play all the notes of the musical scale lying within its range (by quickly changing the length of the tubing by means of the slide), the trombone is not a transposing instrument.

The tuba is the real bass of the brass section with a range similar to that of the string bass. There is usually only one in a symphony orchestra. Its full resonant tone can be mellow as well as heroic and is sometimes used for solo passages.

[2] Techniques of using the tongue to strike against the mouthpiece to achieve rapid articulation.

THE PERCUSSION SECTION

The percussion instruments (see Figure 24) have more variety of tone color than any other section of the orchestra. Composers of this century have experimented with percussion instruments of Latin America, of Spain, of the Orient, of primitive cultures, and with those used in various kinds of jazz. To discuss them all would be beyond the scope of this book, for as long as two materials can be struck together there will be possibilities for new percussion sounds.

Figure 24.

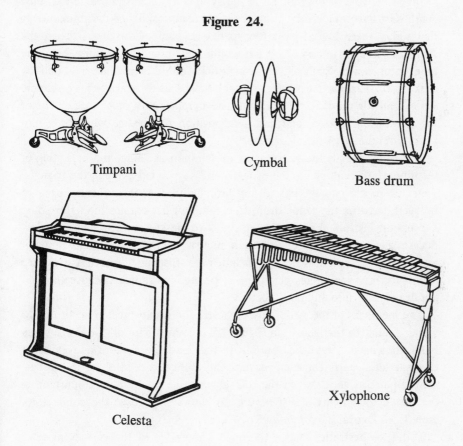

Timpani

Cymbal

Bass drum

Celesta

Xylophone

The only percussion instruments in the eighteenth century orchestra were the timpani. The two timpani of the classical orchestra were always tuned to the tonic and dominant of the key. This meant that at the beginning of each concert and before each different work was performed, the timpanist had to tune his instruments by carefully changing the tension of the heads. Later this task was made much simpler by the invention of the pedal timpani which enabled the player to conveniently change the pitch of the instruments, even during the course of a single movement. This meant that a great variety of pitches could be played, which to some extent changed the role of the timpani in the symphony orchestra. Since that time composers have made increasing demands on the skills of the timpanist so that today there are at least four pedal timpani of varying sizes in the symphony orchestra and any pitch within their range is possible. Also, the tone color can be changed by using sticks of different materials and by striking on various parts of the drum head. Since nearly all symphonic scores call for timpani, the timpanist never plays any other instrument of the percussion section, and enjoys a position of prestige which sets him apart from the other percussionists.

The other percussion instruments in common use since the beginning of the nineteenth century are the cymbals and suspended cymbal, the triangle, the snare drum, and the bass drum. Gradually other instruments began to be used, such as the tenor drum, the tambourine, chimes, and the gong. Percussion instruments are divided into two classes: those which can produce a discernible and definite pitch such as the xylophone and timpani, and those whose pitch is unclear or indefinite. Instruments such as the harp and piano are sometimes classified as percussion simply because they do not fit properly into any other section.

The members of the symphony orchestra are usually seated according to a plan similar to that shown in Figure 25. The music for all the instruments is laid out in an established pattern in the conductor's score as well as in the individual parts for each player. The ability to read all of the instrumental parts as set down in the full score is one of the most important of the conductor's many skills. Figure 26 shows a page of the conductor's score from Dvořák's *Symphony No. 4.*

Today orchestration and a thorough knowledge of the various musical media are an essential part of the composer's art. Some recent composers became so skillful in idiomatic writing for instruments that in some instances (for example, the Bartók String Quartets) the music comes very close to defining the medium. Although one might vary the instrumentation

Figure 25.

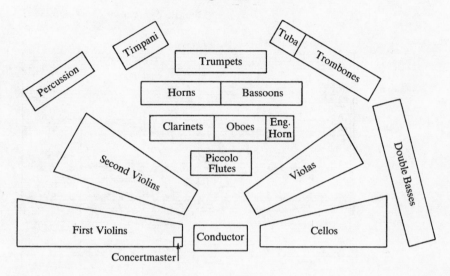

of a baroque trio sonata without changing its essential meaning and significance, more recent compositions by composers such as Berlioz, Rimsky-Korsakov, Ravel, or Stravinsky would be difficult to imagine in any other medium except that indicated by the composer.

LISTENING SUGGESTIONS

Merry Mount Suite	Howard Hanson
Young Peoples' Guide to the Orchestra	Benjamin Britten
Eine Kleine Nachtmusik	Mozart
Symphony No. 41 (Jupiter)	Mozart
Symphony in Three Movements	Stravinsky
Capriccio Espagnol	Rimsky-Korsakov
Daphnis and Chloe Suite No. 2	Ravel
Roman Carnival Overture	Berlioz

SUGGESTED ASSIGNMENTS

1. In listening to the above works, attempt to identify the various instruments heard in the course of the music.
2. Write descriptions of the technical and idiomatic capabilities of the various instruments. For reference use orchestration textbooks recommended by the instructor.
3. Discuss the purpose and function of tone color in various works from the Renaissance to the present.

Figure 26.

Dvořák, *Symphony No. 4*, Op. 88, I

FOUR

INTRODUCTION TO
LARGER FORMS

Music can be thought of as a series of events occurring within a specific duration of time. In this sense music has much in common with the other temporal arts—drama, dance, poetry, and literature—for all of these have the common characteristic of existing within time rather than within space. The physical characteristics of a sculpture or painting can usually be apprehended in a relatively short time, sometimes in a few minutes. Such art exists in space and its form is complete in itself and immediately apparent, although, of course, the fullest significance of the object is usually realized only through a longer period of careful study. Since music is a temporal art, it reaches its final form only after several stages of development. Music is usually written down as notes on a staff but it is not in its written form that it reaches the listener, for after being written down by the composer it must be rehearsed by the performer and then presented in its final form before an audience. Just as a drama must be staged, a choreography must be danced, and a poem or novel read, aloud or silently, so music must be performed.

All this may seem very obvious, but it is important to remember that the events comprising the performance of a piece of music are what give it significant shape or form. The term "significant" implies a great deal in this context, for a series of unconnected or unplanned events would have little or no significance. The events must be connected, one to another, and organized in such a way that the significance of each event is enhanced by the occurrence of the others. In a drama most of the characters are usually presented in the first act. They enter one after another, perhaps more than one at a time, and their relationships to each other begin to be established immediately. Each character plays his part in the plot which begins to unfold and in the second act, when certain characters reappear, their significance is enhanced by the fact that we are already acquainted with them and we wait anxiously to see what they will do next. Sometimes their actions are predictable, sometimes not. If, as sometimes happens, a new character appears in the final act, one who had perhaps been hinted at but not seen previously, then we may experience a moment of intense surprise. The re-appearance in the final act of the other characters produces an effect of completion, of returning at the end to something that had been presented at the beginning. There is an additional significance to the final entrance of these characters for now we see them in a new light, with greater meaning. They may appear in exactly the same setting and costumes in which they first appeared but we view them differently because we have seen their characters develop and reveal themselves throughout the play. We have seen them in action. At the end, every word they say and every motion they make takes on greater significance so that, for some of them, their final appearance may even have the effect of a revelation. All of these things combine with the ultimate unraveling of the plot to give the play its particular shape or form.

Much the same thing happens in a piece of music. Usually most of the basic material of the work is presented near the beginning. These musical ideas immediately begin to establish their role in the total work, each theme or motive playing its part, and as they are developed, they reveal more and more of their potentialities. Sometimes the listener will be able to predict an occurrence in a particular passage, sometimes not; and sometimes a new theme may appear near the end in such a way as to produce a startling or dramatic effect. Near the end the original themes may appear in much the same form in which they appeared at the beginning, but now, because we have seen what these themes are capable of, seen them develop, and seen how they are related to each other, their final appearance takes on a significance far greater than when we first heard them. Again, as in a play, returning at the end to something that happened at the beginning produces a feeling of circular perfection or completion—a kind of consummation of form to be found in all of the temporal arts.

It begins to be apparent that unity in a temporal art rests very strongly upon the principle of *repetition,* but repetition without contrast can produce monotony—like a small child chanting the same melodic fragment over and over again. *Contrast* functions to offset the monotony that would otherwise result from excessive repetition. One of the most important ways to achieve contrast in music is to utilize the element of harmony in various ways. This was demonstrated in a simple way by the Bach chorale discussed in Chapter Two (see Figure 16). In such a short piece very little key contrast or shift of tonal center was necessary. It was achieved simply by moving from the tonic to the subdominant and dominant during the middle section and then returning to the tonic at the end. Since the keys of the dominant and subdominant are closely related to the tonic key, this resulted in a moderate but, in this case, quite adequate degree of key contrast. Works of greater length utilize a more complex harmonic and tonal organization. They may depart from the home key to more distantly related keys and these departures may be more numerous and of greater duration than in a shorter piece.

Another way of securing contrast is by varying the repetitions of a musical idea. We have seen this occur in the second movement of Beethoven's Fifth Symphony where the slow lyrical theme first presented by the violas and cellos was varied in its later presentations. Each of the later presentations is ornamented or embellished, while retaining the length, general contour, and expressive qualities of the original. This is called variation.

A distinction should be made between variation and development. Essentially variation is the process of modifying or changing a musical passage in such a way that the result is recognizable as having been derived from the original, usually retaining its length and general contour. Development, on the other hand, is not so much concerned with the preservation of the identity of a theme as with the gradual elaboration or unfolding of its inherent possibilities. A motive of three or four tones, because of its incompleteness, lends itself well to development, for it can be lengthened, its pitches can be altered, its rhythm can be changed, it can appear in various kinds of harmonic and contrapuntal textures, and can generally be transformed in such a way that its original identity is apparent only by tracing its progress throughout the complete movement. The technique of variation, unlike development, is usually applied not to a short motive but to a longer passage, frequently to a theme or motive that is already complete in itself. This can be seen in the eighteenth and nineteenth century practice of composing complete movements, with the title, "theme and variations." The theme in this type of variation form is usually a simple but complete melody, often a folk song or popular tune familiar to the audience. Each variation which follows preserves the original length and general contour of the theme but varies it by such techniques as adding notes to embellish the melody, changing the accompaniment figure, changing the texture, changing the rhythm, or perhaps changing from the major to the minor mode; the theme and set of variations together forming the complete movement. Such pieces were used as movements of larger works and also as separate movements intended to be performed by themselves. It is hardly appropriate, then, to use the term variation for the developmental techniques used in a movement such as the first movement of Beethoven's Fifth Symphony or the *Hebrides Overture* of Mendelssohn, for each of these works has, as one of its basic elements, a short fragment which evolves or "develops" through many transformations in the course of the complete movement.

Some of the same compositional techniques may be used in both variation and development but the end result is decidedly different. To illustrate this difference let us return to the analogy of drama. We can see the process of development taking place in the audience's view of the main protagonist throughout the course of the play. After he is presented in the first act his character is gradually unfolded and elaborated—in fact, developed—for the audience to see and understand. In some cases his personality and his relationship to the other characters may even undergo a kind of metamorphosis so that at the end of the drama he appears quite differently than at the beginning. Variation, however, could consist of simply changing a character's costume for his reappearances, or varying the lighting in two consecutive scenes. Development is the very essence of the plot, tied up directly with the progress of action in time, while variation is nothing more than a means of achieving contrast which, though useful and important, may not be closely related to the thread of action as it is seen within the total time span of the work. Development is often found in variation forms but it is apparent only in the large view of the complete set of variations rather than in the techniques applied to each separate variation.

So far we have discussed several kinds of contrast in music: harmonic or tonal contrast, contrast by variation, and contrast by development. Much music adds another aspect of contrast by introducing completely new material into the musical structure, comparable to the appearance of a new character in the middle of a drama. A movement or piece of music based essentially on one theme or musical idea, achieving its contrast by harmonic means, by variation, or by development, can be called monothematic. Such movements are usually relatively short, for the amount of contrast that can be achieved without the presentation of new material is limited and might result in monotony if the piece continued for too long a time.

One of the most widely used monothematic forms is binary form. Used a great deal by composers of the seventeenth and eighteenth centuries, it was the most important single-movement instrumental form of the Baroque. Sonatas of four movements, each movement in binary form, were written in profusion by baroque composers such as Corelli, Vivaldi, J. S. Bach, Telemann, and many others. Essentially, as its name indicates, binary form is in two sections, the first section beginning in the tonic, moving toward the key of the dominant and usually ending in the dominant. (In some baroque binary forms the first section ends in the tonic.) The second section continues in the key of the dominant and works back toward the tonic or home tonality (often passing through related keys) and ending in the tonic. This is the usual pattern, although, if the movement is in the minor mode, the secondary key center may be the relative major (also called the mediant or III) rather than the dominant. Figure 27 illustrates the conventional pattern of key relationships in a binary form. Note that each of the two sections is played twice in succession, the repeats indicated by means of the repeat signs in the middle and at the end. In listening to a binary form the progress of the music can be followed more easily by listening for the cadences at the ends of these sections.

Figure 27.

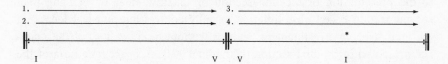

Binary form. The numbers and arrows illustrate the sequence of repeats.

In this, as in all so-called "preconceived" forms, it is important to remember that, although the composer was aware that he was using a form that had been found useful by a large number of his predecessors and contemporaries, nevertheless, if he was a truly creative artist, he modified it to suit his own expressive needs, finding a way to use the form to represent his uniquely personal style. This, in fact, is what is meant by the word "style," the unique combination of practices which together comprise a composer's characteristic personal means of expression, each composer's style being viewed in relation to the common practices of the time.

Often, in a binary form, closely related keys other than those indicated in Figure 27 may be used, particularly in the second section shortly past the middle of the movement. This increases the key contrast and adds variety—very important to a movement that uses only one basic thematic idea. In listening to movements in binary form, particularly those written during the middle of the eighteenth century, you will notice that many of them, at the point indicated by the asterisk in the diagram, contain a clear-cut return to the tonic, presenting the material in almost exactly the same way that it was presented at the beginning of the movement. The material from the beginning of the second section up to this point has the nature of a transition to this return as though its purpose were nothing more than to modulate from the dominant to the tonic so that the material could be presented in this way. Esthetically, this has the effect of rounding out the form, of returning to something that was presented earlier in almost exactly the same manner in which it was first presented. This kind of binary form can be called rounded binary form, and is very important in the evolution of a single-movement form to be discussed later, the sonata form.

Using only one basic motive or thematic idea works well for movements of short duration but for longer movements composers have usually used two or more contrasting themes. One of the simplest forms utilizing two musical ideas is three-part or ternary form. A great many relatively short movements of the eighteenth and nineteenth centuries were written in this form. It is frequently represented by the letters ABA, the first A referring to the presentation of the first section or musical idea, B referring to a second section based on a different, usually contrasting, musical idea, and the final A being a restatement, with or without modification, of the material presented in the first section. If the final A is an exact repetition of the first A, it is usually not written out again in the notated music. Rather, the words *da capo al fine* (Italian: Go to the beginning and then to the end) are placed at the end of the B section, thus directing the performer to return to the beginning and play the final A section from the same music used for the first A section. Movements using this device are sometimes called *da capo* forms and one of the most common of these is the minuet and trio. (Usually its name is shortened to minuet.) It originated during the baroque period as a stylized dance in triple meter, but its use specifically as a dance began to be abandoned during the classical period in favor of a more purely musical function. It is composed in two sections with the first section (minuet) played again after the second section (trio) by means of the da capo device. In the classical minuet and trio each of the two sections is a rounded binary form so that actually it is a composite form built out of two short movements, each like the one diagrammed in Figure 27. In performing the da capo, or final statement of the minuet section, the repeat signs are traditionally not observed so that the final A section is only half as long as it was on its initial presentation. There is a good common-sense reason for this. Having heard both parts of the A section repeated on its first presentation, it would be quite superfluous and perhaps monotonous to play them more than once on the da capo. The numbers and arrows in Figure 28 illustrate the sequence of repetitions in the minuet.

Figure 28.

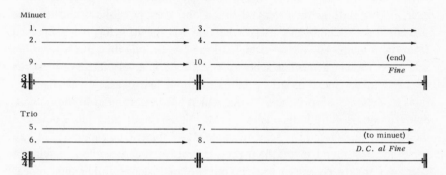

In the classical period the minuet was used most typically as the third movement of four-movement works such as symphonies and string quartets and occasionally as a movement of shorter works. Its typical form can be observed in numerous compositions by Haydn, Mozart, Beethoven, and many other composers of the late eighteenth and early nineteenth centuries. In listening to these movements you will find that you will be able, with a little practice, to follow the progress of the music so that you know exactly where you are at any point in the form. By increasing your perception of the cadence points, the points of full or partial repose, the musical meaning of the phrases and sections will become clearer. The diagram in Figure 28 may be helpful for this. As· your experience with minuets broadens, you will observe that, in spite of the seemingly rigid restrictions of the formal pattern, a minuet can be imbued with a great deal of individuality and character. Haydn, for example, did some truly remarkable things with the minuet form, sometimes, through his rhythmic ingenuity, producing startling or humorous effects, and at other times evoking somber, majestic, or exciting moods by harmonic means or by tempo indications. Beethoven frequently indicated unusually fast tempos for his minuets and generally altered the form so that in his later works a new form evolved from the minuet—the scherzo. During the romantic period this new form began to supplant the minuet in four-movement works and was used in unique ways by composers such as Mendelssohn, Brahms, and Berlioz.

The word "scherzo" is simply the Italian word for joke or jest and was used as a title for pieces of music long before the evolution of the scherzo as a form. Haydn, in a set of six four-movement string quartets composed in 1781 (Op. 33), had applied the title to each of the minuets in the opus. They are not scherzos in the true sense of the word, as used in the romantic period, but are simply rather light, whimsical minuets. The title was, however, appropriate to their general mood and very possibly established the precedent for Beethoven's use of the title for the new form that evolved from the minuet. The line of demarcation in separating the minuet from the scherzo is rather vague. The scherzo is generally in a very fast 3/4 meter as opposed to the more moderate minuet tempo, and characteristically contains elements of surprise and humor which are not essential to the minuet. Scherzos are usually longer than typical minuets and often more developmental in character. In a scherzo some development or modification can sometimes be found in the final presentation of the A section, making it necessary for the composer to write out the final section rather than repeat it by means of the da capo device. Also, in some scherzos, the form incorporates a second statement of the trio, or even a second trio based on new material followed by a third statement of the A section forming an ABABA or ABACA pattern. In some instances the scherzo veers away from the whimsical and playful toward a more serious, even ominous, kind of humor as in the scherzo of Beethoven's Fifth Symphony. Although its internal structure, with a few significant exceptions, is similar to the minuet, one thinks of the scherzo as a phenomenon of the romantic period while the minuet is associated primarily with the eighteenth century.

Before beginning a discussion of the single-movement form known as sonata form, it is important to understand the various meanings and uses of the term sonata. In speaking of "a sonata" the term is used generically to mean an instrumental composition of a more or less serious nature, in several separate movements (usually three or four), the several movements intended to be played consecutively in a set order, together forming the complete composition. In this sense the term is most commonly applied to works for solo instruments or for a single instrument combined with piano. Compositions in three or four movements for larger groups, such as a symphony or string quartet, actually might be called sonatas, though in these cases the name of the medium (symphony or string quartet) is usually applied in place of the term sonata. A Haydn or Mozart symphony is actually a sonata for symphony orchestra, just as a string quartet or trio is actually a sonata for a particular combination of instruments. The term sonata, however, in its normal usage, is applied only to compositions for one or two instruments.

Another usage of the word sonata is in the term "trio sonata." As mentioned earlier, the trio sonata is not a form but a medium, and was used a great deal in baroque chamber music. It consists of two solo instruments, typically a combination of violins, flutes, or oboes, and a continuo group including a keyboard instrument and a bass instrument, so that actually four instruments are involved. The term does not imply any particular form, though certainly the binary form was very typical for chamber music movements of the Baroque.

The terms *sonata da chiesa* (church sonata) and *sonata da camera* (chamber sonata) indicate two specific patterns for the arrangement of movements of sonatas composed during the baroque period. The sonata da chiesa was a sonata of four movements, their tempos alternating, slow-fast-slow-fast. Each of the movements was in binary form with a more or less serious mood prevailing. Typical church sonatas were written by most baroque composers with particularly notable examples to be found in the instrumental music of Vivaldi, Corelli, J. S. Bach, and Handel.

The sonata da camera is more secular in nature. Each of the movements utilizes a specific stylized dance rhythm and for this reason is also called the dance suite or simply "suite." In the eighteenth century it was, like the church sonata, based on an established pattern of four movements, each in binary form. In the late baroque the dances used were the allemande, courante, sarabande, and gigue arranged in that order. Figure 29 shows the meters and rhythmic characteristics of the various dances.

Figure 29.

Allemande:	Duple meter, moderate tempo
Courante:	Triple meter, fast "running" tempo
Sarabande:	Triple meter, slow, with a heavy second beat
Gigue (Jig):	Duple meter with a triplet background or fast triple meter, most typically 6/8, fast

Two additional movements were often used in the suite, a prelude, frequently in a rather free form at the very beginning, and a da capo dance form such as the minuet, gavotte, or bourée inserted between the sarabande and gigue. This brought the total number of movements to six.

The single-movement form called sonata form or sonata-allegro form began its development in the eighteenth century. Its pattern of sections and key relationships remained quite constant throughout the classical period and well into the nineteenth century. This pattern is illustrated in Figure 30.

Figure 30.

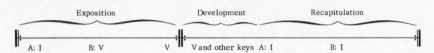

A sonata form in its simplest pattern showing its relationship to binary form

A comparison of the above diagram with the diagram of binary form presented in Figure 27 (p. 59) will show that the sonata form is really a further expansion or evolution of binary form, one important difference being that sonata form, because of its greater length, uses several thematic ideas, whereas a simple binary form often uses only one. The use of a second contrasting thematic group (second tonal group) in the exposition furnishes thematic as well as tonal contrast and, incidentally, results in this section being much longer than it was in the earlier binary form.

The section in Figure 27 from the double bar at the beginning of the second section to the asterisk is also expanded in sonata form to the extent that it becomes something more than simply a transition back to the key of the tonic. In sonata form it becomes a development section—the area in which the real action and conflict of the musical drama takes place. So important does the development section become that, by the beginning of the nineteenth century, the form often appears to be organized in three important sections (exposition, development, and recapitulation) though its origin as a two-part form remains apparent. In the development, the material presented in the exposition is handled in various ways—unfolded, elaborated upon, and transformed by means of the developmental techniques of the composer. Traditionally, the development section begins with the thematic material of the first tonal group, after which the other thematic material of the exposition may gradually be woven into the fabric. Virtually anything may happen in the development, for it is here that the composer demonstrates the finest aspects of his craft as well as the heights and depths of his musical creativity—ideally without losing sight of the esthetic, dramatic, and musical effect of the movement as a whole. At the end of the development it is usual, particularly in Beethoven, to find a more or less sizable section that dwells exclusively upon the dominant of the key in which the sonata is written, thus building up a feeling of suspense and expectation for the recapitulation which follows.

The recapitulation is comparable to the return in a rounded binary form (asterisk in Figure 27) and has the same effect of rounding out the form by returning to the original presentation of the material used in the exposition. The second tonal group and closing group, which were presented in a contrasting key in the exposition, are now in the tonic, emphasizing the home tonality as the movement nears its finish. One of the great beauties of a sonata form is the effect of hearing the basic thematic elements of the movement presented in the recapitulation in almost the identical manner in which they were presented in the exposition, but hearing them *after* the many facets of their character have been presented in the development section. Because we have heard the themes and motives unfold, develop, and reveal their interrelationships, their final appearance acquires a significance far different from that of their first presentation.

Frequently the sonata form is preceded by a slow introduction, particularly when the sonata movement is the first movement of a symphony of large proportions. The introduction invariably ends on the dominant and has the effect of setting the stage for the movement proper, pausing momentarily to enhance the feeling of expectation and suspense before the opening of the sonata-allegro form itself. When a slow introduction is used, it is considered a part of the total movement rather than a separate entity. The first movements of both the First and Second Symphonies of Beethoven are good examples.

At the end of the movement, a section called the coda is often added to the sonata form. It occurs after a logical cadence on the tonic has been reached near the end of the movement and serves to round out the form, even though the movement may seem nearly complete without it. The closing section of Beethoven's Fifth Symphony is a good example of a coda that functions architecturally in the symphony as a whole. There is no doubt that the music reaches a convincing cadence in the home tonality some time before the end of the symphony. The many repetitions of the tonic triad which bring the finale to its triumphant close are necessary in a work of such large proportions to create a feeling of satisfactory culmination in the total work.

Sonata form, evolving from binary form and continuing up to the present, has been the most important single-movement instrumental form for a period of over two hundred years. It is not surprising then, that many composers of today still rely upon it as a basic pattern proven useful by a vast number of their predecessors. In tracing its evolution from the earliest examples, it becomes apparent that several features of the form have remained constant as if they possessed a universal application, though each composer has attempted to bring to the form something that represented his own style.

Some of the earliest examples of sonata form were written during the second quarter of the eighteenth century, referred to as the preclassical or rococo period. The first movement of the *Trio Sonata in G Major* (*Sonata No. 3*) by G. B. Pergolesi (1710–1736) is a good example of a simple preclassical form that has all the characteristics of a rounded binary form as well as those of a classical sonata form. Among the features that make it a sonata form is the presence of a second tonal group (second theme) in the key of the dominant (D major) when it first appears in the exposition (or first section of the binary form), returning at the end of the movement in the home tonality of G major in the classical pattern of the sonata form. It is true that the development section does not really develop the material, but simply restates it in the dominant with a few modifications. Nevertheless, this movement has all the harmonic characteristics of a typical classical sonata movement, for all of the sections are present and all of them are in the traditional key relationships.

In listening to this delightful movement you will find that it is not difficult to follow its form in terms of the diagram in Figure 30. Listen first of all to the phrase structure, noticing the effect of thrust conveyed by the single phrases and the varying effects of the cadences at the ends of the phrases. Then, extending this further, you will begin to hear less obvious features of the structure, for example, a phrase that begins before the preceding phrase is completely finished. An elision like this occurs at the very beginning of the second theme. Remember that music is heard first of all in its smaller components, and only after the phrase structure is understood can the listener go on to experience the fuller meaning of the total movement.

Listen next to a sonata movement by Haydn or Mozart such as the first movement of a symphony or string quartet. It will not be difficult to see how it is related to earlier sonata forms of the type just discussed, but many differences will also be apparent. The Mozart or Haydn movement will have a longer exposition that is expanded by the use of transitional material between the tonal groups and also by the frequent addition of a third thematic group (often called the closing theme) which rounds out the shape of the exposition just before the beginning of the development section. The double bar repeat sign at the end of the exposition continues to be found in sonata forms up to the end of the romantic period, a vestige of the baroque binary form from which it evolved. This, incidentally, is something of a convenience for score readers since the double bar marks the beginning of the development section. The development section also is considerably larger and functions differently for, toward the end of the eighteenth century, composers began to learn how to develop small motives in a manner that was quite new. Haydn particularly developed this skill, and it was through him that the technique of thematic or motivic structure and development was passed on to Beethoven who used it to create effects of tremendous musical and emotional impact.

This technique of motivic development can be seen by examining the first movement of Haydn's *Symphony No. 104,* the *London* symphony. After the slow introduction, the first tonal group begins with a delightfully lyrical theme in the key of D major. Neither this theme nor any other theme from the exposition is actually presented in the development section for it is built, not out of a complete theme, but out of a terse six-note motive extracted from the melody first presented at the beginning of the exposition. Haydn truly unfolds the possibilities inherent in this short fragment for it is passed among many instruments of the orchestra in a highly wrought contrapuntal texture, and it appears in many different harmonic contexts. Then, when the complete lyrical theme returns at the beginning of the recapitulation, it has a different effect than it did in the exposition even though it is presented in exactly the same way. The development section has revealed the multifaceted character of that tiny fragment so that, when we hear it in its original setting, it acquires a new and wonderful meaning.

As we proceed further and examine sonata forms of the romantic period we will see that composers of the nineteenth century, though still using the same basic pattern, expanded the sonata form and attempted to imbue it with greater emotional content, as well as occasional literary and even philosophical overtones. Still, the pattern of key sections and relationships often remained quite close to the classical concept. The first movement of the *Symphony No. 2* by Johannes Brahms (1833–1897) is a good movement to examine from this point of view. Written in the key of D major, the first tonal group is in the home tonality and the second tonal group is in the key of the dominant, A major. The singing, lyrical theme with which the second tonal group begins is easy to follow in its progress throughout the movement and, when it returns in the recapitulation, is back in the home tonality of D major. This and many other features of the movement follow the classical sonata form pattern, even including the double bar repeat sign found at the end of the exposition. In performance this repeat may or may not be observed as the conductor may decide, though it remains in the notated music, reminding us of the simple binary form from which the sonata form evolved.

The expansion of the various sections of sonata form advanced by Beethoven continued through the romantic period so that by the end of the nineteenth century a typical sonata form was considerably longer than in the eighteenth century. Also, the harmonic relationships between the various sections became increasingly free as late nineteenth century composers developed new ways to use the element of harmony. With so many liberties being taken with the form, it would seem likely that the basic pattern might disappear altogether or evolve into a form more suitable to the needs of the newer music. New forms did develop, but the sonata form continued to be used as well. Certain features of the sonata form pattern were found to be so useful that it has continued to be used by many composers even up to the present. Essentially what remained in the twentieth century was the sectional pattern of exposition, development, and recapitulation with the development section frequently being the most important section of the form. The idea of contrasting keys between the thematic groups is such a basic concept that it too continued to influence the practice of twentieth century composers, although this contrast was no longer effected by means of the old tonic-dominant relationship. Rather, it began to be supplanted by new harmonic idioms as the twentieth century, even more than the nineteenth, became fertile ground for harmonic experimentation.

Before discussing the manner in which the sonata form fits into the overall plan of a composition of several movements, it is appropriate to discuss another single-movement form, the rondo. The characteristic unifying feature of a rondo is the repetition of an A section, called the rondo theme, with contrasting material placed between these recurrences. All of the statements of the A section are characteristically in the tonic and are usually almost identical to each other, though contrast is sometimes created by slight modifications in the length or texture of the rondo theme in its repetitions. The material placed between the statements of the rondo theme is usually quite different in character from the rondo theme, and achieves further contrast by being placed in keys which contrast to the home tonality, such as the dominant or relative major. These sections are called episodes and, in addition to furnishing contrast, serve as transitional passages between the recurrences of the rondo theme.

The final movement of J. S. Bach's *Violin Concerto in E Major* is an excellent example of a simple rondo. Its form is particularly clear to the listener because the rondo theme or A section is always played by the full string orchestra while the episodes are played by the solo violin accompanied by only a few instruments. Its form can be diagrammed with the letters ABACADA. After listening to it, examine the structure of the rondo theme. By careful listening you will note that it is a very symmetrical theme, quite self-contained, and similar in form to the folk tune discussed in Chapter Two (Figure 15). Actually it, like the folk tune, is a sixteen-measure double period and, because of its clear outline, seems to stand out in relief against the more freely treated episodic sections. To make some generalizations about rondo themes, they usually have a clear-cut phrase structure, are self-contained, and are often light and simple in character. The rondo is a typically classical form though it continued to be used throughout the nineteenth century and even in the twentieth. Since it is not as serious or complex a form as sonata form, it finds its ideal expression in moods of lightness or wit. It is frequently used as the final movement of compositions of three or four movements.

The diagram in Figure 31 illustrates the pattern of movements frequently used in four-movement sonatas (symphonies, string quartets, trios, etc.) of the eighteenth and nineteenth centuries.

Figure 31.

First Movement: Sonata form, frequently with a slow introduction. Fast tempo.

Second Movement: Slow, lyrical, various forms such as sonatina (a diminutive sonata form), theme and variations, or rondo.

Third Movement: Minuet and trio, often supplanted by the scherzo during the romantic era.

Fourth Movement: Rondo, sonata form, or theme and variations.

A classical symphony or any composition in the classical sonata genre is a single entity or unified group of movements. For this reason there is always a strong tonal relationship between the various movements. The first, third, and fourth movements are usually composed on the same tonal center while the second movement uses a contrasting key, frequently the subdominant. Composers of the romantic period often added another unifying factor by using thematic material from the first movement in later movements, lending a feeling of development from movement to movement. Compositions utilizing this device are said to be cyclical in form. This led to the twentieth century practice of composing symphonies and sonatas in one movement with large divisions corresponding to movements, but with no pause between.

Another important multimovement form is the concerto. Concertos of the classical and romantic periods are usually three-movement compositions, although there are four-movement examples. A concerto is a composition for orchestra and virtuoso soloist (or soloists) featuring the solo instrument to great advantage in brilliant, often very difficult, passage work. To display the skill and artistry of the soloist is only part of the story, however, for the best concertos are also of great musical value. During the nineteenth century many virtuoso performers made a practice of composing concertos intended as vehicles to display their own phenomenal technical skill. As might be expected, many of these works lacked, in varying degrees, the most important fundamental factor—real musical meaning and significance. A few pieces of this sort by composers such as Wieniawski, Czerny, and Bernhard Romberg are still heard occasionally, but are used primarily as training pieces for student performers. Among the works of Mozart, Beethoven, and Brahms are many superb examples of concertos which, though excellent as display pieces, are, more importantly, great pieces of music.

The finest concertos of the classical and romantic periods used the piano, violin, or cello as the solo instrument. The first movement is normally in sonata form, often with a double exposition. Essentially, a double exposition consists of two presentations of the exposition material, the first by the orchestra, and the second, in modified form, by the soloist. Double expositions are much more characteristic of the classical period than of the romantic. The second movement is traditionally in a slow tempo, allowing the solo instrument to demonstrate its lyrical capabilities, while the last movement is often a brilliant rondo. Other features of the form, such as the use of trills and cadenzas, will be discussed later.

As the romantic era reached its height, new forms and harmonic idioms began to develop, many of which were tied up directly with nineteenth century trends in art, literature, and philosophy. Many composers veered away from the purely musical expression of the classical period toward styles that attempted to fuse music with the other arts, particularly with literature. Virtually all composers felt the impact of this movement in one way or another, but it can be seen most clearly in works such as the music dramas of Richard Wagner or in the symphonic tone poems of Berlioz, Liszt, and Richard Strauss. The nineteenth century tone poem was a flexible form in which the arrangement of the musical material and, in fact, the character of the material itself, was dictated by a work of literature or poetry, frequently a piece of fiction or a folk legend. The idea was to evoke literary images in the mind of the listener by purely musical means—to tell a story in music without the use of words. Wagner, in his operas and music dramas, developed a style in which each character was represented by a particular musical motive or theme called a leitmotif. The progress of the drama could then be followed within the musical texture by the action and interaction of these motives. The singers on the stage were merely the exteriorization of the real action which was taking place in the orchestra. This technique was also used by composers of symphonic tone poems, particularly by Richard Strauss, whose music is most representative of the tone poem concept. In order to have greater coloristic and dramatic means, Strauss greatly expanded the orchestra, frequently using woodwinds in fours rather than pairs, sometimes using as many as eight horns, and often doubling the size of the string section.

Although the form of each tone poem was dictated to some extent by the piece of literature upon which it was based, the best examples are works in which principles of musical form are more important than the story or "program" so that the composition has a valid musical meaning as well as a literary basis. In a sense then, the literary aspects of a piece of program music are irrelevant to its musical value. Music is at its best when it is just music and the tone poems in today's symphonic repertoire are, for the most part, works which can be listened to and enjoyed from a purely musical point of view regardless of the fact that they were intended to have an extramusical meaning.

The twentieth century has seen such a diversity of trends and movements in the art of musical composition that it is difficult to make any valid generalizations regarding form in contemporary music. Many composers have clung to the old classical patterns, attempting to infuse them with new meaning by using new harmonic practices or by experimenting with new orchestral combinations and colors. The *Pulcinella Suite* of Stravinsky or the *Classical Symphony* of Prokoviev are good examples of this approach, which has come to be known as neoclassicism. Other twentieth century compositions manifest great freedom of form, the composers abandoning preconceived patterns by applying basic structural principles in refreshing new ways. The twelve-tone or "serial" technique developed by the composer Arnold Schoenberg (1874–1951) has given today's composers a new way to organize harmonic materials, resulting in an increasing abandonment of the triadic concept of harmony. Since all of the forms of the two hundred years preceding this century were in some way governed by the old concept of tonality, the serial technique has necessitated the development of new structural techniques.

It is important to remember that every composition has its own form. Regardless of the fact that many composers began with a basic preconceived pattern that had been used previously, each musical idea demands its own particular kind of treatment and makes its own path through the course of a piece of music. A certain skeletal pattern such as sonata or rondo form may be discernible in the structure, but each piece of music forms its own unique pattern as well. In listening to a piece of music, it is of some value to know whether it should be called a binary form or a rondo. But it is much more important to be aware of the vital musical events that are occurring within the time span of the piece—to feel the flux of tension and relaxation, to perceive the varying effects of the cadences, and to be carried along with the motion of the musical phrase.

LISTENING SUGGESTIONS

Eine Kleine Nachtmusik	Mozart
Trio Sonatas, Op. 6	Corelli
French Suites	J. S. Bach
English Suites	J. S. Bach
Trio Sonata in G Major (*No. 3*)	Pergolesi
String Quartet in G Major, K. 387	Mozart
Symphony No. 104 (*London*)	Haydn
Scherzo from *Symphony No. 9*	Beethoven
Symphony No. 2	Brahms
Violin Concerto in E Major	J. S. Bach
Piano Concerto in C Major, K. 503	Mozart
Tone Poem: *Till Eulenspiegel*	Richard Strauss
Classical Symphony	Prokoviev
Pulcinella Suite	Stravinsky

SUGGESTED ASSIGNMENTS

1. Discuss characteristics that the various temporal arts have in common.
2. Discuss the means of achieving unity and contrast in the temporal arts other than music.
3. Listen to a simple variation form (such as the slow movement of the Haydn String Quartet, Op. 76, No. 3) noting how the theme persists from variation to variation. Attempt to describe the means of varying each successive repetition of the theme.
4. Discuss *development* as it appears in the various temporal arts.
5. In the music we have listened to, find examples of each of the several means of achieving musical contrast.
6. Listen to several binary forms and minuets, following the progress of the music in terms of Figures 27 and 28.
7. Discuss the various usages of the term sonata.
8. Practice listening by carefully following the progress of the music in several sonata-allegro forms.
9. Using reference material recommended by the instructor, investigate the various types of rondo forms.
10. As a special project, try to use the analogy of drama to music in relation to the various musical forms discussed in this chapter.

FIVE

PERFORMANCE, INTERPRETATION, AND MEANING IN MUSIC

The performer, as the final agent in the process of bringing music to its full realization in sound, is the person with whom the audience is most directly concerned. It is not difficult, in the midst of an exciting virtuoso performance, to forget the part played by the other persons involved in the musical process—musicologists, editors, copyists, and many others, all the way back to the composer himself. Perhaps this is as it should be. Certainly it is the end toward which they all are aiming, for music in its final form involves no one except the performer and his audience.

Performers vary in their relationship to their audiences. Some, through their personal charm, are skillful in establishing a mood of rapport or even of intimacy. Others remain completely aloof on the concert stage, letting the music speak for itself, while others are more inclined toward a kind of musical showmanship. There is something to be said in favor of all of these attitudes and some performers use all of them. Ideally, the concert virtuoso is a performer of phenomenal technical skill, deep musical understanding, and consummate artistry.

The virtuoso concept as we know it today began in the nineteenth century as an aspect of romanticism in music, perhaps related to the "hero concept" of that period. There were, of course, numerous performers of earlier centuries whose technical skill and musical excellence were legendary, but none whose attraction could compare with the romantic figure who, in about 1820, began to take Europe by storm, Niccolò Paganini (1782–1840). This great violinist-composer wielded a demoniac power over his audiences unequaled by any performer before or after. It was he who inspired the pianist-composer Franz Liszt (1811–1886) to attempt to bring the same kind of incredible perfection to his art and, if possible, to

74

surpass it. Fabulous, heroic, enchanting figures, these nineteenth century performers—so attractive that even today our audiences tend at times to think of concert artists in highly romanticized terms.

Actually, there is considerable drudgery involved in the art of performing music. Aside from the fact that a performer must spend years perfecting his technical skill and musical understanding, there is a great deal of spade work involved in every separate performance. A performing artist of integrity, in reading a score, will do his best to follow the indications of the composer but, since musical notation often only approximates the intended sound, there are times when the performer must make his own decisions regarding interpretation. Knowledge of the performing practices of the time in which the piece of music was composed can greatly add to his interpretive insight. Thus, writings by musicologists relating to the appropriate period are among the performer's most valuable resources.

While most conscientious performers will to some extent avail themselves of such resources, a completely scholarly approach is undesirable and might possibly result in dry, academic performances. Good performers, through experience, develop also an instinctive approach that can be most valuable in solving problems of interpretation. Both approaches are valid and useful, but neither should exclude the other. The ideal performer achieves a delicate balance between the rational and the intuitive and also brings something of his own creative gift to each performance.

A performer's conception of a piece of music depends upon (1) the objective knowledge that he brings to the printed notation as set down by the composer, (2) his subjective interpretation of the notation in terms of his own musical talent and experience, and (3) the influence of his own unique personality upon that interpretation.

The quality and effect of the actual performance depends upon (1) the technical skill of the performer to bring his conception of the work to its ultimate realization in sound, (2) the acoustical situation, (3) unpredictable but important factors having to do with such things as audience rapport and general mood.

With so many variables it is no wonder that two performances of the same work can differ so radically. This is, of course, one of the exciting aspects of live performances, for audiences would soon grow weary if they were required to hear repeated identical performances of even the greatest pieces of music. On some occasions a gifted performer can bring to even a mediocre composition a meaning that it did not formerly possess. The performer, like the composer, is a creative artist. He knows always that his role is to present the composer's ideas but, since he is a unique personality, he will ofttimes bring a new shading to the composer's original conception. Such shadings, provided that they are conceived with integrity and with responsibility toward the printed notation, make the music come alive and make every performance a unique experience.

Let us examine some of the ways in which musical notation is necessarily restricted to an approximation of the sounds heard in actual performance. Our system of notating pitches is based on the equally tempered scale, that is, a division of the octave into twelve equal half steps. Keyboard instruments today are tuned according to this system. The system, however, is a compromise, for no player of a wind or stringed instrument can possibly adhere strictly to equal temperament when playing in an ensemble. Good intonation (playing in tune) in an ensemble is accomplished by treating each pitch in terms of the whole group of instruments or voices and according to the harmonic context of that pitch. For example, the half step between the seventh and eighth scale degrees in the diatonic scale is normally a smaller half step than that found on the piano, while the whole step between the fourth and fifth scale degrees is larger than the tempered whole step. These differences are slight but exceedingly important to the problem of achieving good intonation in an ensemble. We accept tempered tuning in terms of the piano and organ because our ears are acclimated to hearing this kind of intonation in terms of the timbre of these instruments but we would never accept tempered tuning in, for example, a string quartet. A fine performer develops the skill of playing in tune to the point that it becomes second nature to him, so instinctive that in some instances he cannot define or is perhaps not even aware of the subtle deviations that he makes from the tempered scale. A system of notation incorporating all of these infinitely subtle shadings is not even theoretically possible and would be necessarily so complex as to be totally impractical.

Much the same thing applies to our system of indicating tempo, perhaps to an even greater degree. Tempo markings such as allegro (fast), presto (very fast), or ritard (slow down) are relative terms and it is quite possible to have several interpretations of such markings. A more accurate way to indicate tempo is by using metronome markings which indicate the number of pulses or beats per minute. This also has its shortcomings, for a performance which adhered with mathematical strictness to a metronomic pulse would sound very dry and mechanical. The metronome marking is a great aid to the performer, for it gives him a specific idea of the general range of tempo that the composer had in mind, but it can never be interpreted strictly throughout a given passage. The performer breathes life into the rhythm by taking slight but very meaningful liberties with the beat at certain points. Although the metronome has been in use since the time of Beethoven, the old Italian markings continue to be used, frequently in combination with metronome markings. To musicians, the Italian markings have the advantage of possessing strong connotations of mood and spirit as well as tempo.

The notation of the rhythm of the music—its durations, accents, and cross accents—is relatively accurate but here also it is often desirable that the performer take certain subtle liberties in order that the music will have a kind of vitality much more significant than that which would result from a strictly mechanical interpretation. Dynamic markings, as well, are only relative; and it is up to the performer to decide what the composer means when he indicates *forte, piano,* or *diminuendo.*

With so many approximations in our present system of musical notation, it would seem that the poor composer is at the mercy of the performer, and perhaps sometimes he is; yet it must be remembered that the composer, often a performer as well, is thoroughly acquainted with the traditions and conventions of interpretation practiced by his contemporaries. He knows, within a reasonable range of possibility, what the result will be in performance when he uses a certain indication. Since these traditions and conventions gradually change as they are passed down from generation to generation, it is often important that the performer be acquainted with performance practices of earlier periods. He should know, for example,

that the notation for a dotted rhythm (♩.♪   ) during the baroque period

meant something quite different from what it means today, and that this meaning varied with the context of the music. He should know what Mozart meant when he wrote *dolce* and what Wagner meant when he wrote *Zart*—in addition to the literal translations of these words. Obviously, the area of performance practices is so vast that often the performer's ready knowledge is not sufficient to cope with a problem. In such instances he must form his decision from knowledge furnished by editors or in the writings of musicologists, in combination with his own musical insight.

This does not necessarily mean that today's performers should try to perform a composition of the past in exactly the same manner that it was performed during the composer's lifetime, for this would often be impractical if not impossible. Instruments have changed, in some cases vastly improved, and it would be pointless to perform on an inferior instrument simply for the sake of academic accuracy. Audiences have also changed and we cannot possibly be fully aware of the differences in response between today's concertgoers and those of past generations. Thus, though performance practice of the past is an important consideration, the performer must interpret and modify this factor to achieve a degree of compatibility with the instruments, performers, and audiences of today. The integrity of today's concert artist rests in part upon his ability to maintain an honest link with the past while performing meaningfully for audiences of the present. To do this he must be equipped, ideally, with the ability to see and hear music as the composer does and, in fact, to have a considerable knowledge of the composer's art. Mozart said that the performer should play as if he were the composer. Today, with our vast repertoire spanning several centuries, this is much more difficult to do than in Mozart's time. Today's concert artist must be a kind of paragon who, though primarily a performer, must also have a rather extensive knowledge of the other branches of the science and art of music.

The performer who relies most heavily upon this kind of versatility is the conductor. He stands very high in the musical hierarchy. It is he who is most prominent among the performers at a symphony orchestra concert and it is he who accepts the lion's share of the applause when it is over. Does he deserve such acclaim? What are the duties he performs that entitle him to a position of such distinction?

Actually, for a given performance, most of his work is already done when he appears on the stage at the beginning of a concert. Whether the performing group is a symphony orchestra, a chorus, or a smaller ensemble, a large portion of his time has been spent in rehearsal preparing for the concert. At the rehearsals the conductor's job is one of coordination and interpretation. First, he must see that all the instruments and voices necessary for a specific composition are assembled and prepared to rehearse at the appointed time. He must see that the orchestral and vocal parts are ready and in some cases he must look them over, putting in his own interpretive markings to assist the performer. If the piece to be performed involves an important part for a soloist, either instrumental or vocal, he will usually confer with the artist prior to the first rehearsal in order to understand more fully the soloist's conception of the work, and to reach an understanding regarding tempos and other details of the composition in order to save time at the full rehearsals. For compositions of particularly vast proportions involving an unusually large number of performers, such as an opera, he may rehearse in smaller groups, meeting separately with soloists, chorus, and orchestra before meeting the total group in full rehearsal. He may call upon vocal coaches or assistant conductors to help him by taking over some of these smaller rehearsals. For the more co-ordinative aspects of his work he may also have assistance from persons such as organizational librarians and managers, but he alone is responsible for the final interpretation of the music.

At the rehearsals he must convey his conception of the composition to the performers. Since the instrumentalists themselves may have their own clear-cut conceptions of their own parts as well as of the total work, it is often necessary for the conductor to pull these varying ideas together into a meaningful whole. Obviously, it is important that the conductor be a fluent and articulate man as well as knowledgeable. In a sense he is very much on the spot, presuming, as he does, to stand in front of a large group of his peers and assume the role of leader. Many of the players in our professional orchestras are distinguished virtuosos in their own right and it is understandable that they might be quite critical of the man who stands on the podium of their orchestra. They have been known to demonstrate their opinion of him by very devious means. Many a young conductor has been utterly demolished by such orchestra players' tricks as playing a few slightly wrong notes in order to test his acuity, perception, and knowledge of the score. A successful conductor must command the respect of his orchestra by virtue of his musical knowledge, technical skill, and innate talent. It does not necessarily follow that he must also be well liked by his players, for few professional conductors can say that they are universally esteemed by the members of their orchestras. Many conductors will occa-sionally consult with key players in the orchestra, particularly with the concertmaster, regarding questions of interpretation that pertain directly to the performer's instrument. The concertmaster may often be the con-ductor's right-hand man as well as the primary representative of the orches-tra, often assisting with phrasing and bowing in the strings. One of the most important things achieved at rehearsal is the establishment of a proper dynamic balance between all of the instruments so that the right instrument can be heard at the right time to bring out the most important feature at a given moment. The players themselves will do their best to achieve the proper dynamic level, but seated in the midst of the orchestra it is often difficult to hear everything in the proper perspective. The conductor, from his vantage point, is better able to hear and control the balance among the various sections. Traditionally, he uses his left hand to indicate degrees of loudness while his right hand, holding the baton, is used to beat time. Many conductors depart from this practice in one way or another in their own characteristic conducting style.

After the final rehearsal, most of the conductor's work has already been completed, yet there remains the most important thing of all—the performance. Ideally, the performance should be the final synthesis of everything learned at rehearsals but made more vital and intense by virtue of the fact that it is, indeed, a performance. The presence of the audience adds that extra ounce of nervous energy necessary to infuse the musicians with the kind of artistic vitality that produces first-rate performances. The conductor's function at the performance is primarily to guide the ensemble along the same lines developed at rehearsal, sometimes to inspire by means of his attitude and facial expression, and to "cue" (signal) difficult entries to the players (or, if necessary, to rescue a player who has lost his place in the music).

The professional symphony orchestra conductor of today holds a position of the greatest prestige in the world of music. In many cities much of the musical activity centers around him so that he may become a kind of musical mentor of the community. In addition to his artistic responsibilities, he is often involved in such activities as public relations and personnel for the orchestra. In spite of these demands upon his time, he must continue to study scores in preparation for performances and to maintain a vast repertoire of standard works. Professional conductors today usually conduct without score, which means that every note of each score must be memorized. As a prerequisite, a conductor must be thoroughly familiar with the standard repertoire but in addition there are always new works for him to learn which, in many instances, have interpretive problems far more demanding than those of the standard repertoire.

The difficulties involved in a task so broad and varied are exceeded in no other kind of musical performance except perhaps in that of the solo concert virtuoso. The concert soloist's task is at least as demanding as that of the conductor. The repertoire is just as broad and must be learned just as thoroughly but, in addition, a physical discipline infinitely more complex and refined than that of conducting is required of the instrumental or vocal virtuoso. As a rule he begins to study music in childhood, often at a remarkably early age. This is particularly necessary for the stringed instruments and piano, for without early development of reflex and agility, the more difficult repertoire for these instruments would be completely out of reach. The present concert repertoire is so vast that many of today's concert performers specialize in a relatively small part of it. A pianist, for example, may wish to concentrate his efforts on the keyboard music of J. S. Bach, while a cellist or violinist may be particularly interested in the sonata literature for his instrument. Nevertheless, there are certain standard repertoire pieces for each instrument that every performer on that instrument is expected to learn if he wishes to make a career as a concert virtuoso. As if the physical and mental discipline were not enough, he must also develop the musical maturity and understanding necessary for meaningful communication with his audience.

In performing music for an audience, a soloist or an ensemble establishes a kind of communion between performer and audience. Something of importance or of beauty is communicated to the listener. If the music is by a composer of the past, then this communication extends into the past, usually modified in some way by the interpretation of the performer. In such cases it is safe to assume that the music has a universal appeal, that some aspect of it is as meaningful to present audiences as it was to those of the past. It is very difficult to speak about these universally meaningful aspects of music. Music is not a language in the ordinary sense, for it lacks the precision of meaning conveyed by words. It can, of course, reinforce associated literary or poetic meanings such as the text of a piece of vocal music or the "program" of a symphonic tone poem; but there is a much more significant and powerful meaning in music than that found in its association with words. Music, in fact, is capable of creating an emotional mood or meaning much more efficiently than either words or pictures. It can awaken the most powerful and universal emotions and, in this sense, indeed, music is a language—a language utilizing a powerful, explicit, and colorful vocabulary of tones. In evoking broad images and profound emotions in the mind of the listener, music is supremely eloquent.

Music that relies completely on musical tones unassociated with words is called pure or "absolute" music. Its evocative qualities depend completely on the elements of music and the manner in which they are arranged within the time span of the composition. The fluctuating rhythm, the relation of activity to repose, the degree of harmonic tension, the orchestral color, and, above all, the motion of the musical phrase, all have their function in the vocabulary of so-called absolute music. The listener responds to this music according to the way in which the vocabulary of tones communicates to him.

When music uses words, either as a text in vocal music or as a "program," the composer will often seek to delineate and emphasize the meaning of the words by the use of illustrative devices in the music. The use of such devices in vocal music, when clearly associated with a sung word or phrase, is called text painting. Many fine examples can be seen in both sacred and secular music of the sixteenth century. In renaissance settings of the Catholic Mass, for example, such devices as a rising melodic line on the word *ascendit* or a descending line on the word *descendit* are frequently found.

Figure 32.

Passages from bass and soprano parts from Palestrina's Pope Marcellus Mass

Delightfully naive examples can be found in many renaissance madrigals such as the clever imitation of bird calls in *Les Oiseaux* by Clement Jannequin (circa 1485–1584), the use of a dissonant sonority (augmented triad) on the word "death" in *The Silver Swan* by Orlando Gibbons (1583–1625), and countless other examples by madrigal composers of Europe and England.

Figure 33.

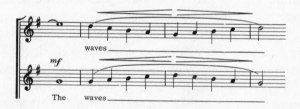

Excerpt showing text painting on "waves" from the five-part madrigal Spring Returns *by Marenzio*

This more or less specific depiction of text, though typical of the Renaissance, can also be found in the music of other periods. Text painting, at its best, has a musical meaning that is often more important than the literal meaning of the depicted word or phrase so that the passage is significant purely as music, unassociated with the text.

Another kind of text illustration, less literal but often more evocative, is present in a great deal of music, both vocal and instrumental. A good example is found in the aria "Dido's Lament" from the opera *Dido and Aeneas* by Henry Purcell (1659–1695). The orchestra accompanying the solo voice of Dido plays an ostinato (melodic figure that is constantly repeated) that beautifully suggests Dido's feelings of sorrow at the departure of Aeneas, her lover. The mood of tragic lament is achieved primarily by the juxtaposition of the voice line to the rhythm and harmony above the bass line. The richly chromatic harmonies are possible because of the chromatic character of the ostinato bass line.

Figure 34.

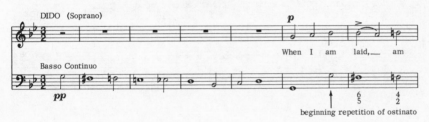

A very similar treatment occurs in the *"Crucifixus"* of the great B Minor Mass of J. S. Bach in which an ostinato bearing a striking likeness to the Dido example is used to create a mood of profound sorrow.

Purely instrumental music, without voices, based on a story or other extramusical association may frequently use similar depictive techniques. From the first notes of Richard Strauss' tone poem *Till Eulenspiegel's Merry Pranks,* one feels the spirit of mischievous exuberance appropriate to the tale of the pranks and follies of a young scapegrace. If the listener knows the story, it can be followed in the music. Sometimes the illustrative devices are conceived quite literally, at other times they are relatively subtle. The long drum roll near the end of *Till Eulenspiegel* is intended to depict Till mounting the gallows but it will have this effect only if the listener is thinking in terms of the story. Otherwise its meaning for each listener depends upon his own individual response and interpretation.

Another of Strauss' tone poems entitled *Don Juan* is based on the story of the hero's many amorous conquests and his final demise and disappear-

84   PERSPECTIVE

Figure 35.

ance into the earth. If the listener's mind is attuned to the sexual overtones of the story there are several frankly sexual symbols apparent in the music. Without the programmatic associations, however, many listeners would undoubtedly interpret the music quite differently. Even when Strauss is being quite literal as in *Don Quixote* where the sound of baaing sheep and the clanking of bells around their necks is actually imitated by the orchestra, it is possible that the listener would not hear it as such unless he was aware of the story.

From this it begins to be apparent that music cannot actually tell a story or evoke a specific image in the way that words or pictures can. The function of the extramusical element in programmatic or vocal music is to narrow the broad image evoked by the music down to a specific situation. The music reinforces the literal image but, at the same time, furnishes a meaning of its own that is purely musical. We apply the term "pure" or "absolute" to music which relies for its effect completely upon the vocabulary of musical sounds but, in a sense, the term is inappropriate, for it implies that all other music is somehow impure or adulterated by the extramusical factor. It also implies a sharp dichotomy between so-called absolute music and all other kinds of music. Actually, no such distinction exists, for nearly all music has a meaning of its own, often unrelated to any text, picture, or story that may be used with it. A text may be quite irrelevant to the real significance of the music, though in a type of music such as the art song the text may be uniquely significant because of its own artistic value.

Music is capable of suggesting broad and profound emotional images and occasionally their effect may be enhanced by means of words or pictures. Often enough, however, this narrowing-down process in no way enriches the meaning of the music. Beethoven's Sixth Symphony, the *Pastorale,* in which each movement purports to depict a country scene, is most meaningful from a purely musical point of view. The pictorial association may enhance our enjoyment of the piece in a very superficial way, but it can also prevent us from seeing beyond into the purely musical meaning of the composition. It should be possible to enjoy a fine piece of program music from the "absolute" standpoint, simply as music, as well as in conjunction with an extramusical association.

The terms "purely musical meaning" and "musical significance" have been used frequently in discussions of esthetic philosophy. What do these terms mean? What does music mean? This is a problem which has puzzled and fascinated philosophers and musicians for centuries and it will continue to do so, for how can one define or discuss emotional and intellectual states that are inherently nonverbal? It is, in fact, well nigh impossible to communicate an emotional experience directly to another person. Music is like a language in that it is a means of communication, but what is this ineffable thing that is being communicated? To say, as some have said, that all music tells a story is to deprive music of its greatest power, that of expressing the unutterable. At the opposite pole are those who say that all art, including music, is meaningful only insofar as its form or design is significant, that its value does not rest upon its evocative qualities but upon the significance of its total pattern. The truth about music is probably somewhere between these two extremes, for music does evoke images and emotions yet it is almost never possible to put this expression into words. The emotional or intellectual character of this expression must remain privately with each individual listener; and it is possible that a given piece of music may have widely varying effects depending upon how each listener responds.

There is no final answer to the question, "What does music mean?" Each listener increases his understanding by experiencing more and more music and thus becomes increasingly capable of answering this question for himself. Ultimately, it is a completely personal matter. The purpose of the succeeding chapters is to expand the beginning listener's knowledge of the literature of music in the hope that his enjoyment and understanding will be proportionately enriched.

LISTENING SUGGESTIONS

Mass: "Pope Marcellus"	Palestrina
Madrigal: "Les Oiseaux"	Jannequin
Madrigal: "The Silver Swan"	Gibbons
"Dido's Lament" from *Dido and Aeneas*	Purcell
"Crucifixus" from the *Mass in B Minor*	J. S. Bach
Don Juan	Richard Strauss
Don Quixote	Richard Strauss
Symphony No. 6	Beethoven

SUGGESTED ASSIGNMENTS

1. Attend a concert and attempt to write a critique of it, keeping in mind the general factors that determine the quality and effect of a performance.
2. Attend several solo recitals and, for each performance, attempt to select the aspects of the artist's attitude and demeanor that contribute positively or negatively to the concert.
3. Attend a rehearsal of a large ensemble, preferably a symphony orchestra, noting the conductor's rehearsal methods, and the many other factors contributing to the final performance.
4. Listen to a number of renaissance vocal compositions, following the text and noting examples of text painting.
5. Class experiment: The instructor plays a piece of unidentified program music that is obscure enough to be unknown to the class. Each student writes down his impression of what the music is "about" in terms of story or program. The results may be revealing as to the ability of music to convey *specific* images.
6. Readings for special projects (discussions or papers) dealing with various esthetic philosophies may be assigned by the instructor.

PART TWO

MUSIC OF THE EIGHTEENTH CENTURY

SIX

JOHANN SEBASTIAN BACH
(1685–1750)

Of all the composers in our musical heritage none stands in a position of greater prestige and distinction than Johann Sebastian Bach. His sheer mastery of the craft of musical composition, applied to all musical forms and media, has never been equaled. Bach's music represents the fusion and, more importantly, the culmination of many different musical styles. By studying and copying the music of his forerunners and contemporaries, he welded the characteristics of many different composers of different nationalities into a style that was uniquely his own. Surprisingly, the music of this exceptional genius was not widely known until the nineteenth century. He composed for himself, his pupils, and the needs of his position as a professional musician. Consequently, though generally known in musical circles, he led a life of relative obscurity—in touch with the times, yet not courting an international career.

He is most eminent as a composer of instrumental music and of religious choral music. With the greatest attention to detail he sought to make every vocal and instrumental part a work of art, yet reached emotional heights that transcend even the remarkable polyphonic intricacies of his music. He wrote a vast amount of solo instrumental music for harpsichord, organ, violin, and cello, as well as much chamber music for various combinations of instruments. His music also includes a number of orchestral suites and overtures but he is best known for his religious choral music. Among these are the large works called Passions, the B Minor Mass, and many smaller sacred works called cantatas.

Bach's church cantatas are relatively short works in several movements composed for specific needs in the church service. They utilize elements of operatic style as well as many other aspects of baroque music. Because so many baroque characteristics are represented in these works, it is appropriate to begin our study of baroque music through a careful examination of a typical Bach cantata, relating characteristics of this work to the period in general.

Cantata No. 140, "Wachet auf"

The very beginning of the opening chorus of the cantata, *"Wachet auf"* ("Sleepers Awake") presents an important aspect of baroque music, the concertato style. The essence of the concertato style is the contrasting of a large group of instruments or voices with a small group, alternating between the two in a sort of musical dialogue. It is seen in the opening measures of this work in the contrast of the strings (first violins, second violins, and violas) with the two oboes and English horn, the first measure dominated by the strings, the second by the double reeds, the third by the strings, and so on through the first eight bars of the piece.

As accompaniment to this, the continuo, consisting of a keyboard instrument (organ or harpsichord) and an instrument or instruments playing the bass line (string basses and/or cellos), furnishes the harmonic background with a steady rhythmic pulse. Continuo is used throughout the cantata, as it is in most of Bach's cantatas, adding the harmonic background as well as the rhythmic pulse. It is an extremely important characteristic of much of the music of this period and we shall see later how its introduction around 1600 marked the beginning of a gradual change from the musical practices of the Renaissance toward those of the Baroque.

After the short section in concertato style, the orchestra continues in a texture dominated by the first violins up to the point where the chorus enters. The chorus consists of the usual sopranos, altos, tenors, and basses, but at first only the sopranos are heard, entering with the chorale tune *"Wachet auf,"* upon which this cantata is based. This entrance is made without any interruption in the flow of the orchestral material. A continuous texture, woven out of the opening material, moves steadily to the very end of the movement. This kind of incessant metrical flow in a contrapuntal fabric is characteristic of much baroque music, particularly that written for instruments.

The chorale tune presented by the sopranos is very important to the cantata as a whole, for in addition to being used as a basic musical idea, the texts of the various verses of the chorale are also used. Chorales are the hymn tunes of the German Protestant church and Bach used them in almost all of his many church cantatas. During the Baroque their importance in the Lutheran service led to their use in many kinds of German church music, serving as a basis for instrumental works such as organ preludes, as well as vocal compositions. The chorales were designed for congregational singing, each tune with its text being appropriate to a particular service in the church calendar. They are derived from several sources, many from Gregorian chant, and others from secular tunes such as folk songs.

As a composer for the church, Bach wrote about 300 cantatas of which 195 have survived. A great many of them end with a four-part harmonization of the chorale tune upon which the cantata is based. Since Bach composed cantatas for specific services of the church year, the chorale tune selected for use in a cantata would be the one that was appropriate to the specific occasion. The text of the chorale, *"Wachet auf"* is appropriate to the twenty-seventh Sunday after Trinity (late in November) and it was for this service that Bach's cantata of the same name was composed.

Returning to the first movement of the cantata—shortly after the entrance of the sopranos on the chorale tune, the altos enter with the first statement of a fugal subject. The subject is answered by the tenors and then the basses, the three lower voices weaving a contrapuntal texture against the firm steady march of the chorale melody intoned by the sopranos. The ancient technique of prolonging the notes of a simple melody, using it as the basis of a polyphonic composition, was a fairly common practice during the baroque period. The melody, when it is used in this way, is called a *cantus firmus*. Bach frequently treated chorale melodies with this technique—in organ works as well as vocal compositions.

An interesting aspect of this fugal exposition is illustrated in Figure 36 by a comparison of the chorale tune as sung by the sopranos with the entrance of the tenors with the fugal subject. The subject is cleverly derived

Figure 36.

from the first three notes of the chorale but ornamented in such a way as to give it a somewhat different character. In fact, the fugue subject without the parenthetical notes (Figure 36) outlines the same pitches as the cantus firmus.

This fugal exposition is quite short, for it lasts only as long as it takes for the sopranos to sing the first phrase of the chorale (*"Wachet auf ruft uns die Stimme"*). The chorus then drops out, leaving the orchestra to emerge with the concertato material that was heard at the very beginning. This material was used as accompaniment to the preceding choral passage but now serves as a *ritornello* leading into the next entrance of the chorus. The term ritornello is used to describe the kind of form used in the baroque period in which the opening section (called the ritornello) recurs throughout a movement with contrasting material placed between these recurrences. This results in the same kind of formal logic and unity as found in the rondo form discussed earlier.

The second entrance of the chorus is similar to the first, the sopranos entering this time with the second phrase of the chorale melody. The material in the lower three voices is again a fugal exposition with the subject based on the cantus firmus that occurs above it. A similar treatment is given to the other phrases of the chorale; but it should be remembered that, although fugal technique is used in the choral passages, this movement cannot be called a fugue. A fugue is usually based on only one subject used in a series of expositions and episodes, and is usually unaccompanied, the fugal voices themselves furnishing the harmonic as well as the contrapuntal aspect of the texture. (See discussion of fugue, Chapter 2, p. 34.) This movement, though not a fugue, consists of a series of fugal expositions, or fugatos, with orchestral accompaniment, the subject of each one based on the chorale phrase used as a cantus firmus above it.

The form of the movement is very simple and clear-cut. There are eleven phrases in the chorale (including, at the end, a repeat of the first three phrases) and each of them is used as a cantus firmus over a polyphonic structure in the three lower voices. The continuous rhythmical flow of the orchestra, emerging as ritornelli between the choral sections, is a strong unifying factor. The final ritornello is an exact repetition of the orchestral material heard at the very beginning. This is accomplished in the notation by means of the da capo device, which occurs frequently in baroque music. In this instance only a short section at the beginning is repeated. In many other instances, however, a longer opening section is repeated by means of the D. C. sign, resulting in an ABA form in which the final A is an exact repetition of the first (i.e., No. 6 of this cantata). Da capo forms originated in the baroque period but continued to be used in later periods, for example, in the minuet of the classical period.

The second movement of this cantata is a recitative, a style which originated around 1600 with the development of the opera. Although recitatives can be musically attractive, their primary function is not musical but dramatic, furnishing the narrative element in operas, oratorios, and cantatas. During the baroque period, recitatives were used for dialogue between characters and also to describe the action of the drama. They were always performed by solo voices, usually accompanied only by the continuo. The rhythm is quite free, following the natural inflections of speech, with the continuo playing a simple chordal accompaniment notated in figured bass. The example in Figure 37 shows how this recitative is notated. The actual pitches on the lower line are played by a bass instrument such as the cello, while the organ or harpsichord plays the harmony by means of the figured bass (numerals appearing over the bass line).

Figure 37.

Translating the figured bass symbols into full harmony, either in musical notation or at the keyboard, is called "realizing" the figured bass. The top line is performed by the voice.

The third movement is an aria in the form of a duet for two solo voices, soprano and bass. In a great deal of baroque opera, particularly a kind called Neapolitan opera, the arias are alternated with the recitatives. The recitatives furnish the dramatic continuity while the arias furnish the musical expression, evoking the mood or feeling of a character in the drama. Arias are always for solo voices and, unlike recitatives, are full-fledged movements in complete, well-rounded form. The recitative preceding this aria announces the coming of Christ, picturing him allegorically as a bridegroom. The aria is in the form of a dialogue between Christ and the Spirit, represented as the bride of Christ. The part of Christ is sung by a bass and the Spirit by a soprano, with the accompaniment furnished by continuo and solo *violino piccolo* (a small violin pitched higher than the ordinary violin, now obsolete) which weaves a continuous independent line above the two solo voices. This kind of solo instrumental accompaniment is called an obbligato.

The aria begins with the solo violin and continuo presenting material that is used throughout the movement. When the voices enter, the instruments continue with the same material, emerging alone four times during the course of the movement. The movement closes with the same material with which it opened, accomplished, as in the first movement, by means of the da capo device.

In the fourth movement the second verse of the chorale is sung by the tenors accompanied by the strings and continuo. The strings play a unison obbligato accompaniment to the chorale tune with the continuo furnishing the harmonic background. The continuous flow of the obbligato melody has a tremendous effect when contrasted with the firm entrances of the tenors on the successive phrases of the chorale.

The fifth movement is an example of accompanied recitative (*recitativo accompagnato*). A recitative, when accompanied only by continuo, as in the second movement of this cantata, is called *recitativo secco* (dry recitative) and is the more frequently used type of recitative. Occasionally, however, when the words are of great dramatic import, a baroque composer might use additional instruments to heighten the dramatic effect. It was Bach's custom, in a recitative representing Christ's voice, to use the full string section for accompaniment, making the recitative uniquely meaningful and distinguishing it from the ordinary secco recitative.

The next movement, No. 6, is another duet for soprano and bass, this time with oboe obbligato, accompanied by continuo. It is a da capo aria and, in keeping with the text, evokes a feeling of deep joy.

The final movement of the cantata is a typical four-part harmonization of the chorale tune accompanied by orchestra, using the third verse of the text. Cantatas were used as an integral part of the church service and most of Bach's cantatas end with a chorale harmonization suitable for congregational singing.

In this cantata we have seen a number of baroque characteristics and, in summarizing them, we may gain a better understanding of the music of this many-faceted period. The term "baroque" was originated by late eighteenth century critics and historians to describe the lavishly extravagant architectural style of the late seventeenth and early eighteenth centuries. Derived from a Portuguese word originally meaning grotesque or misshapen, it soon came to be applied to the music as well as to the other arts of this period. Today, in retrospect, we see that, far from being a period of excess and disproportion, the baroque is artistically one of the richest periods in our history. Musically, the baroque period began in southern Europe with a movement away from the refined polyphonic style of the Renaissance toward the new monodic style.

Monodic music, in the baroque sense, can be described as a single melody with homophonic accompaniment. The second movement of this cantata, with its single voice line and continuo accompaniment, is an example of baroque accompanied monody. The use of continuo typifies the movement away from the practices of the Renaissance, for it is based on a vertical conception of harmony in which a sonority is built of intervals above a bass tone. Renaissance harmony, on the other hand, can be viewed as a texture of several horizontal strands of melody whose relation to each other results in a harmonic texture that can be called polyphonic. This horizontal aspect of renaissance polyphony is incompatible with the baroque concept of continuo. In a nutshell, and to oversimplify for the sake of clarity, the renaissance style is heard primarily in the interrelation of *horizontal* voice lines while baroque music is harmonically organized in *vertical* sonorities. There was, of course, a great deal of polyphonic or contrapuntal music composed during the baroque. Baroque counterpoint, though rooted in sixteenth century polyphonic practices, was strongly influenced by the newer, vertical conception of harmony typical of the Baroque.

Other important aspects of baroque music seen in this cantata are the use of recitative and aria, concertato style, ritornello, da capo form, and the characteristic instrumental style observed in several movements. Bach was a master of instrumental writing and an examination of one of his purely instrumental compositions will be of value in understanding this facet of his art.

Brandenburg Concerto No. 2 in F Major

In 1721 Bach composed a set of six concertos "for several instruments" which today are called the Brandenburg Concertos. At that time Bach was employed as court conductor or *Kapellmeister* in the court of Prince Leopold at Cöthen. Prince Leopold maintained a group of excellent instrumental performers and Bach composed the concertos with these players in mind, dedicating the entire set to the Margrave of Brandenburg, one of the Prince's associates. The fact that this music was intended for specific performers may account for the highly varied instrumentation found among the six concertos. In addition to the usual combination of strings and continuo, they use several different kinds of wind instruments in combinations so unique that they hardly typify standard baroque instrumentation.

From the standpoint of form, however, they are quite typical, representing the kind of three-movement concerto grosso form developed by the Italian composer, Antonio Vivaldi (1676–1741) with whose music Bach was well acquainted. The typical form is usually most apparent in the first and last movements, utilizing the concertato style by contrasting a small group of instruments called the *concertino* with a large group (usually a full string section plus continuo) called the *ripieno*. The result is a sectional form in which the ripieno plays ritornello passages alternating with passages played by the concertino group. Usually the first and last statements of the ritornello are tutti passages played by both the concertino and ripieno.

The frequent shifts from a large group of instruments to a small group result in two basic dynamic levels—loud and soft, with little or no gradation between. The resulting effect is often termed "terrace dynamics" and is characteristic, not only of the concerto grosso, but of other kinds of baroque music as well. Terrace dynamics are exemplified in much of the keyboard music of the period. Both organs and harpsichords conventionally have two or more keyboards or manuals, often set at contrasting dynamic levels (or contrasting timbres). Alternating between the two manuals creates the same effect as that found in the concerto grosso, a sharp contrast of loud and soft. The organ and harpsichord were the two most important keyboard instruments of the period, and it is natural that much keyboard music of the period utilized terrace dynamics.

The Brandenburg Concerto No. 2 is scored for a concertino group of clarino trumpet, flute (recorder), oboe, and solo violin (marked *violino concertato* in the score to distinguish it from the orchestral violins). The clarino trumpet is a valveless instrument, now obsolete, which sounds in the high partials of the overtone series. Music written for clarino trumpet is extremely difficult to play on the modern trumpet because of the very high range of the parts. Consequently, in modern performances, these parts are often played on a valve trumpet specially designed for this music or, infrequently, on a replica of the clarino trumpet. The latter alternative is usually unsatisfactory because the art of playing the very high-pitched diatonic passages found in baroque trumpet parts was kept a closely guarded secret by the trumpeters of that time. A similar situation exists in regard to the flute part, which was intended for the baroque recorder or *Blockflöte*. Today this part is usually played on the modern "transverse" flute. Recently, with the increased interest in authentic performances of old music, much research has been done in these areas so that occasionally it is possible to hear more or less authentic performances of early music played on instruments similar to those used at the time the music was written.

The first movement begins with a triadic motive very typical of the concerto grosso style and after a few measures the trumpet announces a second idea. Out of these two ideas the entire movement evolves. The interplay of the solo instruments with the ripieno is truly fascinating and, through Bach's inexhaustible creative imagination, which repeatedly transforms the simple thematic materials, the listener's interest is retained throughout the movement.

The second movement presents a contrasting mood, deeply romantic in spirit. To establish this mood of intimacy, the trumpet and orchestral strings are not used, leaving only the solo violin, oboe, and flute, plus continuo. The device of canonic imitation appears at the very beginning, utilizing successive entrances of the three instruments, each with the same subject, or thematic idea. As mentioned earlier, the canon is not organized according to the stylized tonal pattern of a fugal exposition discussed in Chapter Two, nor does it utilize the formal organization of the fugue with its pattern of expositions and episodes. Canonic imitation was in common use during the sixteenth century, presaging the fugal practice of the baroque.

The movement opens with an accompaniment figure played by the continuo, over which the solo instruments play the successive entrances of the melodic material. A two-note motive in the form of a descending half step is heard throughout. The descending melodic half step in slow tempo, played with a slight diminuendo from the first note to the second, has a very plaintive quality and for this reason is sometimes called a "sigh figure." The evocative qualities of this movement are, at least in part, created by the presence of this figure.

The final movement is a fugue, rather free in structure, and bubbling over with good spirits. Instead of a pure unaccompanied fugal style, the continuo is used throughout, with the result that the initial statement of the subject is accompanied, rather than played by a single voice line. The exposition is played by the solo instruments with the trumpet announcing the subject at the outset. The ripieno joins the soloists in the episodic sections with one statement of the subject given to the basses near the end of the movement. The movement concludes with a tutti passage in which the final statement of the subject is played by the trumpet.

This final movement of the concerto represents the light side of Bach's musical personality, a kind of lightness that could never be shallow. Profound or fun loving, Bach's musical wit was never superficial. In viewing this work along with the cantata, *"Wachet auf,"* it becomes apparent that Bach's music encompassed a vast range of human experience.

Passacaglia and Fugue in C Minor

In Bach's time a competent professional musician was frequently very well versed in all aspects of the art of music. The idea of specialization, with musicians being trained for performance, conducting, or composition, is a relatively modern concept. Prior to the nineteenth century, a musician in a position such as Kapellmeister or director of music for a court of the nobility was expected not only to write music for specific occasions, but also to prepare it in rehearsal, and finally, to perform it. Bach was no exception, for, within the relatively small area in which he was known, his reputation as a keyboard performer was at least as great as his reputation as a composer. Bach's ability to improvise at the organ or harpsichord is legendary and many of his organ works are brilliantly improvisatory in style. Others are more introspective, as, for example, those based on chorale tunes, while his organ fugues are models of technical excellence without ever sounding dry or academic. As a fine performer he was also a teacher of performance and it was natural that he produce a number of teaching pieces for organ and harpsichord. Examples of this kind of music, such as the six trio sonatas for organ and the two- and three-part inventions, are musically excellent in addition to their pedagogical value.

Although Bach's organ music is the very backbone of the organ repertoire, it comprises only about seven percent of his total output. The organ music can be divided into four general areas, (1) pieces written for a pedagogical purpose such as the six trio sonatas, (2) virtuoso concert pieces such as the *Toccata, Adagio, and Fugue in C Major,* (3) deeply religious pieces such as the eighteen chorale preludes, and (4) mature polyphonic works including the later preludes and fugues. The *Passacaglia and Fugue in C Minor* falls into the last category.

The passacaglia (or chaconne) is a form in which an eight-measure theme in triple meter is used as a cantus firmus, first stated by itself in the bass register and then used in a series of variations. The variations usually differ in their rhythmic and melodic character but each one is composed over a single statement of the eight-bar theme performed in a continuous texture without pause between variations. The chaconne is a variation form almost identical to the passacaglia, their differences being very slight if not ambiguous.

In the first ten variations Bach assigns the theme to the pedals of the organ but in several variations the theme moves to the upper voices. There is a total of twenty variations in all. In a variation form remaining predominantly in the key of the tonic with little or no modulation, a central problem is that of producing contrast between variations in order to maintain interest. Bach achieved this by means of rhythmic variety, each variation being based on a different rhythmic idea to produce a feeling of rhythmic development from variation to variation. A striking feature of the work is the quality of rhythmic accumulation produced in the passacaglia —the effect of starting with slow note values and gradually increasing their speed. In variations 1 to 6 the rhythmic motion moves gradually from quarter notes to sixteenth notes, producing a marvelous momentum in the music. The fast note values then persist through variation 16, after which the rhythmic activity momentarily subsides in variations 17 and 18 in preparation for the final intensity of variations 19 and 20 which return to the fast note values.

Figure 38.

Theme of the Passacaglia in C Minor

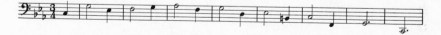

The fugue which follows uses as its subject the first four measures of the passacaglia theme combined in the exposition with two other important thematic ideas. This intense and dramatic fugue is wrought completely from these three subjects.

Contrapuntal skill and facility are demonstrated to varying degrees in any of Bach's compositions, from the simplest chorale harmonization to the most complex fugue. But it is not for technique alone that we admire Bach's music, for his art is possessed of a scope of expression and humanity that transcends mere technical matters. His vast emotional range coupled with his consummate artistry establishes him as the culminating figure of the Baroque, influencing composers of succeeding generations even to the present time.

SUGGESTED ASSIGNMENTS

1. Library orientation: Examine the *Bach Gesellschaft* collection, noting its organization.
2. By means of either scores or recordings, find additional examples of the baroque forms discussed in this chapter.
3. Define the following terms, using supplementary resources as needed:

concertato style	aria	tutti
continuo	da capo	terrace dynamics
cantus firmus	obbligato	passacaglia
ritornello	concertino	chaconne
recitative	ripieno	

4. Using the works discussed in this chapter as a starting point, begin to expand your knowledge of Bach's music, primarily by listening to recordings or attending concerts, but also by doing outside reading as recommended by the instructor.

SEVEN

GEORGE FRIDERIC HANDEL
(*1685–1759*)

It is a remarkable coincidence to find two figures of the stature of Bach and Handel, spanning almost identical periods in music history, and each with an almost equal right to be considered the greatest composer of his time. Their activities as musicians are strongly contrasting, but they are also complementary in many ways. Bach, living his entire life in a small area of Germany, was not widely known; while Handel enjoyed a musical reputation of international scope. Bach is best known for his religious and instrumental music, Handel for his dramatic works such as operas and oratorios. Bach's style, even in vocal music, is oriented to the instrumental idiom; Handel's writing is predominantly vocal in style. The music of Bach shows great attention to detail, while Handel painted on a vast canvas, more concerned with immediate and direct communication than with intricate detail.

Handel's greatest achievements lie in the field of vocal music. From the early chamber cantatas composed in Italy to the mature English oratorios, his style is marked by beautiful melodic lines and tremendous dramatic powers. His melodic writing was influenced by the Italian tradition of lyrically virtuosic vocal lines (the *bel canto* style) and also by the vocal music of Henry Purcell, the most prominent English-born composer of the Baroque. His choral writing is also somewhat influenced by the church cantatas of his native Germany. In addition to his many operas and oratorios, Handel composed a number of shorter vocal works, including church music and a number of incidental choral works such as the *Ode for St. Cecilia's Day* and *Zadock the Priest,* an anthem written for the coronation of George II in 1727 which has been used for every English coronation since that time.

His instrumental works are comparatively few in number, consisting of keyboard works, chamber music, and orchestral works. Handel was well known as an organ virtuoso and his best keyboard music is found among his eighteen organ concertos, many of which are arrangements of his trio sonatas and concerti grossi. The concerti grossi and trio sonatas, in turn, are strongly influenced by the Italian instrumental style developed by Arcangelo Corelli (1653–1713), with whose music Handel was well acquainted. In addition, he produced a number of solo sonatas, as well as several incidental orchestral works such as the famous *Water Music* and the *Royal Fireworks Music.*

Born into a prosperous middle-class German family, the young Handel had the means to travel quite freely and, early in his career, spent three years in Italy, the land of song and the fountainhead of opera. Here he absorbed the Italian baroque operatic style, and began to develop his tremendous melodic gift. Even before the age of twenty-five, he had achieved a considerable reputation as an opera composer, primarily through the success of his opera *Agrippina,* which was premiered in Venice in 1709. Successfully launched on a most remarkable career, in 1710 he arrived in London, the city which became his home for the remaining fifty years of his life; and where, even today, he is viewed as a national celebrity.

All did not go smoothly for him in London, however. With many ups and downs, he produced opera after opera, financed and sponsored, for the most part, by the Royal Academy of Music, which was founded in 1720 and of which he was a musical director. Within a period of thirty years he produced forty operas. Unfortunately, the English middle-class audiences were becoming increasingly disenchanted with the aristocratic, Italian-style *opera seria* (serious opera) used by Handel. The fact that they were performed in the Italian language did not help matters in spite of the fact that fluency in Italian was a fashionable affectation among the aristocracy. Also, Handel's characters tended to be of an allegorical or prototype nature, not unlike the characters in Greek drama. His heroes were likely to loom larger than life, to represent the epitome of heroism rather than lifelike, realistic figures. The audiences of that time preferred greater realism and found it—not in Handel's music, but in the ballad opera, the eighteenth century counterpart of modern musical comedy. Humorous, direct, and sung in English, these ballad operas strongly appealed to the knowledge and experience of middle-class London. One of the most successful, *The Beggars Opera,* was effective in discouraging Handel's efforts in serious opera.

With much reluctance, and only after a desperate struggle in which both his health and financial status were in grave danger, Handel began to give less attention to opera in Italian and turned increasingly to the composition of oratorios in English. The oratorios were designed as entertainments, not as religious works, and their musical style is similar in many ways to opera. Like the opera seria, the oratorio is in three acts with the narrative element furnished by the recitatives. Arias and choruses alternate with the recitatives to add the dramatic and theatrical elements.

Because the oratorios were presented in concert form rather than acted out like opera, it was possible for Handel to increase the importance of the chorus—a major factor in the subsequent success of the Handelian oratorio, for the English have always held choral singing in great affection. The chorus, which is to say, the people, became the center of the drama and functioned in a manner similar to the chorus in the Greek theater, commenting and reflecting on the action, as well as occasionally taking an active part in the plot.

Handel wrote both sacred and secular oratorios and there is no difference in style between the two types. The sacred oratorio librettos, with the exception of the *Messiah,* are drawn from the Old Testament. Towering biblical figures such as Saul, Deborah, Joshua, Jeptha, and Judas Maccabaeus were ideal characters for Handel's unique dramatic gift. One of the reasons for the success of his oratorios is that, because they were not so elaborately staged, with foreign singers and lavish scenery, they were much less expensive to produce than operas. Ultimately, the English middle class accepted Handel as their chosen composer. Certainly, for the English-speaking peoples, there is no choral work that has achieved greater renown and popularity than the *Messiah.*

The *Messiah* is unique among Handel's oratorios. The choice of a New Testament subject, the life of Christ, is in itself unusual (parts of the text are drawn from the Old Testament). The contemplative, even philosophical mood is quite dissimilar to the power and dramatic conflict found in the other oratorios. Today there is no large choral work heard more frequently. In many musical communities, in the United States as well as in English countries, a performance of this work is considered a necessary adjunct to every Christmas season. Handel's reputation rests in large part upon this renowned and beloved work, yet it is only a tiny portion of his total output. It was first performed in Dublin in 1742 and met with immediate success.

Because of changing tastes, Handel's operas are not nearly as popular nor as well-known as his oratorios. The aristocratic theater audiences of the seventeenth and early eighteenth centuries, schooled in the tradition of classical tragedians such as Corneille and Racine, were able to accept the heroic, larger-than-life characters of Handelian opera. Even in Handel's time, however, as the bourgeois class became increasingly dominant, this tradition began to give way to a preference for greater realism in theater as well as in opera. In a sense, a social change vital to eighteenth century political and philosophical thought is represented by Handel's switch from opera to oratorio. It is a symbol of the new middle-class culture and loss of power for the aristocracy—a harbinger of the romantic era.

Today's opera companies present, almost exclusively, works drawn from the late eighteenth and nineteenth century repertoire, finding that baroque opera does not satisfy the tastes of present-day audiences. The modern opera impresario will run the gamut from Mozart to Puccini, but will not or cannot produce any of the excellent operas of the baroque period. Baroque oratorios, on the other hand, since they were not designed primarily as theatrical presentations, have been more successful in enduring. Handel's oratorios are as powerful and dramatic as his operas, but in a more purely musical way so that their ultimate place in the musical repertoire relies primarily upon their musical value rather than upon their theatrical interest.

Oratorio: *Judas Maccabaeus*

The oratorio *Judas Maccabaeus* is one of the very finest of Handel's great vocal works and is a representative example of his last and most mature oratorios. Composed in 1746, it deals with the exploits of the Old Testament hero, Judas Maccabaeus, a great Jewish military leader who lived around 160 B.C.

Part I of the three parts or acts deals with the lamentations for the death of Mattathias (father of Judas Maccabaeus and Simon) who had roused the Jewish people to resist the cruelties and oppressions of Antiochus Epiphanes, the king of Syria. The people appeal for divine favor and the young Judas is recognized as the new leader. He arouses the patriotic resolve of the people and they prepare for war.

Part II opens with a celebration of certain victories but is shortly quelled by a new attack of the Syrians. Judas again arouses the failing courage of his people and the armies of Israel set out once more. Those who remain behind show their hatred of the heathen idols which have been imposed upon them in the sanctuary at Jerusalem and they resolve to destroy them. In Part III Judas, upon his victorious return, restores the sanctuary to its appropriate form and the people celebrate with a feast of dedication. The liberties of the country having been reestablished, Israel rejoices.

The oratorio is scored for strings, timpani, continuo, four-part chorus, children's choir, and a full complement of soloists, each taking the role of a particular character in the drama. (Judas: tenor; Simon: bass; the Israelitish Woman: soprano; the Priest: alto; etc.)

Handel, as an inveterate traveler, was acquainted with the music of many nationalities, and, in fact, borrowed quite freely from much of it. As a result his music may be said to be a coordination of many national styles, of which one aspect is found in the overture of this oratorio. It is of the type developed by the distinguished French opera composer, J. B. Lully (1632–1687) and is called the French overture. The typical French overture consists of a slow, majestic introduction utilizing dotted rhythms, usually in a minor key, closing with an incomplete or suspensive cadence (frequently on the dominant), and followed by a fast movement in fugal style. Many eighteenth century French overtures, including this one, return to the majestic mood of the introduction after the completion of the fugal section, although this is not an essential feature of the form (see Figure 39).

Figure 39.

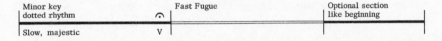

Minor key dotted rhythm		Fast Fugue	Optional section like beginning
Slow, majestic	V		

Diagram of a French overture

In listening to the fugal section of the overture, note that the character of the fugal subject, with its repeated notes, creates a harmonic effect totally different from that found in most of the fugues of J. S. Bach. Handel's fugues (Figure 40) are inclined toward a homophonic style with measured changes of harmony, the motion of each voice being strictly con-

Figure 40.

trolled by the prevailing sonority. In Bach's fugal style the voices give the effect of great melodic freedom, weaving a polyphonic web in which the harmonies appear to be the incidental result of the linear motion—quite different from the predominantly homophonic effect produced in a typical fugue of Handel.

The first chorus, No. 2, immediately following the overture, opens with the words, "Mourn, ye afflicted children," a lamentation on the death of the hero's father. The mood of sorrow is created by beautiful delineation of the text within the framework of a slow, expressive tempo. As evidenced in this chorus, Handel's typical harmonic idiom is predominantly diatonic and does not incline toward the use of highly colored chromatic sonorities for expressive purposes. The emotional and expressive qualities of his vocal music are achieved by means of melodic inflection and by his superb treatment of the text. Handel did not adopt the type of harmonic expression used, for example, in the *"Crucifixus"* of Bach's B Minor Mass. In keeping with the Italian tradition, he preferred diatonic homophony to chromaticism and contrapuntal intricacy.

Handel did not concern himself with the fine detail involved in complex polyphonic textures. Often, in a movement which is ostensibly contrapuntal, he would abandon a fugal or canonic texture for the sake of a particular dramatic device appropriate to the text at that point.

Such a device occurs in the opening chorus of Part II (No. 18 "Fall'n is the foe"). Shortly after the beginning, a canonic section begins with the words, "Where war-like Judas wields his righteous sword." The thematic material is presented by each of the voices in turn in what promises to be a true canonic texture. For dramatic emphasis, however, he soon superimposes striking unison passages on the words "Fall'n is the foe." Such abrupt changes of texture within a relatively short time span contribute immensely to the dramatic impact of his choral style. The variety of textures, even within a single chorus, is most remarkable and shows Handel's ingenuity in finding new resources for dramatic effect.

The bel canto style is evident in many of Handel's arias. No. 21 ("From mighty kings he took the spoil"), an aria sung by the Israelitish Woman, and No. 31 ("Father of heaven, from thy eternal throne"), the opening number of Part III, sung by the Priest (originally a male alto part) are both representative examples. The bel canto influence shows Handel's link with Italian baroque opera and is seen in emphasis on vocal technique, beauty of sound, and brilliance of performance rather than upon excessive emotional expression. The virtuoso or "coloratura" aspects of the style are seen in the use of long florid lines to a single syllable of text and other technically demanding vocal devices. The characteristic simplicity of the harmonic background delineates the text and further enhances the beauty of the vocal line.

Frequently, in arias as well as in choruses, Handel finds unique means for illustration of the text. A delightful example of Handel's text painting is found in No. 24, a da capo aria sung by Judas. The text of the first section (and also, by means of the da capo, of the final section) is, "How vain is man who boasts in fight the valour of gigantic might." Typical of bel canto arias, the text is repeated several times, and each time, on the word "gigan-tic," there occurs a truly gigantic embellishment of the second syllable of the word. The longest of these is presented in Figure 41. Other text painting devices are found throughout the oratorio.

Figure 41.

No. 35, "See, the conqu'ring hero comes," one of the most famous choruses in the oratorio, is sung by the children's choir with the full choir added near the end of the movement. No. 36, a march for the orchestra alone, is based on a five-note motive derived from the preceding chorus, a type of connective device that was infrequently used during the Baroque. It serves the dramatic function of sustaining the victorious mood established in No. 35 (see Figure 42).

Figure 42.

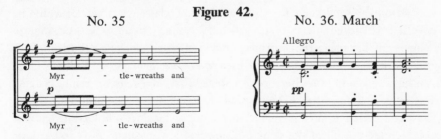

Excerpts from Numbers 35 and 36 of Judas Maccabaeus *showing melodic relationship*

No. 41, the final movement of the oratorio, concludes triumphantly with the famous "Hallelujah, Amen" chorus, representing Israel's rejoicing for their restored liberties. Throughout the oratorio the chorus represents the mass of Jewish people, and typical of Handel's late oratorios, plays an active part in the plot.

The Concerto Grosso

Handel's most significant contribution to the instrumental repertoire is found in his highly varied concerti grossi. In addition to the eighteen organ concertos mentioned earlier, he composed a set of twelve concertos for strings alone (Op. 6) which, in the tradition of Corelli and Vivaldi, use a concertino of two violins plus continuo (the trio sonata group), and a ripieno consisting of full string orchestra. In addition, he composed a number of separate concertos, many of which use wind instruments in combination with the strings. The concertato style, discussed in Chapter Six, is utilized in various ways throughout these works.

The set of six concertos, Op. 3, often called the Oboe Concertos, were composed at various times, perhaps over a period of nearly twenty years. Handel collected them into a set for publication in 1734. In keeping with the baroque practices of revising existing compositions and reusing them, many of the movements appear in different form in other compositions. Number 6 of this set, which will be discussed in some detail, is a prime example of the composer borrowing from himself. The concerto is in two movements, of which the first is a version of a movement appearing in the opera *Ottone,* composed in 1723.

Versions of the second movement appear in the overture to the opera *Il Pastor Fido,* in the third suite for harpsichord, and later in the organ concerto, Op. 7, No. 4. Handel borrowed freely, not only from himself, but also from the music of other composers. It was the custom to do this, and the baroque period knew no copyright laws. Today such practices would be decried as plagiaristic but, in justice to Handel, it must be said that in almost all instances the borrowed material was somehow transformed—revised and elevated so that it fit its new environment. So skillful was he in putting his stamp upon borrowed material that, in a sense, it really became his own. Seldom does the borrowed material sound inappropriate to the new context. It is very probable that modern musical scholarship has not yet ferreted out all of the delightful musical larceny that exists in baroque music.

The concerto, Op. 3, No. 6, is scored for two oboes, strings, and continuo. Although it is commonly called an oboe concerto, the two oboes are used as solo instruments only in the first movement. In the second movement they are used to double the first and second violins for additional color and sonority.

The first movement opens with the ripieno strings and continuo playing a triadic theme, partly in a unison doubling and quite typical of the concerto grosso style. The continuo traditionally consists of either harpsichord or organ plus a bass instrument. In listening to this movement, the contrast of the solo instruments to the tutti passages will be readily apparent. In their first entrances the oboes are totally unaccompanied, standing out in sharp relief to the entrances of the strings. The contrasts achieved by the various instrumental combinations is a fascinating feature of the concerto grosso style. Although the instrumental means are quite modest, it is possible to hear a number of strikingly different colors and dynamic levels: the oboes by themselves, in combination with the continuo for a trio sonata effect, in solo passages against the full ensemble, in unison with the strings, and in several other ways, all of which add color and contrast to the total effect. The movement concludes with a tutti section in which the two oboes play in unison with the first violins.

The second movement utilizes the oboes as part of the ripieno, doubling the first and second violins. The concertato effect is achieved by using the keyboard instrument (organ or harpsichord) as a solo instrument, the rest of the ensemble furnishing the ritornelli. The movement is in binary form and the ritornello material recurs in almost the same form throughout, although in varying keys. Contrast is furnished by the extensive solo passages for the keyboard performer. Moderate key contrast is also achieved by casting the second movement in the key of D minor, "parallel minor" to the key of the first movement. The work is unusual in that it has only two movements, neither of which is a slow movement.

Corelli, who strongly influenced Handel's instrumental style, frequently wrote concertos of five or more movements. The late baroque practice, instituted by Vivaldi, was to use a three-movement form: fast, slow, fast. Handel generally followed the older practice of five (or more) movements, while Bach, as seen in his *Brandenburg Concertos,* favored the more modern three-movement form.

The concerto, Op. 6, No. 5, is more typical of Handel's concerto grosso style. It is in five movements—the four movements of the da chiesa form plus a minuet. The scoring is for a standard concertino of two violins and cello with a tutti or ripieno consisting of a full complement of strings. With the ever-present keyboard instrument as a part of the continuo group, this concertino group is essentially the same as the trio sonata medium—two solo instruments plus continuo.

The first movement is a French overture, the slow, massive introduction ending on a half cadence and followed by a sprightly fugue. Unlike the overture to *Judas Maccabaeus,* this example of the French overture does not return to the slow introductory material after the completion of the fugue.

The second movement, marked presto, moves like the wind. It is a simple, clear-cut, rounded binary form. All of the characteristics of this form, as discussed in Chapter Four, are apparent here. It is monothematic, the cadence of the first section (at the repeat sign) is in the key of the dominant, the second section begins in the dominant and, after several excursions into closely related keys, swings back to the tonic for a restatement of the opening material. This return is varied by the use of canonic imitation but is, nevertheless, very similar to the opening material.

The third movement, slow and somber in mood, contributes tonal contrast to the concerto by the use of the relative minor key, B minor. All of the other movements are in D major. In keeping with the improvisatory practices of the time, the two solo violin parts in eighteenth century performances might have been decorated with improvised embellishments. The practice of extemporizing figurations in both instrumental and vocal music was very common in the baroque period, particularly in slow movements. Such movements, when performed exactly as written, have a very reserved and somber quality which, although endowed with a kind of stark beauty, is probably not the intended effect. With the stylized improvisations of the baroque period, the mood was, no doubt, quite different—probably quite unlike the austere quality frequently achieved by present-day performers in playing the same music.

The fourth movement, marked allegro, does not use the solo instruments at all. The two solo violins return in the fifth movement, but only to double the orchestral violin I part at the unison. This final movement, called a "Menuet," is unlike the classical minuet form discussed in Chapter Four in that it is not a da capo form and does not have a trio. Many minuets of this nature were written during the Baroque and can be considered ancestors of the fully developed minuet form used as the third movement of classical symphonies and string quartets.

In listening to Handel's music, instrumental as well as vocal, the remarkable use of textural and dynamic contrast is most striking. His sense of the dramatic is unsurpassed and for this reason his greatest strengths lay in theatrical media such as the opera and oratorio. In his oratorios he left a standard of excellence in choral writing to which many have aspired but few have reached, establishing a tradition of the large choral work that has influenced composers ever since.

Like Milton, whom he admired, and like Bach, Handel became blind in his last years. The affliction scarcely impaired his activities, for he continued to compose by dictation and even to conduct. His irrepressible energy and ambition remained to the very end. From the English, as well as from the entire musical world, he achieved a distinction afforded to few composers, that of being renowned and deeply honored before his death as well as after.

Suggested Assignments

1. Compare Bach and Handel from various points of view: their musical styles, their lives and relationships to society, their output, their professional activities, etc.
2. Listen to a recording of *The Beggars Opera,* noting the features which may have been particularly attractive to eighteenth century English theater audiences.
3. Research project: The orchestration normally used in today's performances of the *Messiah* differs in many respects from the original. Using resources suggested by the instructor, investigate the history of this changed orchestral arrangement.
4. Begin to expand your acquaintance with Handel's music by listening to an oratorio not discussed in this chapter and by listening to instrumental works such as his organ concertos, violin sonatas, etc.

EIGHT

JOSEPH HAYDN
(*1732–1809*)

"The free arts and the beautiful science of composition will not tolerate technical chains. The mind and soul must be free." Thus, in a letter to a group of Viennese composers [1] in the year 1779, did Franz Joseph Haydn express the spirit of the age. It was, indeed, a time of breaking chains—an era that saw the beginning of new attitudes and philosophies in the arts as well as in the political world. In the world of letters, philosophers such as Locke and Voltaire were spokesmen for a complex movement called "the Enlightenment." Generating the movement was a spirit of revolt that reached into all areas of human activity and questioned all preexisting standards. Out of it came such vital developments as the political and industrial revolutions, public education, and the empirical method in science.

The impact of the Enlightenment upon the art of music was felt in an increased concern for communicating with a mass audience. No longer was fine music to be limited to the knowledgeable, well educated, aristocratic classes. Public concerts came into vogue along with larger and less sophisticated audiences. The popular ideal became a kind of music that was free of needless technical complication and capable of being easily understood by the average listener—entertaining, but, at the same time, nobly expressive. Obviously not all the music written during the classical period (1750–1820) subscribed to these standards. At the same time, no composer could be completely untouched by them.

Haydn, living a large part of his productive life in the relatively secluded atmosphere of a wealthy aristocratic household, was able to view the period with a degree of equanimity. Yet he, perhaps more than any other composer, represents the spirit of the classical period in music. It is he who

[1] The *Tonkünstlersocietät*.

112

brought to eminence such typically classical forms as the four-movement symphony and the string quartet. As heir to all that the baroque period had achieved, he fused its diverse elements into a unified style that not only epitomized the classical period but led forcefully into the romantic era.

A certain homogeneity of style existed during the classical period, more so than during either the baroque or the romantic periods. Consequently, it is possible to make several valid generalizations regarding technical features of classical music. The harmonic vocabulary remained much the same as that used during the baroque but its treatment in the classical period is characterized by slower harmonic rhythm (meaning that the sonorities change or progress at a slower rate, not necessarily that the music is at a slower tempo) and by clear, decorative textures. Within the framework of each sonority there is often a great deal of rhythmic motion—active melodic lines moving above relatively slow moving and conventional harmonies. The sonorities are less weighty and more transparent in texture, frequently arpeggiated or broken into figures like the *Alberti* bass shown in Figure 43. By means of such devices a single sonority could be retained for a relatively long period, maintaining inter-

Figure 43.

Excerpt with left hand only from finale of Haydn Sonata

est by means of the motion among the various tones of the chord. Similar techniques had been used during the baroque but not so prevalently and not in so simple and obvious a manner. As shown in Figure 44, the addition of a melody above the Alberti bass produces a typical piano texture of the classical period. Such devices were particularly characteristic of piano music but were also used in other instrumental media.

Phrase structure of the classical period became simpler and more clear-cut than that of the Baroque. Simple structures such as the double period became standard building blocks for new single-movement forms such as sonata allegro form, rondo, and minuet. (The student should review these forms, as discussed in Chapter Four, prior to beginning the study of the music of this period.)

Figure 44.

Complete version of excerpt in Figure 43

In general, textures became less polyphonic and inclined toward simple homophonic style. Fugal technique, however, was not forgotten, and there are many examples of fine contrapuntal writing in the music of the period.

There evolved a standard instrumentation for the symphony orchestra which, with considerable expansion, remains with us to the present (see Chapter Three). Other new media appeared, such as the string quartet and the piano trio (piano, violin, and cello), and the newly developed pianoforte began to supplant the harpsichord in both solo and ensemble music. Figured bass and continuo practices slowly died, though vestiges of them remained well into the nineteenth century.

The period of 1720–1750, concurrent with the late Baroque, is known as the Rococo. It is a time of transition in which many of the practices of the classical period were anticipated. A number of composers in this period, notably C. P. E. Bach (the most famous son of J. S. Bach) and Domenico Scarlatti (a distinguished harpsichord composer), were important in the development of the new style and set the stage for the classical period.

The most representative composers of the classical period are Haydn, Mozart, and Beethoven, all of whose careers centered in the city of Vienna. Haydn arrived in that city as a child to become a choir boy in St. Stephen's Cathedral. When he left the Cathedral choir school at the age of seventeen, he entered an environment well suited to the development of his great musical gifts. For Vienna, then as now, is a city rich in musical tradition.

The musical community of Vienna, largely controlled by the aristocracy, soon became aware of his talent and he was variously employed as a musician in several Viennese households. In 1761 he entered the service of the Esterhazys, fabulously wealthy patrons of the arts, where he remained for a period of almost thirty years.

As director of the musical activities in a noble household, his position was that of a servant, a role which he accepted with good grace. In moderate seclusion, and with a professional orchestra at his disposal he was in many ways ideally situated. During this period he established an international reputation that rivals and, in some ways, parallels that of the great Handel. In 1790, when he was retired on a pension from his position at Esterhazy, he was engaged by Salomon, an English impresario, to compose and conduct in the city of London. The visit was most successful and a return engagement in 1794–1795 so greatly enhanced his reputation that he returned to Europe as the most distinguished composer of his time.

Haydn's achievements center in his symphonies, over a hundred of them, and in his string quartets. These works were composed throughout his life and show the development of his personal style, as well as the musical evolution of the classical period. His works in both media strongly influenced the music of Beethoven and, to a lesser degree, that of Mozart.

In the area of church music he was quite prolific, producing fourteen Masses for chorus, orchestra, and soloists, and several shorter works. Today his Masses are ordinarily performed in concert form rather than in the church service.

An eminent place among Haydn's compositions must go to his two monumental oratorios, *The Creation* and *The Seasons*. The choral writing in these works is somewhat in the tradition of the Handelian oratorio and is filled with imaginative text painting that is both profound and delightful. He wrote much piano music and a vast amount of chamber music for various instruments, including a number of piano trios—some of the first distinguished compositions for that medium. He also enriched the concerto literature, composing solo works for cello, piano, and violin, some of which are staples of today's concert repertoire. He did not particularly excel in the area of musical drama, though he wrote a number of operas and some incidental music for the theater of the Esterhazy court.

Haydn's latter years were spent in the seclusion of semiretirement, during which time his output declined in volume but not in quality. Some of his finest works, including the two great oratorios, were produced around the turn of the century.

String Quartet, Op. 76, No. 3 (Emperor)

Haydn composed over eighty string quartets, spanning the full length of his productive life. Within them can be seen not only the evolution of the new string quartet medium, but also the beginnings of a new method of development, a technique that became an important aspect of Beethoven's style. The very first quartets, the sets of Op. 1, 2, and 3, are little more than entertaining baroque trio sonatas realized for four stringed instruments. Pieces of this sort were written by many composers around the middle of the eighteenth century. Often in five movements with two minuets, they went by such titles as divertimento or serenade.

The young Haydn, during his freelance years in Vienna, was frequently employed to compose and perform music for incidental entertainments presented by the wealthy Viennese aristocracy. Many of these affairs were outdoor entertainments in which an unwieldy keyboard instrument would have been most awkward if not impossible to use. Perhaps this was an incentive for the young composer to begin to develop a style that did not rely on the continuo for harmonic support. Removing the harpsichord from the trio sonata group and replacing it with a viola made the instrumentation that of the string quartet.

These first string quartets showed the influence of the baroque and rococo trio sonata in that the lower instruments were almost completely relegated to a supporting role, simply furnishing the harmonic background for the two violins. Even the second violin often functioned supportively so that, for the most part, the first violin was heard as an accompanied solo part.

Gradually in the course of Haydn's quartet writing there developed a texture unique to the medium of the string quartet, establishing an ideal that has inspired quartet composers from that time to the present. The lower instruments began to play a more important role in the texture, with important thematic material assigned to all four instruments. The first violin still dominated the melodic activity but did so within a fabric woven of both polyphonic and homophonic elements. The result was a highly organized and beautifully integrated fusion of four instruments, each treated idiomatically according to its own capabilities.

Of particular importance in the development of the new quartet idiom was a set of six quartets, Op. 33, composed in 1781. Haydn himself spoke of these quartets as being "composed in a new and special manner." They marked the inception of what can be termed "motivic development," the breaking up of phrases into motivic fragments and developing them contrapuntally. The technique can be seen particularly in the first movements (sonata forms) of the Op. 33 quartets where it is found not only in the development sections but also within the expositions. Haydn continued to use the technique consistently in sonata forms and it was later to become one of the most striking aspects of Beethoven's art.

Haydn composed string quartets for over fifty years, continually experimenting with contrapuntal devices, daring key relationships, and developmental techniques. The high point was perhaps reached in his set of six quartets, Op. 76. Composed during the years 1797–1798, they contain some of his most famous quartet movements—the "Witches' Minuet," a minuet in the form of a strict two-part canon (from Op. 76, No. 2); and the "Fantasia" (from Op. 76, No. 6), containing some of the wildest modulations in all of his music.

The quartet, Op. 76, No. 3, in C major is nicknamed the *Emperor* because its second movement is a set of variations on the famous hymn "God Save Our Emperor." The hymn was composed by Haydn, later became the Austrian National Anthem and, even later, the hymn of Nazi Germany, "Deutschland, Deutschland über Alles," a part of its checkered career that is best forgotten. The quartet is in four movements and represents the typical pattern of movements for string quartets and symphonies of the classical period.

The first movement of Op. 76, No. 3 is in sonata form opening in the first four bars with two phrases that typify the clear-cut phrase structure of the classical period. After the strong cadence in the fourth bar, the viola and cello play the first five notes of the opening theme, presenting the motive that becomes a prime element of the total movement (see Figure 45). Against this motive the second violin superimposes an ascending scale passage in a driving dotted rhythm which begins to be developed immediately in the other instruments, and becomes another important element in

Figure 45.

the quartet. Most of the developmental activity in the quarter is generated by these two fragments, a good example of the kind of motivic development that first appeared in the Op. 33 Quartets.

The second tonal group is a new thematic idea, rigid and angular in character, assigned to the cello (see Figure 46). Presented in the key of

Figure 46.

the dominant, it represents the typical key relationship between first and second tonal groups in the exposition of a classical sonata form. It is not an important element in the developmental progress of the movement but serves as a moment of thematic contrast in the exposition. Within the second tonal group are heard frequent references to the opening five-note motive.

The exposition concludes traditionally on the dominant. The repeat sign, marking the end of the exposition in the score, may or may not be observed. Classical composers almost always indicated a repeat at this point, but the performers themselves decide whether or not it is essential to the effect of the movement. In this instance, because of the brevity of the exposition, the repeat is usually observed.

After the repeat of the exposition, the development section opens with material derived from bar 5 of the exposition, containing the two important building blocks—the five-note motive and the scale passage in dotted rhythm (see Figure 45). Out of these two motives the complete development section is wrought—fragmented, extended, transformed, and passing through various keys. Midway through the development section the viola and cello set up a heavily accented drone bass, repeating the same tones in an incessant pedal point. (A pedal point is a tone or group of tones, often in the bass, that is sustained while other harmonic progressions, often dissonant to the pedal point, continue above it.) Above the bagpipelike sounds of the low instruments the violins play a sturdy, rustic tune suggestive of a folk dance. This tune, too, is cleverly derived from the five-note motive and also contains the dotted rhythm. Folk elements such as this appear quite often in Haydn's music, reminding us of the peasant stock from which he sprang. Their use, however, is always fully integrated with his style, and seldom produces an incongruous effect (except when it is done intentionally for a touch of humor).

Out of this folklike section evolves the preparation for the recapitulation. Pedal points are frequently used in such preparations. They create a feeling of stationary harmony so that when the recapitulation begins in the home tonality it arrives with a feeling of fresh activity in contrast to the static quality of the preparation. Most typically (though not in this case) the pedal point preceding the recapitulation is on the dominant, producing a logical progression of dominant to tonic for the start of the new section.

The recapitulation opens exactly like the beginning of the movement but soon veers into other keys in order that the theme of the second tonal group can be presented in its proper key. The second tonal group is presented in the same setting as in the exposition except that now it is in the tonic. This demonstrates the traditional key patterns of the second tonal group in sonata form—dominant (or relative major) in the exposition, tonic in the recapitulation.

At the end of the second tonal group the momentum of the movement is interrupted momentarily by two pauses in preparation for the coda. The coda, marked *piu presto,* is played at a faster tempo and uses material from both the first and second tonal groups. The movement ends in a burst of controlled energy. (In listening to this movement it is important to note that the whole second section, from the development to the end, is sometimes repeated as in a binary form. When this is done the piu presto is observed only on the repetition, the faster tempo being heard only at the very end of the movement.)

The second movement, from which the quartet derives its name, is a set of cantus firmus variations. This means that the theme is kept intact from variation to variation with the varied elements occurring in the surrounding texture rather than in the theme itself. It differs from the passacaglia or chaconne in that the theme is a complete, well-rounded entity, in this instance twenty measures in length, rather than being a brief eight-bar theme as in the baroque ostinato variation. Also, the classical theme and variations come to a complete stop after the theme and between the variations, whereas the passacaglia and chaconne are continuous in texture with no pause separating the variations.

The movement is in the key of G major, a tonality that is moderately contrasting but closely related to the home tonality of C major. It is normal, in classical symphonies and string quartets, for the second movement to be in a contrasting key, frequently the subdominant, while the first, third, and fourth movements are in the key of the tonic. The theme is first presented in a hymnlike setting of four parts with the first violin playing the melody. In variation I this melody is given to the second violin while the first violin weaves a fabric of rapid arpeggios against the slow, lyrical progress of the theme.

In variation II the cello, in its rich tenor register, plays the theme while the other instruments, particularly the first violin, interlace a contrapuntal texture against it. The viola has its turn at the melody in variation III in a texture that begins with only two instruments. The others are added in the course of the variation, ending with all four parts.

Variation IV returns the melody once again to the first violin. This final variation is often played at a slightly slower tempo than the preceding and, with rich, poignant harmonies, serves as an epilogue to the movement. It ends very quietly with four measures added after the melody is completed.

The minuet, third movement of the quartet, opens in striking contrast to the reflective mood of the slow movement. Again, as in the first movement, we see a short motive used to generate larger sections. In listening, note that the first three tones played by the first violin develop and recur in various forms throughout the movement (see Figure 47). In the Trio the relative minor furnishes an element of key contrast.

Figure 47.

The movement is, in every way, a typical classical minuet. (Refer to the discussion of this form in Chapter Four.) One characteristic of classicism (in the abstract) is its interest in reworking and refining existing forms—striving to reach new pinnacles of excellence within a preexisting framework. From the standpoint of form this minuet is exactly like hundreds of others composed during the late eighteenth century. Its sectional character, defined by important cadence points, is totally predictable. Its beauty lies not in the use of striking dissonances or formal innovations, but in its extraordinary polish, economy of means, and sheer mastery of the form. (It must be added that some of Haydn's minuets are not so predictable, for he occasionally capitalized on the stereotype to add humorous touches and the element of surprise.)

The final movement is an intensely virtuosic sonata form. It is in the parallel minor and opens with three dramatic chords, sounding as hammer strokes to begin the movement. The three-note motive used at the beginning of the minuet is also heard here but, because of the minor key, evokes a strikingly different mood (see Figure 48). Very soon the cello bursts

Figure 48.

forth with a series of fast arpeggio figures in its lowest register against
the return of the three hammer strokes. The fast notes are then passed to
the first violin and later to the other instruments. The emancipation of the
lower instruments from the supportive role they played in the earliest
quartets is clearly shown in this movement. All four of the instruments
have virtuoso passages to play and, although the first violin still dominates,
the other three instruments are almost as important.

The first tonal group is largely built of the three-note motive heard in the
third and fourth measures (see Figure 48) along with several recurrences
of the three hammer strokes. The second tonal group does not present a
new theme but is defined by its contrasting tonality, the relative major. As
explained in Chapter Four, this is the traditional tonality for the second
tonal group when the movement is in a minor key. This section, too, begins
with the three hammer strokes played by the three lower instruments while
the first violin plays running scale and arpeggio passages above.

The development section builds a tremendous amount of impetus using
all of the instruments in fast running figures. It moves energetically and
without pause into another statement of the three hammer strokes to begin
the recapitulation.

The recapitulation is different in many ways from the exposition. There is
no apparent return of the second tonal group and a developmental character
is maintained throughout. The fast notes, when they begin again, continue

unrelentingly to build momentum, finally arriving at an abrupt cadence on the dominant. After a slight pause the coda begins in the sunny key of C major with which the quartet opened.

The coda is quite long and serves to round out the complete quartet as well as the final movement. Codas of remarkable length later became a hallmark of Beethoven's style and often served, as this one of Haydn's does, an architectural function—to establish a feeling of completion at the end of a large work in several movements. In this, as in other aspects of his music, Haydn opened pathways that were of vital importance to the development of Beethoven's style.

Symphony No. 104 in D Major (London)

Haydn's symphonies, like his quartets, span the full length of his career; and the twelve composed during his visits to London represent the summit of his achievement in this form. Among these "London" symphonies are the famous *Clock* symphony (No. 101), the *Surprise* (No. 94), and the *Military* (No. 100). Salomon, the impresario who brought him to England, represented him to the British as "the greatest composer in the world," an epithet that no doubt spurred him to supreme efforts, for these works are unsurpassed from the standpoint of pure musical craft.

The twelfth in the set, and the last of his symphonies, is known as the *London*. It is scored for a typical classical symphony orchestra of woodwinds in pairs (including clarinets), two horns, two trumpets, timpani, and strings. The first movement is preceded by a slow introduction in which the choice of the somber key of D minor enhances the effect of the brilliant key of D major which follows.

The classical symphony is descended from the trisectional overture called the *sinfonia* used in Italian baroque (Neapolitan) opera. Slow introductions such as this one, however, owe their heritage to the French overture and often possess many characteristics of that baroque form. In the *London* symphony this influence is shown in the use of spacious dotted rhythms, the minor key, and the cadence on the dominant. As in the French overture, the effect is one of majestic preparation for the movement that follows.

After the introduction, the movement opens briskly but quietly, with a mood of brightness created by the use of the major mode in contrast to the minor introduction. The opening theme, played by the first violins, is a choice example of the double period. Shown in Figure 49, it is sixteen measures long with a half cadence at the end of the eighth bar. The second

Figure 49.

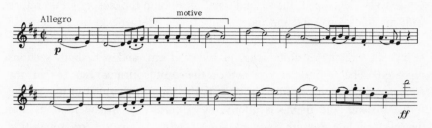

half is identical to the first except at the end where it is altered to cadence on the tonic. Well contoured and symmetrical, the theme forms a complete musical thought. So beautifully self-contained is this melody that Haydn did not develop it as a whole, but chose rather to extract from it a single motive that becomes the primary thematic element for the development section. This motive, taken from the third and fourth measures of the theme, is indicated by the bracket in Figure 49.

The second tonal groups in Haydn's sonata forms seldom produce an effect of great contrast to the preceding material. In this movement, in fact, the theme of the second tonal group is identical to that of the first, simply transposed to the key of the dominant. Some thematic contrast is introduced in the closing theme, just preceding the development.

The main theme of the exposition, having been used in both the first and second tonal groups, does not appear at all in the development section. The development is built almost completely out of the terse six-note motive shown in Figure 49. By passing it among many instruments of the orchestra in contrapuntal development, and by presenting it in various harmonic contexts, Haydn reveals the fragment to be endowed with a potential that was only hinted at in the exposition. The development section functions as the climax of the movement; for, with increasing rhythmic and dynamic intensity, a crescendo is built that utilizes the full resources of the classical orchestra. The height of the crescendo is reached at the dominant preparation just preceding the recapitulation. One of the striking moments in this movement is the restatement of the theme at the beginning of the recapitulation; for now, because the development section has revealed the multi-faceted character of the six-note motive, its return as a part of the original theme lends it a new and wonderful significance.

In comparing the recapitulation with the exposition, a number of distinctions are to be noted. The first eight-bar period is identical to its original presentation, but in the second period both orchestration and contrapuntal treatment are varied, producing a fresh effect. The six-note motive continues to be developed, the second tonal group and the closing group return with modifications, and the movement strides energetically to its close.

The slow movement is a theme with three variations, but treated very freely. The theme is quite long, in binary form, and with both sections repeated. The variations are not of the cantus firmus type as in the *Emperor* quartet, for in none of them is the theme presented in its original form. Instead, the theme is altered by a variety of ornamentations and figurations. The texture is continuous, with no pause for separation between variations.

The theme, in the key of G major, is followed by a variation in the parallel minor. The introduction of the key of G minor at this point is a striking bit of key contrast and permits the use of colorful chromatic sonorities in this variation. Further variety is achieved by the use of repeated notes and arpeggios in faster note values. The second variation, which returns to the key of G major, is more clearly related to the theme. Near the end of this variation the flute, accompanied by other woodwinds, effects a transition based on material from the first notes of the theme, setting the stage for the final variation. The final variation decorates the theme with interlaced scale and repeated note passages and concludes with a quiet coda. In listening to this movement, try to follow the progress of the theme from variation to variation, noting the devices that are used to embellish it.

The minuet which follows is one of Haydn's truly ingenious achievements in this form. The first eight-bar section is repeated as usual, but not by means of a repeat sign. The repeat is written out in full with changes in orchestration that allow the repeat to be played very softly, in sharp contrast to the full sturdy sound of the first statement.

A real surprise and a marvelous musical effect is heard near the end of the second section of the minuet (and on the repeats, as well). Here the upper woodwinds and violins interject a heavily accented chord on the third beat of the measure. Because of the rhythmic context the chord sounds as though it should be followed by another chord on the downbeat of the next measure. It sounds like an upbeat but is, in fact, an upbeat to nothing, for it is followed by two measures of total silence. The effect of surprise is enhanced by the regularity of the rhythm throughout and by the fact that, just preceding this remarkable upbeat, there is a series of accented third beats that behave quite normally. The listener expects this one to behave normally, as well; and when it doesn't, the effect is delightful.

The trio is lighter in texture and in the key of B flat major, quite distant from the home tonality of D major. Haydn's daring use of tonal relationships, particularly in his maturest works, forecast harmonic innovations of the romantic era. At the end of the trio a short section is added to effect the modulation back to D major for the da capo.

The exuberant finale begins quietly over a tonic pedal point in the cellos. Again, as in many of his sonata forms from Op. 33 on, the technique of fragmentation and motivic development is apparent. The most prominent fragment is the three-note motive shown in Figure 50. Even prior to the development section it passes through a number of interesting metamorphoses. Of particular interest in the exposition is the technique of diminution (discussed in Chapter Two) that is applied to this motive. This occurs near the end of the exposition just after the soft lyrical passage scored for strings and bassoons. At this point a comparison of the original motive

Figure 50.

(Figure 50) with the passage containing the diminution (Figure 51) will reveal how the technique is applied.

Figure 51.

The development opens quietly with an imitative treatment of the three-note motive presented against the rhythm of another motive from the opening theme. Soon other fragments from the exposition appear and the tightly knit development section gradually builds momentum; finally culminating, at the point of greatest intensity, in a moment of complete silence. There follows a soft lyrical passage that, by a fascinating and unorthodox harmonic progression, leads directly into the quiet opening of the recapitulation.

The recapitulation is slightly longer than the exposition and, as might be expected, contains further development of motives worked out earlier. With striking dynamic contrasts in a coda built over a tonic pedal, the movement surges to a close.

Haydn continued to produce masterworks even after the turn of the century. His last composition is the unfinished string quartet, Op. 103. (Only two movements were completed.) Rooted in the tradition of the eighteenth century, he was, nevertheless, an innovator of remarkable genius. The paths that he opened for Beethoven and for the beginnings of the romantic era must be recognized. But, quite aside from historical perspective, he is most distinguished for his own personal style, manifest particularly in his mastery of purely instrumental idioms. Although he was influenced by others, as others were by him, he trod a path that was uniquely his own, developing a superbly polished style that was not only nobly sophisticated but eminently human.

SUGGESTED ASSIGNMENTS

1. Summarize stylistic traits of the classical period.
2. Discuss the ways in which music of the classical period was influenced by activities of the Enlightenment movement.
3. Listen to a very early quartet of Haydn (Op. 1, 2, or 3) noting its relationship to the trio sonata and other baroque instrumental music.
4. Using resource material recommended by the instructor, investigate the various types of variation forms that have existed in the various periods of music history.
5. Listen to other instrumental works of Haydn, noting the use of motivic development and other techniques and devices discussed in this chapter.
6. As a special project investigate the use of text painting in *The Creation* or *The Seasons.*

NINE

WOLFGANG AMADEUS MOZART
(*1756–1791*)

Mozart played almost as important a part as Haydn in perfecting the characteristic means of expression for the instrumental forms of the late eighteenth century. Viewed together, their music represents every significant aspect of the classical style. Mozart, perhaps second to Haydn as a composer of symphonies and string quartets, surely excelled him in the media of the opera and concerto.

In contrast to the works of Haydn, Mozart's music overflows with lyrical thematic material, for he was one of the great creators of spontaneous melody. Where Haydn built complete movements from only a few concise motives, organized and unified with prodigious developmental skill, Mozart, in an exposition alone, used as many as four or more full-fledged, singing melodies. Their differences in melodic style partially account for the fact that Haydn's development sections tend to be longer than Mozart's. Haydn's terse thematic germs, often fragmented from longer themes, are capable of more extended development than Mozart's self-contained, beautifully contoured melodies.

In listening to such works as Mozart's G Minor Quintet (for two violins, two violas, and cello) or the *String Quartet in C Major* (the *Dissonance,* K. 465 [1]), a certain unique harmonic quality will be apparent which can be described as the dramatic use of dissonance and chromaticism. Haydn's harmonic daring was manifest more in the use of striking tonal relationships (between sections of considerable length) than in the use of Mozart's brand of chromaticism. Mozart's richness of harmony comes also from the greater contrapuntal and melodic activity in the inner voices.

During the years 1781 to 1783 Haydn and Mozart met in Vienna and

---

[1] The "K" (Köchel) numbers refer to the numbering in a catalog of Mozart's works made by Ludwig Köchel in 1862, revised by Alfred Einstein in 1937.

established a relationship of mutual respect that lasted until Mozart's death in 1791. That each learned from the other is seen in Haydn's increased use of chromaticism in the years just preceding Mozart's death, and in Mozart's increased use of motivic development in such mature works as his last symphonies and in many of his string quartets.

In the minds of many, Mozart enjoys a distinction that sets him above all others; for he was endowed with gifts of inventive musicality, dramatic instinct, and sheer creative genius to a degree that is perhaps unparalleled in the history of music. He demonstrated these remarkable gifts almost in infancy, composing at the age of five and performing as a concert pianist at the age of six. His enterprising father, a violinist-composer of considerable distinction named Leopold Mozart, took the child prodigy at the age of seven on a concert tour that included all the principal musical centers of Europe. He arrived at young manhood with an assurance and mastery of his art that is unrivaled. He was one of the few composers of all time who was able, not only to envision the total pattern of a composition in his mind prior to beginning work on it, but also to mentally work out every note—every detail of the composition. According to his own testimony, the act of notating his music was often nothing more than setting down on paper what was already complete in his mind.

His adult career began as a musician employed in the household of the Prince-Archbishop of Salzburg. Constantly rebelling at his role as a servant, he left Salzburg at the age of twenty-five to pursue his career in Vienna, hoping there to find greater artistic freedom. The remaining ten years of his life were tormented by a constant, futile struggle for financial security.

In his short career he composed more than a dozen operas, forty-one symphonies (plus several that are unnumbered), nearly forty concertos (about half of them for piano and orchestra), more than twenty string quartets, thirty-seven violin sonatas, seventeen piano sonatas, a vast amount of chamber music for various combinations, much sacred music for chorus and orchestra, and many incidental compositions.

Of his symphonies the most famous are among the numbers 31 to 41 including the *Haffner* (No. 35), the *Prague* (No. 38), No. 39 in E flat major, No. 40 in G minor, and the *Jupiter* (No. 41). His best-known quartets are a set of six dedicated to Haydn, although others are often performed as well. It is difficult to say where his greatest achievements lie, for his infallible command of design, sureness of technique, and keen dramatic sense penetrated to all musical media.

Concerto for Piano and Orchestra in D Minor, K. 466

Evolved from the concerto grosso and solo concerto of the Baroque, the classical concerto is a three-movement form for symphony orchestra and instrumental soloist. The first movement is normally in sonata form with certain stylized modifications, the second is a slow movement allowing the soloist to demonstrate the lyrical capabilities of his instrument, and the third is a brilliant fast movement, crowning the work with a display of musical virtuosity.

Most typically, the solo instrument is piano or violin, although there exists a sizable repertoire of cello concertos as well as isolated examples of concertos for other instruments. Occasionally composers have used more than one solo instrument, distinguished examples being Mozart's *Sinfonia Concertante* with solo violin and solo viola, and, in the nineteenth century, Brahms' *Concerto in A Minor* with both solo violin and solo cello.

The double exposition, a distinguishing feature of the sonata form as used in the classical concerto, begins with a complete exposition for the orchestra alone. It consists of two tonal groups with the usual key relationships and presents some of the main thematic material of the movement. This sets the stage for the second exposition which begins with the entrance of the solo instrument, usually accompanied by the orchestra. This also contains two tonal groups with the same relationships as in the first exposition. Very often, particularly in Mozart's concertos, the second exposition allows the solo instrument to present new thematic material. After the development section, the recapitulation presents the orchestra and soloist on a more or less equal basis, without the divided character of the double exposition.

Trills played by the solo instrument are used in a very stylized manner in classical concertos. They serve to delineate the sections of the form and are characteristically used at the end of each large section played by the solo instrument. As a mannerism of the style, a tutti entrance of the orchestra is heard after almost every extended trill of the solo. Trills of this sort are often found near the end of the exposition, near the end of the development, and near the end of the recapitulation.

The cadenza is an important element in the form and is usually located at the end of the recapitulation just preceding the coda. Historically it originated as an improvised embellishment of the final cadence (hence the name cadenza, Italian for cadence). In the classical concerto the solo performer used it as a vehicle to demonstrate skill in improvisation and technical virtuosity. Although a solo performer of the classical period might conceivably prepare his cadenza prior to performance, it was not normally written out by the composer. The cadenza is usually preceded by an orchestral crescendo culminating in a stereotyped cadence. The orchestra then cuts off and the soloist proceeds with a brilliant improvisation, using thematic material from the movement and concluding with a final trill, usually over a dominant sonority, to signal the orchestra to prepare for the coda. These trills serve as milestones in the form and aid the listener in following the music. In many eighteenth century concertos the coda following the cadenza is remarkably short, thus avoiding an effect of anticlimax after the culminating passages of the cadenza. The solo is not normally used in the coda.

The second movement is invariably a slow movement, often in rondo form, while the finale is either a sonata form or a rondo. Each of these movements might also contain a cadenza, although its characteristic location is in the first movement.

Most of Mozart's piano concertos were written for specific occasions in which the composer himself was soloist. In such performances the improvised cadenza was no doubt fully integrated with the rest of the movement, properly balanced and with appropriate treatment of the thematic material. In the nineteenth century increased specialization resulted in a separation of the activities of composition and performance. Composers began to write out their cadenzas in order to be assured that the musical effect would not be destroyed by an inappropriate cadenza. Other changes in the subsequent development of the concerto form will be discussed later.

A fine concerto is much more than a display piece for the virtuoso. It is also a beautifully wrought piece of orchestral music. In Mozart's concertos the soloist is always displayed to good advantage—this is essential to the ideal character of a concerto. But there is also a delicate balance achieved between orchestra and solo, realized in a variety of textures in which sometimes the soloist comes to the fore, sometimes the instruments of the orchestra. A concerto composed for the sole purpose of virtuosic display, relying upon bombast and empty theatrics for its effect, is likely to be lacking in genuine expression and musical meaning. Such is not the case in Mozart's concertos.

Figure 52 presents a diagram of a typical first-movement concerto form of the classical period.

Figure 52.

Exposition 1	Exposition 2	Solo trill	Development	Solo trill	Recapitulation	Cadenza	Solo trill	Coda
I V (III in minor)	I V (III in minor)		V and other keys		I I I⁶₄	V		I
Orchestra	Piano and Orch.		Piano and Orch.		Orch. (Piano)	Piano		Orch.

The first movement of the D Minor Piano Concerto, K. 466, is a representative example of the classical first-movement concerto form. The first part of the double exposition opens quietly but intensely with the orchestra alone. The second tonal group of the orchestral exposition is in the key of F major (the relative major), typifying the usual key relationship for sonata forms in the minor mode. The second portion of the double exposition begins with the piano alone in D minor, immediately presenting a melody that was not heard in the orchestral exposition (see Figure 53). As the orchestra joins the piano, the solo plays the first tonal group material heard at the beginning, but in a somewhat modified form. This is followed by the second tonal group, in F major.

Figure 53.

The development section opens with the melody shown in Figure 53 alternating with material from the beginning of the movement. The recapitulation begins with both piano and orchestra presenting the thematic material as it was heard at the beginning of the movement. The second tonal group is recapitulated in D minor followed shortly by an orchestral transition with a crescendo that leads directly to the cadenza.

In present-day performances of eighteenth century concertos for which the composer has not written out a cadenza, it is very rare for the soloist to actually improvise one. For most well-known concertos, there are a number of published cadenzas composed by various concert artists for use by other performers. A performer may choose to modify such a cadenza to suit his own tastes, or he may wish to compose a new one. Even during the classical period it is probable that cadenzas were often partially prepared beforehand rather than extemporized at the performance.

The second movement, entitled "Romanze," is a lyrical rondo in B flat major. The first eight measures of the rondo theme are played by the piano alone at the beginning of the movement. This melody, typical of rondo themes, is a double period, of which the second half is played by the orchestra. The form of the movement can be diagrammed with the letters ABACA plus a coda. The coda also begins with the piano alone, the orchestra entering near the end.

The final movement is a rather free rondo, with a very strong resemblance to sonata form. There are three appearances of the rondo theme, the first phrase of which is shown in Figure 54. These are always presented by the piano alone. In addition, there is an indication in the score that

Figure 54.

cadenzas should be improvised before the second and third appearances of the rondo theme, thus separating the A sections from the episodes that precede them. Both the B and C sections are quite long and tuneful, with a variety of thematic material. Just after the final return of the rondo theme, the key shifts from D minor to D major to present a coda which concludes the concerto in a mood of lyrical brilliance, a striking contrast to the pervasive minor atmosphere created earlier.

In listening to this concerto compare its style to that of the baroque concertos studied earlier. When he wished, Mozart was perfectly able to use characteristics of the baroque concertato style but, in addition, he infused the concerto form with a new subtlety of texture. The delicate balance of lyrical and virtuoso styles, the beautiful shadings of orchestral color, and the exquisite balance of materials are some of the features that rank the piano concertos among Mozart's greatest achievements. Nineteenth century concerto composers were profoundly influenced by these works.

The Magic Flute, an Opera in Two Acts

The versatility demonstrated by Mozart's achievements in all musical forms and media is nowhere more striking than in the area of music drama. Opera—since it demands great skill in writing for the orchestra, for solo voices, and for chorus, and since it requires the masterful manipulation of a variety of musical forms—was the ideal vehicle for a composer of Mozart's varied talents. The ability to coordinate these diverse musical factors in the service of the libretto is what makes Mozart a great composer of opera.

Not the least of his talents was his gift of dramatic characterization, his ability to penetrate the depths of each individual character. So unerring was his psychological and dramatic instinct that his characters come alive in a manner unparalleled in the history of opera. Baroque opera composers were often satisfied with prototype characters—stereotyped lovers, typically tragic heroes, and the like. With Mozart's operas, however, there begins an emphasis on musical characterization of unique, individual personalities—a kind of realism that comes from the spirit of the Enlightenment and which presages realism in nineteenth century opera. This is seen partly in the orchestral accompaniment to the voices and partly in the vocal lines themselves. In large ensembles involving several characters Mozart portrays individuals by using distinctly different melodic styles for each. By these and other means the listener is left with a clear and unforgettable impression of each character in the drama.

Mozart's mature operas fall into three general categories—(1) opera buffa, (2) opera seria, and (3) German Singspiel opera. Opera buffa is a type of comic opera that originated as entertainments presented between the acts of opera seria. They were originally called intermezzi and were in two acts, one performed between acts one and two of the opera seria, the other between acts two and three. A superb example of an early intermezzo is Pergolesi's La Serva Padrona, first performed in 1737. It is in two acts, uses three characters (one a mute), and its organization consists of the alternation of arias and duets with secco recitative. During the classical period the intermezzo idea developed into the full-length comic opera style called opera buffa. Mozart's most distinguished examples in this form are Cosi fan tutte and The Marriage of Figaro. Their complex plots are typical of the style, involving love triangles and intrigue in a deliciously subtle musical fabric.

Opera seria, the dominating eighteenth century opera style, is seen in

Mozart's *Idomeneo* and *La Clemenza di Tito*. *Idomeneo* is notable for its superb orchestration, seen particularly in the colorful and expressive use of the brass and woodwinds. Experimentation with orchestral color is more prominent in Mozart's dramatic works than in his symphonies, possibly because of the stylized and restricted instrumentation of the classical symphony and also because of the greater expressive demands of the theatrical idiom.

Singspiel (sung drama) is a term describing opera in the German language, usually comic, in which the recitatives are replaced by spoken dialogue. It characteristically uses indigenous material such as folk song or legend along with a mixture of various operatic styles and, in many ways, is the German counterpart of the English ballad opera. Mozart's link with the older Italian opera tradition is seen in his use of the Italian language in opera seria and buffa. Nevertheless, he did not neglect the German language, for an important contribution to native German opera is found in his singspiel *Die Entführung aus dem Serail* (The Abduction from the Seraglio). A further and more profound development in this direction is seen in *Die Zauberflöte* (The Magic Flute), the most enigmatic of Mozart's operas, completed and premiered in 1791.

The libretto of *The Magic Flute* was written by Emmanuel Schikaneder, an enterprising Viennese theatrical manager whom Mozart had met in Salzburg in 1780. The opera is in two acts with a fantastic and complex plot containing allegorical references to the current Austrian political situation as well as to Freemasonry. Both Mozart and Schikaneder were members of the Masonic organization which wielded considerable influence in eighteenth century politics, including in its ranks such distinguished figures as Frederick the Great, Goethe, Haydn, and Voltaire.

The plot of *The Magic Flute* can be summarized as follows: Prince Tamino falls in love with a picture of Pamina, daughter of the Queen of Night. Pamina, however, is under the protection of Sarastro, high priest of Isis and Osiris. The Queen attempts to use Tamino to get her daughter back. The Moor Monostatos, a treacherous priest in Sarastro's Temple, intrigues with the Queen, hoping to acquire Pamina for himself. Tamino, before setting out to reach Pamina, receives a magic flute as protection against evil, and the bird-catcher Papageno who accompanies him is given a set of magic bells. In Act Two, when Tamino is at the gates of the Temple, he discovers that Sarastro is wise and good and that the Queen of Night is the evil one. Tamino and Papageno pass through several ordeals (possibly veiled references to Masonic ritual) and finally Tamino and Pamina are united. The Queen of Night and Monostatos are defeated and Papageno, who has been seeking a wife, is rewarded with a bride, Papagena.

The music of *The Magic Flute* is characterized by a variety of musical forms and by great diversity of musical textures. The overture is a sonata form with a slow introduction and contains fugal development of the principal theme. The three fortissimo chords heard at the outset are a mystical symbol of Freemasonry as is also the principal key of E flat major. These three chords recur in various forms at crucial points throughout the drama.

Papageno's opening number (No. 2, *"Der Vogelfänger bin ich ja"*) in the form of a simple strophic song (meaning that the same music is used for each verse of text) represents the folk element in singspiel. Little more than a simple street song, Mozart's wit and brilliant instrumentation elevate it to a level of artistic significance. Throughout the opera Papageno's part represents the influence of the German folk song—transformed by Mozart's genius. The parts sung by the Queen of the Night, on the other hand, represent the Italian opera style. No. 14 (*"Der Holle Räche kocht in meinem Herzen"*), for example, with its elaborate coloratura passages, is typical of Mozart's opera seria style; but, at the same time, serves to characterize the blind passion of the evil Queen. Hers is the most technically demanding part in the opera, requiring a coloratura voice of great agility.

Much of the music in *The Magic Flute* lies between these two extremes of German folk song and sophisticated Italian opera. The duet for Pamina and Papageno (No. 7, *"Bei Männern, welche liebe fühlen"*) is a charming example of the fusion of the two styles. The first strophe is simple and folk-like in character while the second is varied with restrained coloratura passages.

The thread of action in the drama is carried primarily by spoken dialogue but accompanied recitative is also used. Such recitatives function to depict the personalities of the characters by musical means as well as to carry on the plot. A good example of this is found in the finale of Act One (No. 8—Tamino's recitative just following the trio of the Three Spirits when he first sees the Temple) (see Figure 55).

An aspect of the opera that is unusual for Mozart is the use of motives and even entire phrases that are repeated throughout the course of the work. Papageno's whistle and the three Masonic chords are cases in point.

Figure 55.

Die Weis heits leh - re die-ser Kna-ben   sei e - wig mir ins Herz ge-gra-ben.
These words of wis-dom tru-ly spo-ken   Be in my heart en-graved as to - ken.

Such devices anticipate Wagner's leitmotif practices, one of a number of ways in which Mozart contributed to the establishment of a native German opera.

The finales of Mozart's operas are uniquely successful. No one knew better than he the effect of a striking curtain scene. Yet at the same time his finales are as musically unified as his finest symphonic works. In many of his operas the ultimate unraveling of the plot takes place in the finale of the last act, lending a dramatic significance to a section that, in the hands of lesser composers, was often nothing more than a final musical set-piece. In *The Magic Flute* the finale opens in the key of E flat major with the trio of Spirits. They come upon Pamina, torn by sadness because Tamino would not speak. (Unknown to her, part of his ordeal at the Temple was to maintain silence.) She is about to end her life when the Spirits convince her that Tamino loves her and together they proceed to find him. The scene shifts and (in the relative minor) two men in armor intone a chorale melody. Tamino is brought to them and while they speak together Pamina's voice is heard offstage calling to Tamino. It is decided that she, along with Tamino, is worthy to be ordained and the lovers are brought together. With the help of Tamino's magic flute, they survive the final ordeals, passing through the caves of fire and water into the Temple. The offstage chorus rejoices their triumph.

In the meantime, Papageno has broken his vow of silence and fears that he will not find a wife. In an extended solo passage he lugubriously bemoans his folly until finally the Three Spirits exhort him to use his magic bells. He does, it works, and there follows a joyous duet between Papageno and Papagena, comically using the syllables pa-pa-pa.

Outside the Temple the villainous Queen with her attendants and the Moor Monostatos are foiled in a final attempt to abduct Pamina. Amid thunder and lightning they sink into the earth. In the Temple, Sarastro stands before Pamina and Tamino as the opera concludes with the full chorus and orchestra.

To understand and appreciate an opera it is, of course, necessary to understand the words that are being sung on the stage. Because of the practice of performing opera in its original language (a practice which, hopefully, is on the decline) it is important that the listener avail himself of a translation of the libretto. With this, and with an acceptance of the conventions of opera (for opera cannot be appreciated from the same point of view as legitimate theater), splendid worlds of dramatic and musical fantasy are opened to the listener.

During the last year of his life Mozart was mysteriously commissioned to compose a Requiem Mass. Poverty stricken, in poor health, and obsessed with the notion that this funeral mass was to be his own, he worked feverishly to fulfill the commission. The *Requiem,* nearly completed, was finished after his death by one of his pupils and ranks among his greatest works. Never achieving the recognition that he richly deserved, he died in his thirty-fifth year, leaving an incomparable legacy of musical masterworks.

SUGGESTED ASSIGNMENTS

1. Summarize the important differences in style between the works of Haydn and Mozart.
2. Investigate the history and evolution of concerto forms from the mid-Baroque to Mozart.
3. Investigate the history of the piano, noting the type of instrument used by Mozart. How might this information be used by present-day interpreters of Mozart's piano concertos?
4. Listen to Pergolesi's *La Serva Padrona* and compare it to *The Magic Flute.* Note the differences in operatic style and dramatic characterization between the two works.
5. As a special project investigate the use of symbolism in *The Magic Flute.* Use resources recommended by the instructor.
6. Expand your knowledge of Mozart's music by listening to a major work from each of the media in which he excelled: symphony, concerto, opera, chamber music, choral works, etc.

PART THREE

MUSIC OF THE NINETEENTH CENTURY

TEN

LUDWIG VAN BEETHOVEN
(*1770–1827*)

Beethoven entered a world bristling with new ideas. The beginning of the romantic era was teeming with activity and thought. New worlds of art, science, and philosophy were beginning to be explored and it was a time of conflicts—absolutism versus freedom of the individual, flourishing capitalism versus emerging socialism, religious faith versus scientific thought. Much of what was new in the nineteenth century, however, was the logical result and continuation of attitudes, events, and circumstances of the eighteenth. The cataclysmic political upheavals and philosophical changes taking place around the turn of the century could not conceal the fact that the seeds of revolt were planted long before the beginnings of the romantic era.

In music the romantic movement is generally said to begin around 1815 or 1820 and extend to the end of the century. Yet composers such as Haydn and Mozart had composed music during the eighteenth century that was, in many ways, strongly romantic in character, using techniques that later developed into stylistic traits of romantic music. In the other arts— for example, in the poetry of William Blake or the paintings of Jacques Louis David—there is much prophecy of artistic and philosophical trends of the succeeding century. In all human activities the nineteenth century must be viewed as the child of the eighteenth.

For the artist the early nineteenth century was a time of the decline of aristocratic and ecclesiastical patronage, a time of his emergence as a free individual. The figure of Beethoven, more than any other, provided the romantic period with a model for its conception of the "artist." In his relationship to society Beethoven played a role quite different from that of his predecessors. Haydn could play the part of the "esteemed musical factotum" with a degree of good grace. Mozart, though rebelling against the

141

patronage system, failed to establish himself as an independent artist. Beethoven, however, would accept no part of the role of servant. As an artist he yielded no precedence to mere noblemen. He accepted their patronage when he required it, but in return demanded that he be treated not as an equal but as the superior individual that he was. The increasing middle-class audience and the growth of music publishing gradually freed him from absolute dependence upon patrons so that he was able to maintain himself financially and compose in whatever manner he wished.

Beethoven was firmly grounded in the techniques of the classical period. He apparently learned a great deal from Haydn, with whom he studied for a short time in Vienna, for his use of thematic fragmentation and motivic development became very highly refined. He inherited all the forms and techniques of the eighteenth century and, at first, used them in very classical ways. His first two symphonies and his Op. 18 string quartets are superb examples of the culmination of the classical style. They are representative of his so-called first period (to 1804) but, at the same time, contain elements that are suggestive of the later Beethoven.

After the turn of the century, Beethoven increasingly infused his music with a meaning and significance that transcended the classical style. The works of his middle period (from 1804 to around 1816) stretch the classical forms to the breaking point. To contain his spacious, sweeping, and tumultuous ideas, it was necessary for him to expand the framework of the classical symphony. This was done in many ways (some already mentioned in our discussion of the Fifth Symphony) and reached a peak in the Ninth Symphony which calls for a larger orchestra than had ever been used in a symphony and, additionally, requires the vocal forces of a full choir and four soloists. Many features of his music served as ideals for the musical expression of the romantic era.

Beethoven was the first to adopt the principle of "art for art's sake." He did not cater to a limited public but seemed, in works such as the Fifth Symphony, to address a universal audience—perhaps an audience of the future, but certainly not one that was limited by social levels or political boundaries. In other instances, the last string quartets, for example, he wrote only for himself or for those few who could understand him—the profound reflections of a solitary genius.

Perhaps it is putting it too strongly to say that Beethoven was "the man who freed music," but in many ways he established important precedents for the musical trends of the romantic movement. Prominent among these is the vastness of symphonic expression seen in the greater length of his symphonies (as compared to those of Haydn and Mozart) and in the proportionately greater length and importance of his development sections. Presaging the concept of the symphonic tone poem are such works as his Sixth Symphony and the *Coriolanus* and *Egmont* overtures, all of which are more or less programmatic in nature. A further contribution is seen in the evolution of the scherzo from the classical minuet. In this Beethoven opened the way for unique scherzo movements in the works of Brahms, Chopin, Mendelssohn, Berlioz, and a number of other nineteenth century composers.

Beethoven's freer use of the variation form is another aspect of the genesis of the romantic movement. This is seen particularly in his *Diabelli Variations,* Op. 120, a set of thirty-three variations for piano solo based on a theme by the publisher Diabelli. In this work the variations hold a much freer relationship to the theme than in the classical theme-and-variation form. Each variation has its own particular mood or character, producing great contrast within the total work and giving rise to the term "character variation," a free and typically romantic concept of the variation technique.

Yet another innovation is seen in his set of solo songs, *"An die ferne Geliebte"* ("To the Distant Beloved"), a work that is often referred to as the first romantic song cycle. Cycles (sets) of German art songs (nineteenth century *lieder*) occupy a central position in the works of such distinguished romantics as Schubert, Schumann, Brahms, and Wolf. The solo song with piano accompaniment is the medium through which the romantic period expressed itself most purely and freely, and it wielded a strong influence on the instrumental music of the period. The lied also represents a salient feature of romanticism in general, the blending and overlapping of the arts—in this case the ideal fusion of poetry and music.

The most striking feature of Beethoven's music, particularly that of his middle period, is its character of intense and boundless energy. This can be seen in the volcanic outbursts such as in the finale of the Fifth Symphony or in the trio of the same symphony where it takes on the quality of humorous bombast. Sharp dynamic contrasts and sudden accents also mark his music but there is a gentle side as well. This can be seen in his slow movements, which are often endowed with a hymnic lyricism that can be tender, yearning, sad, or profoundly reflective.

So vast a range of human expression required new and broader concepts of musical architecture. Manifesting the classical heritage, his musical structures are strongly balanced and superbly cohesive; yet in scope and grandeur of conception they are supremely romantic. Movements of epic length are built with great economy of means, often constructed completely from a few terse motives painstakingly woven into a fabric of tremendous dramatic and expressive qualities. Sections of the first-movement form, such as the introduction and the coda, became longer, while his development sections showed even greater expansion as compared with the classical models. In this he set the precedent for the romantic concept of the development as the dominating section of the sonata form. Many of his sketchbooks have been preserved—a vivid testimony to the assiduous and self-critical manner in which he approached problems of form and the art of composition in general.

Over a period of about twenty years Beethoven gradually lost his hearing, becoming almost totally deaf in 1820. The works of the last period (from about 1816 till his death) show an increased quality of meditation. The dynamic, impassioned outbursts of his middle period are replaced by calm affirmation—reflective assurance. To his contemporaries, some of the music of this period was beyond comprehension. Critics of the time attributed certain enigmatic musical effects to his deafness, saying that he went too far in sacrificing musical practicability to the ideal conceptions heard in his inner ear. In listening to certain of these works, such as the String Quartet, Op. 133 (*Grosse Fuge*) or parts of the Ninth Symphony, it is not difficult to understand this attitude. Yet it is quite possible that Beethoven would have explored the same obscure worlds of sound had he not been deaf. The abstract or absolute qualities of the music of this period are the result of his concern with purely musical matters—a preoccupation with contrapuntal textures, motivic development, and thematic variation. The essence of his third period is heard in his last string quartets where, with few exceptions, resemblances to the classical forms of Haydn and Mozart are heard only as vestiges.

Beethoven's works include nine symphonies as opposed to Mozart's forty-one and Haydn's one hundred and four; and sixteen string quartets against Mozart's twenty and Haydn's eighty. This disparity in musical output is explained partly by the relatively greater length of Beethoven's compositions and partly by his slow, painstaking work habits. More significant, however, is the indication of a changing relationship between the artist and society. Haydn composed such large quantities of music primarily because he was employed to do so. Retained as an employee in an aristocratic household, it was his obligation to compose, rehearse, and perform music for any incidental occasion that might arise. Beethoven, since he was not

employed as a court composer or Kapellmeister, produced as his inclination led him. He accepted commissions, but only on his own terms. He
hoped for public response, even for immortality; but he maintained a status
quite different from that of the eighteenth century composer—a relationship of artist to society that persists even to the present day.

In addition to his symphonies and string quartets, Beethoven produced a
number of overtures and incidental orchestral pieces, a violin concerto and
five piano concertos, nine piano trios and other chamber music for various
combinations, ten violin sonatas, five cello sonatas, thirty-two piano sonatas, an opera, various choral works, and numerous other compositions.
Works in all of these varied media have maintained a lasting popularity in
the concert repertoire. The piano sonatas hold a place in the keyboard literature paralleled only by the *Well-Tempered Clavier* of Bach. Many of
his works maintain similar positions of prestige, for he is perhaps the first
musical spokesman of the age in which we live. His music sings of freedom
and self-asserting individuality, bridging the transition from the old society
to the new.

Symphony No. 1 in C Major, Op. 26

The list of movements of Beethoven's First Symphony (see Figure 56)
shows the characteristic four-movement pattern used in the symphonies of
Haydn and Mozart. Essentially, it is a classical symphony, but one that
contains a number of features typifying Beethoven's unique style. The first
of these is seen in the opening chord of the slow introduction At the first

Figure 56.

1. Adagio molto: Allegro con brio
2. Andante cantabile con moto
3. Menuetto e Trio
4. Adagio: Allegro molto e vivace

performance in 1800 critics took special exception to the fact that this sonority was a dissonance. Today our ears hear it not particularly as a dissonance, but as a chord of unrest, a sonority requiring resolution like a dominant seventh. Indeed, it is a seventh chord but not in the home tonality of C
major. Rather it is the dominant seventh of the key of F major, closely related to C major. Symphonic works of the eighteenth century normally began on the tonic or with some member of the tonic triad. For Beethoven to

ignore this tradition and begin with a sonority not even in the same key as the symphony was a daring innovation. To the ear it has the effect of creating a false tonal center, of obscuring the key feeling. This ambiguity of tonality is gradually clarified so that just before the allegro con brio there is a strong feeling of dominant in the key of C major progressing to the tonic at the beginning of the fast movement.

The fast movement opens with a three-note motive (shown in Figure 57) out of which the entire first tonal group is wrought. After a well-defined cadence at the end of the first tonal group, the second tonal group proceeds in the key of the dominant. The contrasting thematic fragment presented here is tossed back and forth between the oboe and flute accompanied by the violins playing a five-note figure that later becomes important

Figure 57.

in the development section (see Figure 58). This material is passed to the other instruments of the orchestra and then, shortly before the end of the exposition, the three-note motive is heard again, this time in combination with other material.

Figure 58.

The development section is built out of several fragmentary ideas from the exposition. In addition to the three-note motive of the first tonal group, the fragment shown in Figure 58 is also prominent. Introduced very unobtrusively at the beginning of the second tonal group, it now becomes an important element of the development section, demonstrating Beethoven's ingenuity in endowing seemingly insignificant thematic germs with great musical meaning.

The recapitulation is more heavily orchestrated than the exposition but follows the classical pattern of key relationships. *Sforzandi* (heavy accents) are heard throughout the movement and are even more prominent near the end. The movement concludes with an expanded coda.

The slow movement is a sonata form in the key of F major opening with a fugal exposition of the subject shown in Figure 59. Note the manner in which the beginning of the subject is built out of successive repetitions of the opening three-note motive (shown in brackets). This motive plus the dotted rhythm in the third measure are the primary building blocks of the

Figure 59.

movement. The theme at the beginning of the second tonal group, for example, is derived from the first two notes of the opening motive (see Figure 60) and later becomes a significant element of the development. In the course of the movement the dotted rhythm is heard in a number of varying forms.

Figure 60.

Development of the two-note motive shown in Figure 60 occurs at the beginning of the development section, soon combining with the dotted rhythm. After a series of sforzandi, the timpani enters on the dominant tone, marking the beginning of a long dominant preparation (transition and preparation for the recapitulation) that is most characteristic of Beethoven's style.

The recapitulation begins like the exposition except for the added element of a gently running scale passage that is first presented by the cellos against the opening subject played by the second violins. This continues to be used against entrances of the subject, producing the effect of a fugal exposition with two subjects presented simultaneously. A substantial coda effectively combines the various thematic elements of the movement as it reaches a quiet ending.

The classical minuet pattern is closely followed in the third movement. Its quality of intense energy, and the speed of the movement foretells the later development of the scherzo form. Again, as in so much of Beethoven's music, it is built out of a few short motives tightly woven into a fabric of remarkable unity.

In the final movement the dominant tone played fortissimo by the entire orchestra heralds the beginning of the slow introduction. The introduction is quite short and uses only the first violins in a gradual unfolding of a seven-note scale passage (see Figure 61). The violins begin with just three notes of the scale: G, A, B. On each halting repetition another note

Figure 61.

is added, finally arriving at the F above. The fast movement then begins with the violins playing the full eight-note scale, completing the scale begun in the introduction. The most prominent thematic characteristic of the movement is the use of scale passages—ascending, descending, and in various rhythmic and contrapuntal contexts. By gradually unfolding the scale passage in the introduction, Beethoven, at the outset, presents the essence of the entire movement.

The movement is in sonata form and possesses a feeling of intense but highly controlled energy. The contrasting second tonal group is clearly apparent in the exposition. The development section is woven almost entirely out of scale passages leading into a fairly long dominant preparation. The recapitulation is almost identical to the exposition (except for the usual key change in the second tonal group) while the coda is of architectonic proportions, almost equal in length to the exposition. The movement concludes with Beethoven's typical reiteration of the tonic triad.

Beethoven's use of the sonata form instead of the rondo for this movement is indicative of the increased importance of the finale in Beethoven's symphonies, as well as of his predilection for the sonata form. (Three of the four movements of this symphony are in sonata form.) In many of the nine symphonies the finale is the longest of the movements and always concludes with an extended coda that has the effect of rounding out the total work like a builder balancing structural units of a massive edifice. The emphasis upon rationality of formal design marks Beethoven as a classicist, but in his later works the scope of design reached such new and imposing heights that the restrictive classical practices became inadequate. It has been said that an important trait of the romantic movement is the subjugation of form to content. As applied to Beethoven, it should be rephrased. In regard to form, the important trait is *expansion*—the consummation of old techniques and the development of new ones. Only thus could his magnificent ideas be contained.

String Quartet in F Major, Op. 59, No. 1

The three string quartets of Op. 59 were commissioned by a Russian nobleman, Count Rasoumovsky. The Count, who maintained his own string quartet with himself as second violinist, had asked that each of the quartets contain a Russian folk tune, but Beethoven observed this request only in the first two.

The *Rasoumovsky Quartets,* as they are called, fall into Beethoven's second period and exhibit a consummate mastery of the string quartet medium. No longer does the first violin dominate as in most of the quartets of Haydn and Mozart, and in Beethoven's Op. 18 quartets. Virtuoso writing abounds in all four parts, woven into a great variety of textures with the four instruments treated almost equally. There is much dialogue between the instruments, a wide range of expression, and abundant use of short rhythmic motives. Great economy of means is demonstrated by his frequent emphasis upon one or two musical ideas, sometimes building complete movements in this way. On the other hand, there are a number of instances of movements utilizing many themes and fragments woven into structures of perfect unity. (The two middle movements of Op. 59, No. 1 are admirable examples of the latter.)

The Op. 59 quartets were written in 1806 and, in spite of Beethoven's increasing deafness, are perhaps the greatest string quartets in existence. The superlative qualities of the last quartets (Op. 127, 130, 131, 132, 133, and 135) as pure music cannot be disputed. Yet for sheer mastery of the instrumental idiom, the *Rasoumovsky Quartets* are unsurpassed.

Op. 59, No. 1 begins with the cello playing the melody in the deep, rich register of the G string accompanied by repeated notes in the second violin and viola. The melody (shown in Figure 62) is flowing and lyrical in quality but it contains two motives (indicated by brackets) that are the main thematic fragments of the first movement. At the end of the exposition there is no double bar or repeat sign, but Beethoven gives the impression of a repeat by pretending to begin the development section exactly like the exposition, then surprises the listener by going off on a tan-

Figure 62.

gent with much development of both motives of the opening theme. Throughout the development section there is a great deal of contrapuntal activity concluding with a fugato which leads smoothly into the recapitulation which begins with the cello playing the melody as at the beginning of the movement. The tonal relationships in the recapitulation are quite standard with the second tonal group being recapitulated on the tonic. As a whole, the movement is a striking example of the use of fragments to develop longer, more flowing ideas.

The scherzo which follows is remarkable in a number of ways. For one thing, the placement of the scherzo as the second movement is unusual, although both Haydn and Mozart occasionally used the minuet as the second movement. Also, the classical practice usually followed by Beethoven was for the slow movement to be in a contrasting key with the minuet or scherzo cast in the home tonality. In this work Beethoven reverses this procedure by putting the scherzo in the key of B flat and the slow movement in F minor.

To all intents and purposes this is a scherzo but it is also a full-fledged sonata form. It opens in a most remarkable manner with the cello alone for the first four measures, defining a rhythmic pattern on a single tone, B flat. The second violin then enters alone, followed by the viola and then the first violin in a droll dialogue effect. The large number of short thematic ideas used in this movement is unusual for Beethoven, who often built movements out of only one or two short motives. It is perhaps because of this that its range of emotional expression is so astonishingly wide, yet the movement is completely unified. The practice of endowing the scherzo with traits of sonata form increased in later works of Beethoven.

Against a sustained chordal accompaniment, the first violin opens the slow movement with a profoundly tragic melody. The theme is immediately repeated by the cello, sustaining and intensifying the somber mood. The movement is characterized by tremendous evocative qualities and by a great deal of rhythmic activity. This is the longest of the four movements and the feeling of sublime sorrow is preserved with absolute mastery throughout. The movement concludes with a trill on the dominant tone played by the first violin. Under this inverted pedal point the cello begins the finale with a "Theme Russe," satisfying the Count's request for a Russian folk song (see Figure 63). By connecting the third and fourth movements in this way, Beethoven achieves a greater feeling of continuity as the

Figure 63.

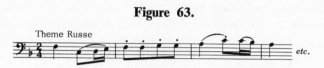

quartet nears its finish—another instance of breaking ties with the classical tradition.

The fourth movement is a typical Beethoven finale—a sonata form with rondo characteristics. Most of the thematic material of the movement is extracted from the Russian theme first played by the cello, although other material, including a prominent dotted rhythm, is used as well. The exposition concludes on the dominant with a violin trill identical to that at the end of the third movement. This sets the stage for the repeat of the exposition as well as for the beginning of the development section after the repeat. The development uses various fragments from the Russian theme and presents the dotted rhythm in a complex structure that builds a tremendous amount of rhythmic intensity. This is then developed even further in the recapitulation.

Following a pause and a descending arpeggio in the first violin, the coda begins with a fugato treatment of the last part of the Russian theme. It gradually dies away and is immediately followed by a few brilliant measures in a very fast tempo, concluding the quartet.

In listening to this work, as in any fine example of chamber music, it is best to remember that the drama in this sort of music is of an inward kind. Here we find neither the thunderous grandeur of the symphony nor the melodramatic gesture of the operatic stage. Everything is on a smaller scale—more intricately chiseled, more highly polished. Chamber music differs from orchestral music in that there is only one player to a part. Each performer is solely responsible for his part. The ideal chamber music player is able to subjugate his musical personality to serve the total ensemble or, when necessary, to come to the fore as a soloist. The definition of chamber music usually restricts the number of players to a minimum of two or three and a maximum of eight or nine performers. Fewer than three is usually too soloistic to suit the characteristic language of chamber music while more than nine begins to sound like an orchestra.

Ideally, chamber music is played for a small audience; its most natural setting is perhaps the home. Because of this, composers of chamber music have traditionally addressed themselves to a select audience of connoisseurs, musical amateurs, and the like. Their most personal musical thoughts are best expressed in chamber music media, for here the composer can speak in a more refined vocabulary than in music designed for vast public audiences; and here also, he can test his most profound musical ideas and be assured of an understanding audience.

The classical and early romantic periods saw the creation of a vast chamber music literature. The most important chamber music medium of the time was the string quartet, and so it remains to the present. For string players it is the ideal form of music. Among composers of string quartets, Beethoven is preeminent, but he is closely attended by Haydn, Mozart, Schubert, and Brahms. Music of these composers remains the backbone of our chamber music literature—a vast wellspring for the chamber music player as well as for the understanding listener.

Mass in D, Missa Solemnis, Op. 123

Beethoven's third period is characterized by greater use of contrapuntal devices and polyphonic textures. Undoubtedly his deep admiration for the music of J. S. Bach was an important factor in this culmination of his contrapuntal style. Fugatos, canons, as well as complete fugues are found in the last piano sonatas, in the late quartets, in the Ninth Symphony, and in the *Missa Solemnis*.

His introspective concern with purely musical effects during the last ten years of his life caused him to be increasingly occupied in experimentation with new textures and sonorities. Effects such as very wide vertical spacing between voice lines and unusual sonorities resulting from contrapuntal motion are found among these last works. It is possible that his almost total loss of hearing contributed to the abstract qualities of the music of this period, causing him to attempt to bring to full realization sounds that existed only within his imagination.

The *Missa Solemnis* is divided into five movements corresponding to the five sections of the Ordinary of the Roman Catholic Mass: [1] 1. *Kyrie;* 2. *Gloria;* 3. *Credo;* 4. *Sanctus* and *Benedictus;* 5. *Agnus Dei.* The work

[1] The Ordinary is that part of the Mass which remains the same for every occasion of the church year. An exception is the Gloria, second section of the Ordinary, which is conventionally omitted in certain seasons. The remainder of the text of the Mass, placed between sections of the Ordinary, varies according to the church calendar and is called the Proper.

was intended for the coronation of Archduke Rudolph as Archbishop of Ölmutz in 1820 but was not completed in time for the ceremony. Work on the Mass began in 1818 but it was not completed until the end of 1822. It was neither published nor performed in its entirety until after Beethoven's death.

The Mass is pervaded with Beethoven's very personal and unorthodox religious attitudes. Like Bach's B Minor Mass, it is not particularly appropriate for liturgical use, although it has been performed in the church service. Scored for full orchestra (including four horns and three trombones), organ, soloists, and chorus, it is like a vast choral symphony in five movements. The choral style shows the influence of Handel whose music Beethoven particularly admired; but there are no independent solo numbers as in most operas and oratorios. Rather, the chorus and solo quartet alternate and interweave within each of the five movements, thus preserving the five sections of the Mass.

In all of the movements Beethoven evolves a logical musical form from the organization of the text itself, and, at the same time, endows the music with the inner meaning of the words. The three parts of the *Kyrie* (*"Kyrie eleison"*—*"Christe eleison"*—*"Kyrie eleison"*) furnish the outline of a simple ABA form; and this ternary pattern, expanded to grandiose proportions, is the basic form of the first movement. As in most Mass settings, repetitions of each part of the text furnish additional length. It opens with the orchestra alone and soon the chorus enters with material already presented. Brief entrances of the tenor, soprano, and alto soloists are presented in this A section but a more striking use of the solo voices is heard at the beginning of the middle section. This B portion is set off from the preceding section by the change from chorus to soloists, from duple to triple meter, and by the introduction of a new motive. This is the motive to the word *"Christe,"* consisting of a descending third (see Figure 64). It is the most prominent thematic fragment of this section and recurs in later movements as a unifying factor in the total work. At the end of the B section the meter changes back to duple for the return of the A material. The extended final A section

Figure 64.

Chri - ste

uses the soloists sparingly in a texture dominated by the chorus and orchestra. Contrast to the first A section is achieved by varying and extending the material on its final presentations. Much imitation is heard in this movement and a wonderfully smooth contrapuntal texture is maintained throughout.

The *Gloria* is also organized in a spacious three-part structure. It opens jubilantly, like a shout of joy, with imitative treatment of the words *"Gloria in excelsis Deo."* The first section begins in D major, passes through B flat major and concludes in F major, furnishing intense harmonic contrast. The use of powerful harmonic progressions to depict the meaning of the text is demonstrated at the climactic point of the first section on the words *"Pater omnipotens."*

The middle section of the *Gloria* opens in F major with the words *"Qui tollis peccata mundi."* Mood, tempo, texture, and meter are all changed, furnishing great contrast to the first section. The intensely personal interpretation that Beethoven attaches to the words of this section is seen in his use of the solo voices—a means of deepening the quality of intimacy. In the final presentation of the words *"miserere nobis,"* Beethoven precedes each statement with the exclamatory syllables "ah" and "oh," thus heightening the intensity of emotional expression. The final section of the movement beginning with the word *"Quoniam,"* returns to the mood of the opening and then culminates in a tremendous fugue.

The central tonality of both the first and second movements is D major. For the *Credo* he chose B flat major, demonstrating a key relationship characteristic of the romantic period, that of two tonal centers separated by a major third (often called the "third relation"). This also serves to distinguish the *Credo* from the other movements, setting it off as the very core of the Mass—the affirmation of faith and the longest text of the five movements. Again the expansive three-part form is used, and again the middle section is set off by a slower tempo and a change of key (back to D major). The middle section begins with the words *"et homo factus est"* and presents the descending third motive that was used in the first movement on the word *"Christe"* (Figure 64). The use of cyclical devices (tying movements together by the use of the same thematic material) increases in Beethoven's third period. This is particularly apparent in the Ninth Symphony where it sets a precedent for the use of cyclical devices by later symphonic composers.

The climactic section of the movement begins on the words *"et ascendit"* in an imitative setting using ascending scale passages. On the words *"Credo in spiritum sanctum,"* Beethoven treats the word *"Credo"* in the same way that he did at the beginning of the movement, thus returning to the final A section of the ternary form. The final portion of this section, beginning with the words *"et vitam venturi,"* returns to the key of B flat major in an inspired choral fugue of great dramatic impact, utilizing the full resources of chorus, orchestra, and soloists.

The *Sanctus* begins quietly, and the contrast of D major to the preceding key of B flat contributes much to the effect of this opening—one of the most beautiful moments in all of Beethoven's music. Here we see the truly romantic practice of utilizing orchestral color for expressive purposes— the emphasis on sheer sonority for its evocative qualities. The rich fabric woven in the low strings, low woodwinds, and trombones creates an effect of unearthly beauty that is further enhanced by the entrance of the solo voices on the word *"Sanctus."* The mood of enraptured meditation is preserved throughout the opening section. It is followed by a striking contrast as the soprano solo begins the *"pleni sunt coeli"* section treated as a fugato in the solo quartet. On the words *"Hosanna in excelsis"* the solo voices continue with another fugato at a very fast tempo, building a mood of tremendous jubilation.

Then abruptly, the mood changes, and in the rich lower depths of the orchestra is heard a solemn passage in preparation for the *Benedictus*—the transubstantiation, a most sacred moment in the Mass. Beethoven emphasizes its importance by writing the word *"Praeludium"* in the score for the instrumental section preceding the *Benedictus*. The basses of the chorus begin softly, intoning the opening lines of the text like a chant. Above this, and from here to the end of the movement, the solo violin plays an ethereal obbligato melody in its very highest register. The solo quartet figures very prominently in this section although the chorus takes over near the end of the repetition of the *Hosanna,* this time with a new theme and with a more restrained feeling of jubilation than in the first section.

The *Agnus Dei* opens with the bass solo alternating with the men's voices of the chorus in a sort of concertato effect. The dark tonality of B minor (relative to D major) contrasts to the key of G major in which the fourth movement ended and again demonstrates the striking third relation —a distinguishing feature of the harmonic practice of the romantic period. The middle section begins with the words *"Dona nobis pacem."* In the score at this point Beethoven wrote the words, "Prayer for inner and outer peace," indicating a personal significance that he attached to these words. The soloists are used very little in this section, perhaps suggesting that this is a prayer for peace among the masses of humanity symbolized by the chorus.

The descending third motive, prominent in the first movement and in the *Credo,* is also woven into the thematic material of the *Agnus Dei.* It appears in the opening bass solo on the word *"miserere,"* again in the recitativelike passages following the *"Dona nobis pacem,"* and repeatedly throughout the movement. It may be indicative of Beethoven's religious beliefs that this, the most prominent unifying thematic fragment of the total work, first appears on the word *"Christe"* in the opening movement of the Mass.

The final section of the *Agnus Dei* begins with a long orchestral passage in the home tonality of D major. The chorus again introduces the contrasting key of B flat major, but the bright, hopeful key of D major returns in a gigantic coda on the words *"Dona nobis pacem."* The chorus and orchestra dominate the concluding passages with great emphasis upon the single word *pacem.*

On the first page of the score of the *Missa Solemnis* Beethoven wrote the words, "From the heart—may it go to the heart." From this it must be assumed that the musical expression of this work is of a deeply personal nature. So it is with most of Beethoven's music; for in his art, more than in the music of any earlier composer, is found the direct outpouring of the individual personality. This is one of the most important characteristics of the romantic period, a trait that accounts for the tremendous diversity in nineteenth century music. Composers viewed themselves differently than in the classical period, and each strove to make his contribution in a uniquely personal way.

Individuality and diversity in the arts were not totally new. Baroque painters were sometimes given to free display and the same kind of freedom is found in the improvisatory style of such works as the organ fantasias and toccatas of J. S. Bach. Mozart's *Magic Flute* may be said to possess some of these same qualities and there are many similar examples in periods preceding the nineteenth century. As seen in the romantic period, however, this uniqueness of style, rich diversity, and free display became the rule rather than the exception, as each composer delved into the depths of his soul in search of new thoughts, emotions, and the means of expressing them.

It is understandable that the romantics claimed Beethoven as their own.

Responding to the monumental sweep of his music, they believed that he had broken the bonds of the classical period—freed music from the tyranny of restrictive forms. In this they were wrong, for every note of Beethoven's music is conceived with utmost musical and formal logic. It is true that after Beethoven the symphonic forms demanded strikingly different treatment, but not for the reasons given during the nineteenth century. Beethoven did not "break form asunder"; he simply brought classical forms to the pinnacle of their development, proceeding on pathways that had already been laid by Haydn and Mozart. The fact that throughout his life his music was inspired by the philosophies of a new era perhaps marks him as the first true romantic in music; but there is a magnificence in his art that cannot be defined by chronological limits. In addition to its tremendous historical importance, his music lives today—the supreme testimony to its universal appeal.

Suggested Assignments

1. Investigate the cultural and political activity taking place at the end of the eighteenth century. Attempt to draw specific conclusions regarding its influence upon the beginnings of the romantic era and upon the art of music.
2. Contrast Beethoven's role in society with that of Haydn.
3. Compare Haydn's *Symphony No. 104* with Beethoven's First Symphony.
4. In outline form summarize the ways in which Beethoven's music presaged musical phenomena of the romantic era.
5. In outline form summarize the characteristics of the music of Beethoven's three periods.
6. Expand your knowledge of Beethoven's music by listening to works not studied thus far.

ELEVEN

TOWARD A DEFINITION OF
ROMANTICISM IN MUSIC

In the preceding chapter a number of specific aspects of Beethoven's music were mentioned as precedents for important musical trends of the romantic movement. These included the expansion of symphonic forms, the use of a larger orchestra, occasional programmatic tendencies, a less restrictive treatment of the variation form, the beginning development of the song cycle, and certain harmonic innovations. The direct outpouring of his innermost feelings was manifest in greater freedom, variety, and diversity of musical form, but always within the framework of formal and musical logic. The continuance of these musical phenomena will be exemplified in the study of specific nineteenth century compositions, but before this is done let us examine some of the elements of romantic thought as they might be applied to music.

The romantic movement, in its origins and in its later development, can be more clearly viewed in poetry and literature than in any of the other arts. It is best defined in the work of such figures as Blake, Wordsworth, Shelley, Keats, Coleridge, Poe, Goethe, Heine, Schiller, and other late eighteenth and nineteenth century writers. Because of music's inherently nonverbal character, it is difficult to relate it to the literary arts. Nevertheless, some aspects of romantic thought as presented in nineteenth century literature and poetry can, at least outwardly, be linked with musical trends of the nineteenth century.

The character of "boundless yearning," so often ascribed to the romantic attitude, is in reality nothing more than a symptom of a more essential trait of nineteenth century thought, the response of the *individual* to his new role in society. While it is true that surface aspects of romanticism such as the idealization of the past in the novels of Scott and Dumas or the theme of social injustice dominating the works of Hugo and Dickens reflect

158

a general dissatisfaction with the world as it is—a yearning for an ineffable ideal and the desire for escape to strange, faraway places, these are really only the exteriorization of deep conflicts rising within the spirit of man. Prior to the nineteenth century, men had viewed themselves typically as being small but integral parts of a highly organized society—a complex hierarchy at the very summit of which was found the church and the aristocracy. As a part of this society musicians such as Bach and Haydn moved within more or less prescribed limits. Their greatness is not diminished by the fact that they were content with their roles; for their music not only fulfilled the needs of their society but also spoke across the centuries in a more universal language.

Beethoven, more than any other nineteenth century artist, typified man in the new society, who viewed himself not as standing on one rung of a very long and carefully built ladder, but as being in a position accessible to all of society, and able to exert his influence upon any part of it. This presented numerous conflicts to the artist, for no longer could he permit himself to accept society's solutions to his problems. He felt inwardly obliged to come to grips with things that the eighteenth century artist was willing to accept as unchangeable. In Beethoven this is strikingly illustrated by his impassioned musical outbursts in such works as the Third and Fifth Symphonies. An essential aspect of both of these works is the conflict resulting from the dramatic working out of an inner problem—coming to grips with fate—a titanic struggle to resolve opposites. This element of conflict contributes greatly to the unique character of Beethoven's music. It is the desire to express the most strongly felt, inward feelings that produces such diversity and contrast in nineteenth century art.

In William Blake's *The Marriage of Heaven and Hell,* completed in 1793, is found the following passage:

> Without Contraries is no progression. Attraction and Repulsion, Reason and Energy, Love and Hate, are necessary to Human existence.

The philosophy implied here has to do with man's new view of himself as a unique individual capable of dealing with the conflicts and problems of human existence in his own way. Throughout the ages man has contemplated opposites and this speculation has taken many forms. As seen in the music of the romantic period, contraries or antitheses are not mutually exclusive like darkness and light, heat and cold, or up and down. Rather, they are complementary, like the positive and negative poles of an electric battery between which a constant state of tension exists—a tension that results from the ever-present flow of current from one pole to the other. This peculiar character of contrast in romanticism has given rise to the use of the term "polarity."

One example of polarity is found in the relationship of the composer to his audience. A characteristic attitude of the romantic composer was to reject the past and even the present by the belief that he was, at least in part, composing for audiences of the future. At first glance this attitude of the prophet or "visionary" seems incompatible with the fact that, at the beginning of the nineteenth century, a mass bourgeois audience was becoming a reality, an audience much larger and considerably less knowledgeable than that of Bach, Handel, Haydn, and Mozart. The concept of immortality inherent in the idea of composing for the future had to be accommodated to the fact that the new mass audience was also a consideration, and an important one. The composer's newfound freedom enabled him to have a more idealistic attitude toward his art, but it also made it necessary for him to have a very realistic attitude toward his survival as an artist. Although composers were interested in the future, they must also be interested in the past; for inherent in the idea that they were writing for future audiences is the idea that they themselves were the audiences for which "immortal" composers of the past had written. The revived interest in J. S. Bach's music during the nineteenth century was a manifestation of this. Mendelssohn, Schumann, and Brahms were members of the great *Bach Gesellschaft* which, around the middle of the nineteenth century, undertook to publish all of the works of Bach, most of which had fallen into obscurity after his death. The appeal that Bach's music had for the nineteenth century is found in its expressive qualities, its free use of chromaticism, and its profoundly universal and diverse character.

The difficulty in defining romanticism in music derives largely from the great diversity of styles found in the period—a diversity that resulted, directly or indirectly, from the composer's changed view of himself. In listing a few of the composers of the era it becomes apparent that here, within a single frame, are the greatest of contrasts: Carl Maria Von Weber, whose greatest efforts were in the opera; Schubert, whose attempts at opera were failures but whose greatest contribution was to the solo song literature; Berlioz, whose fantastic flights of fancy required vast instrumental resources; Chopin, who wrote almost exclusively for solo piano; Wagner, whose music dramas aimed at an impossible fusion of the arts; and a host of others. Since these are all composers of the romantic period, it is logical to assume that they had something in common, yet so striking are their contrasts that it is not readily apparent where this common ground lies. The extremes of introversion to extroversion, of subjectivity to objectivity are so great that sometimes, even within the work of a single composer, it is difficult to find unifying stylistic traits.

What then is the close connection between these nineteenth century composers whom we group together and label as romantics? What are their affinities? The first is found in their relationship to sheer sound. To understand this, let us compare music of an earlier period to that of the nineteenth century. The fact that Bach did not specify the keyboard instrument intended for certain of his keyboard compositions (the *Well-Tempered Clavier,* for example, which could have been performed on the harpsichord, clavichord, or organ) strongly suggests that he was not particularly concerned with this problem, and that tone quality or timbre was not a primary element in his music. His music is certainly not abstract, yet the expressive use of specific tone qualities is not an important facet of his art. Again, in *The Art of Fugue,* Bach did not bother to indicate the instrumentation. In fact, the idea of specifying instruments for the various voices or parts of the music and treating the instruments idiomatically was, even in Bach's time, a relatively new concept. During the classical period the instruments had a more or less standardized role in the orchestra. In the symphonies of Haydn, Mozart, and even the early works of Beethoven, orchestration was not yet a serious problem, was not a uniquely expressive element of the music. It was part of the composer's craft, and the workmanship of classical orchestration is as fine as that of the romantic era; but it did not differ substantially from one composition to another. Brass, timpani, woodwinds, and strings, all had a relatively fixed relationship to each other.

Nothing could be further from the truth in the orchestra of the romantic period. New possibilities for instrumental sounds were discovered by combining the instruments in new and different ways. Weber and Schubert were among the first to do this and, as a by-product, textbooks on orchestration began to appear. Berlioz' *Treatise on Instrumentation* and, at the end of the century, Rimsky-Korsakov's *Principles of Orchestration* are cases in point. Both are still used today as standard textbooks of orchestration. Significantly, books of this sort had not been written before the nineteenth century

Sonority and the careful treatment of timbre were important not only in the orchestra but in the other musical media as well. Even music for piano solo was profoundly affected. Composers such as Chopin, Schumann, and Liszt made such demands upon the coloristic and dynamic capabilities of the piano that it evolved into quite a different instrument from its eighteenth century counterpart. It became much larger, and new pedal techniques were developed which enabled the pianist to achieve effects that rivaled the diversity of colors and dynamics found in the symphony orchestra. Thus, sound itself became a tremendously important factor in the expressive qualities of romantic music, a role that it had perhaps played in primitive music but not significantly in the music of the Renaissance and Baroque.

Another great "contrary" is apparent in this, for the use of timbre as an expressive element is both new and old—new in the sense that it is a further refinement of the art of music, and old because it returns to a primitive relationship that man had to music—to the evocative qualities of a tone, the darkly mysterious, the magically exciting. As a result of the new use of sonority, the symphony orchestra became considerably enlarged in the nineteenth century, a process of expansion that began with the symphonies of Beethoven and culminated in the tremendous proportions of the orchestra of Richard Strauss. Berlioz and Strauss even went so far as to specify the number of instruments that were to be used in each of the string sections in order to be sure that they would be sufficiently strong to balance the increased sonority of the wind sections.

Directly opposing the grandiose expression of the vast symphony orchestra is the typically romantic interest in the miniature. Many short simple piano pieces, often less than a page in length, were written by Schumann, Mendelssohn, Chopin, and others. Such pieces are sometimes called "character pieces" and were frequently grouped together to form collections such as the Schumann *Scenes from Childhood,* the Mendelssohn *Songs Without Words,* and the Chopin *Preludes.*

A more significant manifestation of the interest in small-scale works is seen in the development of the romantic song cycle—collections of solo songs with piano accompaniment. The solo song, particularly the German art song or lied (pl. lieder), wielded a strong influence on all of the music of the period. In instrumental music this influence was seen in the increased use of long songlike melodies in preference to structures built from short motives. As a result it became less possible to construct long movements with the high degree of organic unity and economy of means characteristic of the classical composers. Certain composers, notably Schubert, Schumann, Mendelssohn, and Brahms, managed in some of their large-scale works to combine the technique of motivic structure with romantic lyricism. More often, however, organic unity was sacrificed to greater freedom of expression—to long flights of deeply expressive melody or extravagant display.

The romantic striving for individuality was further manifest in the growth of nationalistic feeling. It became common for the artist to identify himself with his homeland—and to express this identity in his work. The interest in subjects in nature is, in a sense, an extension of nationalism. A tree, a landscape, or a river became appropriate material for subjective interpretation in a painting, a poem, or a piece of music—particularly when it was clearly a part of the artist's national heritage.

One important means of nationalistic expression was to use folk music, or folklike melodies, in serious compositions. This perhaps reached its highest development at the end of the nineteenth century in the music of the Bohemian composer, Antonin Dvořák, but it is also a distinguished feature of the music of others, such as Grieg, Sibelius, Smetana, and a group of Russian composers known as "The Five." Nationalism and other extramusical elements found their best musical expression in the programmatic symphony or symphonic tone poem. Berlioz and Liszt were most prominent in the early development of the tone poem and it reached its culmination in the symphonic works of Richard Strauss.

The romantic composer's interest in extramusical elements proceeded in the direction of erasing clear-cut boundaries between the arts; and, as a side effect, musicians and all artists became very verbal creatures. Berlioz, Schumann, Liszt, Wagner, and many others wrote profusely on all of the arts and on the position of music among them. Human existence itself seemed secondary to art as dozens of esthetic philosophies were propounded and dissected. Fusion of the arts found its ideal form in the German art song—the union of poetry and music through which the romantic spirit was most purely and freely expressed. For the most part, lieder composers selected the finest poetry for their song cycles; and neither music nor poetry sacrificed anything to the alliance. Other attempts at fusion of the arts were less successful. Wagner's music dramas, organized along the lines of his *Gesamtkunstwerk* theories, excessively emphasized orchestral sonority, with a proportionate loss to the arts of poetry, drama, and scenic design.

Just as tone color was harnessed to express the moods and emotions of the romantic spirit, so harmony began to be used in striking new ways. New tonal relationships appeared, such as the third relation seen in the

Missa Solemnis. But, above all, nineteenth century musicians experimented with the power of dissonant harmony to create states of great emotional intensity. Chopin, Liszt, and Wagner were foremost among the many composers who made contributions to the vocabulary of dissonance. Indeed, Wagner is considered by many to be the forerunner of the twentieth century harmonic concept known as the twelve-tone system. Coincidental with these new harmonic developments was a slowly decreasing emphasis on the fifth relation (relationship of two triads with roots a fifth apart), the beginning demise of the tonic-dominant concept. The evocative qualities of chromatic dissonance were explored so fully that a new and uniquely expressive harmonic language developed—a language that led to the shifting harmonic colors of Debussy and Ravel and to the many diverse harmonic expressions of the twentieth century.

Throughout the romantic era the greatest of contrasts continued to exist side by side—imposing symphonies beside simple character pieces and the grandiloquent gestures of opera beside the intimate lyricism of the art song. There remains today an intense excitement about the romantic period. The music of no other time is more popular with present-day audiences. We are drawn to its individualistic strivings, its great diversity, and its idealism— evidence to the fact that what we call the romantic spirit is a universal state of mind, common to mankind in every era.

Suggested Assignments

1. List significant examples of polarity in nineteenth century music.
2. As a special project look further into the "Doctrine of Contraries" expressed in Blake's *The Marriage of Heaven and Hell.*
3. Read biographical sketches of the lives of composers such as Schumann, Chopin, Liszt, and Wagner. Compare their roles in society to those of eighteenth century composers such as J. S. Bach, Haydn, and Mozart.
4. By examining orchestration textbooks and scores of the eighteenth and nineteenth centuries, attempt to pick out specific stylistic differences between the orchestral music of the two periods.
5. Citing specific instruments, compare a typical classical orchestra to the symphony orchestra used in late nineteenth century works such as the Strauss tone poems.
6. List several examples of nineteenth century compositions that make use of romantic literature or poetry. Note the variety of ways in which this was done.

TWELVE

THE EARLY ROMANTIC PERIOD

FRANZ SCHUBERT (1797–1828)

Schubert's short, unhappy, and improvident life epitomizes the popular image of the romantic composer. Born near Vienna, he lived his life in the shadow of his great contemporary, Ludwig van Beethoven. Like Beethoven, Schubert had a strong connection with the classical heritage, a link that is particularly apparent in his symphonies and chamber music. Unlike Beethoven, Schubert possessed a melodic gift that was purely romantic in nature. Throughout his music are found lyrical passages of magical charm—finely wrought, self-contained melodic phrases of surpassing beauty. The presence of these moments of ecstatic lyricism is a saving feature in much of his symphonic and chamber music; for only in his last works, such as the "Great" C Major Symphony and the *Quintet in C Major* (for string quartet plus a second cello) can he be said to have mastered the classical forms. Much of his earlier music in large forms suffers from lack of unity and a developmental technique which, though adequate, does not quite match that of the classical masters.

Nevertheless, in the area of chamber music Schubert ranks among the elect. His fifteen string quartets continued the Viennese tradition established by Haydn, Mozart, and Beethoven. The two trios for violin, cello, and piano are among the great works for that medium; while his *Trout* Quintet (for violin, viola, cello, double bass, and piano) has maintained a lasting popularity. His chamber music is enhanced by frequent melodic passages of pronounced romantic character. Of particular interest in his chamber music as well as in his symphonic works is his use of striking key relationships—sudden shifts to distantly related keys, particularly between keys separated by a major third.

Although Schubert composed eight symphonies, seven Masses, and a

165

number of other works of considerable length in addition to his chamber music, his greatest excellence lies in short lyrical forms. Brief movements for piano with titles such as *Moment Musicale* and *Impromptu* represent the beginning of the romantic character piece. These and his dance movements for piano led the way for achievements in similar forms by Schumann, Mendelssohn, Liszt, and, above all, by Chopin.

Schubert's gift for short lyrical forms is particularly striking in his solo songs, for here we find the musical poet in his natural element. He wrote nearly six hundred songs for voice and piano, and wrote them quickly, spontaneously—as many as a dozen in a single day. His talent for evoking poetic images by means of the piano as well as the voice is at times almost miraculous. Verses which have been set by Schubert never again seem complete without his music. Some of his songs are complex and sophisticated while others have the direct appeal of folk song. Most of them are strophic in form, meaning that the same music is used for each verse of the poem, sometimes slightly modified to suit the words of a specific verse. Occasionally he used a through-composed form (German: *Durchkomponiert*) using new musical material for each verse.

One of the most famous of Schubert's works for solo voice and piano is the song cycle *Die Winterreise* (The Winter Journey), written near the end of his life during a period of deep darkness and despair. The mournful, even lugubrious, images of Wilhelm Müller's rather mediocre poetry must have appealed strongly to the composer in his state of poverty and illness, for it is one of his most expressive works.

At almost the same time that Schubert was conceiving *Die Winterreise* he was also working on the B Flat Major Trio, Op. 99. The contrast between the two works is most remarkable, for the trio, ranging from a mood of triumphant joy to tender lyricism, preserves an air of optimism that is almost incredible when viewed alongside the tragic qualities of *Die Winterreise*.

Trio in B Flat Major for Violin, Cello, and Piano, Op. 99

The first movement is in sonata form and opens with a unison statement of the theme, the piano furnishing the harmonic background. Within this theme (shown in Figure 65) are heard the two germinating motives of the movement: (1) the dotted rhythm heard in the left hand of the piano and (2) the triplet motive heard in bars two and three. The use of the third relation is apparent quite early in the first tonal group, for the music care-

Figure 65.

fully gravitates from the home tonality of B flat major toward D major. After some alternation between the two keys, the tonality settles on F major, the expected key for the second tonal group.

Although the key of the second tonal group is quite traditional, the manner of approach to it is uniquely Schubertian. By ending the first tonal group on the dominant of D major (A) a striking third relation between the F major triad and the A major triad is made possible. The cello effects the shift in tonality by sustaining an unaccompanied A (common to both triads) and then proceeding in the key of F major. The device is simple but the result is breathtaking, for the key of F major sounds magically fresh in contrast to the A major triad heard just before.

The melody continues in the high singing register of the cello and demonstrates the influence that lieder wielded upon the instrumental music of the period. So lyrical and self-contained is this melody that it could conceivably be removed from its context and used as the basis for an art song. It is quite typical to find songlike melodies of this type used as the theme of the second tonal group in nineteenth century sonata forms. As mentioned earlier, such themes do not usually lend themselves well to development but seem to exist within themselves for their own intrinsic beauty rather than for their organic potential in the total movement. In some instances Schubert carried the influence of lieder so far as to use complete examples from his own songs as the basis for movements of his chamber works, frequently as the theme for a set of variations. The String Quartet *Death and the Maiden* and the *Trout* Quintet are cases in point, both of which derive their titles from the names of the songs used within the works.

The exposition does not end with a cadence but leads directly into the development or, when the repeat is taken, back to the beginning of the movement. The development deals primarily with the main theme of the first tonal group, moving through a sequence of rather distantly related keys: B flat minor, E major, G flat major, and D flat major. The recapitulation is quite traditional, bringing back the exposition material in a manner very similar to its first presentation. The movement culminates in a brilliant coda.

The melodic opulence of the second movement places it among the most attractive movements in nineteenth century chamber music. It opens with the cello playing the melody shown in Figure 66. A hallmark of Schubert's style seen in this melody is his subtle use of variation technique. Note that

Figure 66.

bar 4 is a variation of bar 3, a type of spinning out device often used by Schubert.

Near the end of this melody the cello begins a new idea that serves as a countersubject to the violin's entrance with the original theme. The interweaving of these two melodic instruments furnishes contrapuntal interest as well as maintaining the songlike character of the movement. The middle section shows the piano to great advantage in melodic passages accompanied by a tense, syncopated figuration. As in the first movement, there are a number of touching key relationships with A flat, G flat, C, and E serving as important secondary tonal centers. This is the most chromatic of the four movements and admirably demonstrates the romantic use of harmony as a strongly communicative element.

From the standpoint of form, the scherzo is quite ordinary. It is in the key of B flat major with a leisurely and melodic trio in E flat major. The movement opens with repetitions of the thematic fragment shown in Figure 67, clearly showing the influence of Beethoven in its motivic structure.

The fourth movement is a rondo, bubbling and gay with delightfully contrasting episodes. The listener can readily trace the progress of the music by the recurrences of the rondo theme. The coda, marked presto, is

Figure 67.

somewhat of a surprise, for it is based primarily on the material of the vigorous first episode rather than upon the rondo theme.

The length, pattern of movements, and developmental character of this work shows Schubert's link with Viennese classicism—with Haydn and Mozart, but particularly with Beethoven. Uniquely romantic traits are found in Schubert's way of precipitating sharp key contrasts, in his expressive use of color and sonority, and, above all, in his spontaneous and flowing melodic utterances.

HECTOR BERLIOZ (1803–1869)

Berlioz is perhaps the most enigmatic composer of his time. He seems to have been viewed in various ways by his contemporaries as well as by succeeding generations. Musicians of the early romantic period only partially recognized his talents and, at the same time, viewed him as an incurable radical. To the later nineteenth century, from Wagner's point of view, for example, he may have seemed old fashioned. Today we recognize that, in addition to being the very embodiment of his own time, he was a kind of musical visionary—a composer who spoke to the twentieth century in a way that few composers of the past have done. On the other hand, his music also evokes images of antiquity, for there is something almost primitive in certain of his harmonic progressions as well as in some of his melodic lines.

The single aspect of his music that is most admired today is the audacious brilliance of its orchestration. Berlioz dared to combine instruments in such a way as to produce sounds that had never before been set down on paper. This, combined with his unique gift of writing for the instruments in their most rewarding registers and his unprecedented demands on the performer's technical skill, resulted in an orchestral metier that is awesome even today.

Examples of his orchestral boldness are found in almost all of his compositions. Some of the more notable instances are (1) the opening flourish of the *Roman Carnival Overture,* (2) the mixture of strings with low flutes at the opening of the "Love Scene" from the *Romeo and Juliet* Symphony, (3) the use of unique percussion instruments in "Queen Mab," also from *Romeo and Juliet,* (4) a chordal passage for four timpani at the end of "Scene in the Country" from *Symphonie Fantastique,* and (5) from the same work, the double basses *divisi* in four-part pizzicato at the beginning of "March to the Gallows."

The fact that Berlioz was a French musician living at a time when the art of music was dominated by Germany and Austria accounts in part for the unique place that he holds in romantic music. Proof of his genius, and perhaps of the universality of his music, is found in his attainment of a stature unequaled by any other French composer of his time. He was apparently quite conscious of his singular position for he wrote a great deal about himself, his music, and the work of his contemporaries. For a period of nearly thirty years the main part of his livelihood came from his position as a music critic. His *Memoirs,* published in 1870, make fascinating reading but are not completely reliable as autobiography.

Although the term symphonic poem was invented by Liszt, the concept begins with Berlioz and culminates in the works of Richard Strauss. Almost all of Berlioz' compositions contain some programmatic elements. They bear descriptive titles and most of them are supplied with program notes furnishing the audience with a key to the extramusical associations of the music. They can, however, be heard purely as music, for Berlioz was endowed with a sure (albeit unorthodox) sense of musical logic. By employing a device known as the *idée fixe* he was able to unify diffuse musical ideas in long works. The idée fixe is a specific melody that recurs throughout an extended work, often from movement to movement, serving to bind the music together. Usually it bears dramatic significance, symbolizing an important character or event in the story or program. In *Symphonie Fantastique* the idée fixe (Figure 68) is a melody representing the young artist's beloved and is heard in each of the symphony's five movements. The

Figure 68.

idée fixe is one of Berlioz' most significant innovations for it led to similar devices in the work of other programmatic composers (notably Liszt and Strauss) and to the development of Wagner's leitmotif principles.

A characteristic outlet for Berlioz' extravagant imagination was the combining of large forces of instruments and voices in new ways. This is apparent in many of his works but is most striking in his *Requiem,* a vast work which, in addition to a large chorus, orchestra, and soloists, uses four separate brass choirs and eight pairs of timpani. His symphonic work entitled *Harold in Italy* contains an extended solo part for the viola, an instrument which up to that time had seldom been used for solo passages.

Opera was a most appropriate medium for his unique talents and it was inevitable that he produce major works in this area. His operas (*Beatrice and Benedict, Benvenuto Cellini,* and *The Trojans*) have not, however, established significant places in the operatic repertoire. The *Damnation of Faust* has been performed as an opera but is more properly viewed as a secular oratorio. Berlioz also wrote a number of programmatic concert overtures such as *Rob Roy* (after Sir Walter Scott) and *The Corsair* (after Byron).

The Roman Carnival Overture, Op. 9

This overture has been variously described as a rondo, an Italian overture, and as a sonata form. It shows traces of all three but in actuality none of these terms is completely appropriate for, like much of Berlioz' music, the work is quite free in form and probably was not conceived in terms of a preexisting formal pattern. It was written as an overture to the second act of *Benvenuto Cellini* and is based on two extracts from that work. The first is a love duet from Act I, heard in the overture as a prominent English horn solo just after the brilliant opening flourish (Figure 69), while the second is drawn from a festival scene in Act II. This second idea is heard just after the slow section containing the English horn solo. It is

Figure 69.

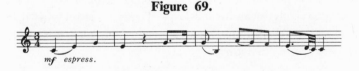

marked Allegro vivace and is characterized by a fast 6/8 rhythm very similar in style to an Italian folk dance called the *saltarello* (Figure 70). As both of these ideas are developed, the love theme is heard in augmentation against the saltarello rhythm.

The theme heard at the very beginning of the overture (Figure 71) is heard later in fugato form, at one point building an imitative texture that

Figure 70.

starts in the low instruments and successively adds higher instruments to produce a terraced effect. Canonic imitation is used also in the slow section following the opening flourish. After the English horn presents the melody

Figure 71.

shown in Figure 69, it is taken up first by the violas, then the cellos, and then by woodwinds, brass, and percussion, all blended into a marvelous bit of contrapuntal scoring.

The masterly and imaginative orchestration of this work was a marvel for the period and remains unsurpassed even today. The listener can gain much insight into modern orchestration by listening to this work with the score in hand, attempting to relate these flamboyant orchestral colors to the printed notation. Berlioz upset all previous notions of orchestral technique, exerting a profound influence on such later composers as Rimsky-Korsakov and Richard Strauss. With the current widespread revival of Berlioz' music, contemporary audiences are becoming increasingly aware of the genius of this vitally inventive musician. Today he is recognized as a romantic composer of the first rank, a man of his own time who spoke eloquently to future generations.

FELIX MENDELSSOHN (1809–1847)

Mendelssohn's development and career were attended throughout by favorable circumstances. Born into a wealthy and highly cultured family, he spent his childhood in an environment well suited to intellectual and cultural pursuits. Such persons as Goethe and Hegel were among the intellectual elite with whom his family associated during his youth, while his childhood efforts as a composer enjoyed the critical appraisal of some of Europe's most distinguished musicians. He was endowed with considerable musical talent and became a thoroughly mature and well-rounded musician at a remarkably early age.

His overture to *A Midsummer Night's Dream,* an acknowledged masterpiece, was presented to an enraptured audience of household guests when the young composer was seventeen. It would seem that such auspicious beginnings might predict a future of titanic achievement, but this did not quite come to pass. Most of Mendelssohn's music is so highly polished, so nearly perfect in form and musical detail, that it is almost too elegant to be profoundly expressive. It is said that he never surpassed the achievements of his earliest years of maturity. There are several reasons why this is so.

First of all, Mendelssohn excelled in a number of different roles. In addition to his activities as a composer, he spent much time as a concert pianist and organist, as a conductor, as a musical entrepreneur, and as a teacher. Active in virtually all musical fields, he was unable to devote the time and effort necessary to transcend the limitations of his natural fluency as a composer. He was so astonishingly good with so little effort that it apparently never occurred to him that he might be *profoundly* expressive if he were able to reach beyond his own glibness. The passionate outbursts of a Berlioz or the deeply poetic expression of a Schubert or Schumann were foreign to his character.

It was natural that his orderly and conservative mind would be strongly linked with the classical tradition. He was an enthusiastic organizer of performances of Bach, Mozart, and Beethoven. In 1829 he presented a performance of the *St. Matthew Passion* that was a significant event in the Bach revival taking place during the nineteenth century. It was his aim to preserve the classical ideals against the ravages of the romantic movement. That he achieved technical mastery of all classical forms and media is undeniable; but, in addition, there are strong elements of romanticism in his music. In our brief discussion of Mendelssohn's *Hebrides Overture* (Chapter One) it was mentioned that the composer was attempting to convey his idea of a subject in nature. Preoccupation with nature is a romantic trait appearing frequently in Mendelssohn's music, often achieved by means of typically romantic orchestration. His scoring is marked by the use of the French horn and clarinet as melodic instruments, by blending of the woodwinds to achieve subtle new colors, by expanding the role of the brass instruments so that they do more than simply give rhythmic and dynamic support in tutti passages, and by the use of strings in a variety of new ways, particularly in harmonic accompaniment figures, arpeggiating chords, etc. The relatively limited orchestral style of the classical symphonists was expanded by Mendelssohn, though not in the flamboyant manner practiced by Berlioz.

Mendelssohn's ability to create moods of sparkling lightness is particularly worthy of note. A magical kind of witty effervescence is found in his scherzos and other passages in scherzando style. Good examples are the scherzo from the incidental music to *A Midsummer Night's Dream* and the scherzo from the String Quartet in E Minor. Similar passages are found throughout his music, often relying partly on the orchestration to produce the desired effect.

Mendelssohn was sometimes pictorial, even programmatic, but his highly refined sensibility preferred not to be revolutionary. He represents the extension of classical trends into the nineteenth century. The conflict and struggle that we associate with romantic expression are found in his music only in a highly refined form, somewhat lacking in emotional impact. Perhaps this is because conflict and struggle were not realities in his well-organized life. His music is not bland, but quite homogeneous.

He wrote five symphonies, of which the *Scotch* (No. 3) and the *Italian* (No. 4) are the most famous, a sizable quantity of chamber music, including six string quartets, two piano trios, and the famous Octet for Strings, several large choral works, including the oratorio *Elijah,* overtures, concertos, and other vocal and instrumental works. His numerous short piano pieces called *Songs Without Words* are standard fare for students of the piano. Many of his works, by virtue of their pleasing melodies and superb organization, have maintained lasting places in the concert repertoire.

Concerto for Violin and Orchestra in E Minor, Op. 64

Let us compare the first movement of this work to the Mozart Piano Concerto studied earlier (Chapter Nine) noting differences and similarities between the romantic work and the classical concerto form. One difference will be immediately apparent, for the violin concerto does not contain a double exposition. Instead, the solo violin enters immediately with a melody played entirely on its highest string (Figure 72). This is the main theme of the movement, but there are two other important thematic ideas heard in the exposition.

Figure 72.

After an expansion of the first idea into brilliant passage work for the solo, and after a restatement of the theme by the full orchestra, a second (transitional) idea appears. This then leads into the theme of the second tonal group presented softly by the woodwinds over a pedal point held by the solo violin on its lowest tone, the open G string (Figure 73). Note that the key of this theme is the usual key for the second tonal group of a

Figure 73.

classical sonata form. That is, since the movement is in a minor key, the second tonal group is in the relative major.

As noted in the discussion of the classical concerto form, it is usual to find the solo instrument playing trills at crucial points in the form, at the end of the exposition, the end of the development, etc. A vestige of this practice is found in this work. The trills, however, are presented not by the solo violin but by the orchestra, particularly the woodwinds. These orchestral trills function much as do the solo trills in a classical concerto form, marking the important sections of the first movement and serving as roadmarks to the listener's understanding of the form.

Another departure from the classical concerto form is found in the location of the cadenza. In the eighteenth century it was typical to find it at the end of the recapitulation just preceding a short coda. Mendelssohn chose to use it as a link between the development and the recapitulation. Also, it was completely written out by the composer, not left to the improvisatory skills of the performer. This was the practice in most nineteenth century concertos, for it assured that the cadenza would have an organic function in the music and avoided meaningless virtuoso display. This cadenza culminates in rapid arpeggio passages played by moving the bow rapidly from string to string. The recapitulation then begins with a woodwind entrance of the main theme, the violin continuing the arpeggio passages. The classical key pattern is found in the recapitulation and the movement concludes in a brilliant coda.

The second movement, which follows without a break, is in ABA form and presents the violin at the outset in a tender melody of truly romantic sentiment. This melody (shown in Figure 74) demonstrates Mendelssohn's ability to create an atmosphere of calm, even ethereal, meditation. It is

Figure 74.

melodies such as this that have made his *Songs Without Words* so popular. The form of the movement is simple and clear, with a rather somber middle section.

After an opening brassy flourish, the final movement commences with a rondo theme that is typical of Mendelssohn's best scherzando style. The form of the movement is easily traced by the listener; but the real excitement lies in the brilliant virtuoso passage work for the solo violin. To compose music of this sort, that is demanding and rewarding from the standpoint of virtuoso display, as well as being musically meaningful, requires an intimate knowledge of the solo instrument's capabilities. To help him in this part of his task, Mendelssohn enlisted the counsel of Ferdinand David, a well-known violinist of the period. That David's advice was well given and wisely used is demonstrated by the great success of this work, for violinists as well as concert audiences rank it among the five or six great violin concertos.

In this work the classical spirit is blended with romantic expression. It is clearly related to the classical concerto but there are a number of notable departures from the earlier form. Among these are (1) the absence of the double exposition, (2) the novel use of orchestral trills in place of the solo trills, (3) the cadenza, its location, and the fact that it was written by the composer, and (4) the elimination of the pause between movements by the use of connective material. The scoring is conservative, though typical of the nineteenth century, while the melodic writing is representative of Mendelssohn's best romantic style.

FREDERIC CHOPIN (1810–1849)

Chopin's art is closely linked with the technique and development of the pianoforte. Piano music of the early nineteenth century, particularly that of Beethoven and Schubert, revealed a trend away from the classical keyboard style and was accompanied by important changes in the instrument's construction. Chief among these was the increased size of the instrument. Longer strings and larger sound boards tremendously increased the amount of sound that the piano could produce. In addition, by Chopin's time, the range or compass of the instrument was extended to over seven octaves, the size of the present-day piano. An improved key action incorporated a device called the double escapement which allowed quicker repetitions of the same tone. The damper pedal (which had been in use earlier) also became very important to the romantic piano style.

Chopin capitalized on these structural innovations in a number of ways. The fact that the damper pedal allowed a tone to be sustained after the key was released made it possible for him to spread and sustain the tones of a single arpeggiated sonority over a much wider range than previously. This is reflected in the style of his left-hand accompaniment figures, almost all of which span a larger range than can normally be encompassed by the pianist's hand. Typical eighteenth century left-hand figurations were restricted to a range that could easily be contained within the hand. Tones within the figuration were sustained by holding the keys down rather than by the use of the damper pedal. Figure 75 illustrates the difference between a typical Chopin accompaniment figure and the Alberti bass figuration typical of the eighteenth century. Chopin was the first to consistently use these widely spaced figurations and the great variety of piano textures that he was able to produce with them is a hallmark of his style.

The damper pedal was also important in certain harmonic innovations in Chopin's music. In accompaniment passages an arpeggiated sonority might shift to another within the same figuration so that, by means of the damper pedal, a momentary overlapping of the two chords would occur. Thus new sonorities became possible—mixtures of chords, combinations of one harmony with another. This, in addition to his marked tendency toward chromaticism, resulted in a unique harmonic idiom. Contemporary reports of Chopin's performances of his own music state that he had a subtle way of blending and fusing his harmonies so that they did not sound as dissonant as they appeared to be on paper.

Chopin's melodic style is completely his own and is characterized, above

Figure 75.

Excerpt from the left hand of a Chopin Nocturne

*The same harmonic pattern in the typical left-hand
piano style of the classical period*

all, by great rhythmic freedom—a trait that endows his music with a strong improvisatory feeling. His music contains frequent rapid melodic flourishes in which a seemingly unmeasured number of notes are set against a strictly metered left-hand accompaniment. Melodies encompassing an unusually wide range are also found in his piano style, as well as melodic passages of a highly chromatic character.

He was at his best in miniature forms of short duration. In Chopin's hands, the romantic character piece reached a pinnacle of gemlike perfection. Collections of these short pieces comprise a large part of his output, including the twenty-four Preludes, the Nocturnes, the Etudes, the Waltzes, the Mazurkas, and the Polonaises. The last two represent the nationalistic element in his art, showing marked influences of the folk music of his native Poland. (Chopin was born in Poland of French and Polish parentage but spent most of his productive life in the aristocratic and artistic circles of Paris.)

Chopin's particular gifts were not shown to the best advantage in the larger forms. The two piano concertos, however, in spite of their deficiencies in orchestration, are worthy of note because of the brilliant writing for the solo instrument. The four *Ballades,* for piano solo, are exceptional examples of his ability to compose works of more extended duration; while his piano sonatas and his sonata for cello and piano have also retained their popularity.

Chopin was closely associated with nineteenth century French salon society. He preferred to perform for small intimate groups of the cultured elite of Paris rather than for large public audiences. It was said that he seldom played loudly but achieved considerable dynamic contrast within the framework of a relatively low dynamic level. He was also known for his use of *rubato*, for his free and sometimes whimsical interpretation of the rhythm, particularly in the melodic line. This led to frequent abuses in later interpretations of his music. Chopin himself advocated a strict metrical approach to piano playing. He allowed considerable rhythmic freedom and imaginative interpretation of the melody but always within the metrical framework of the accompaniment figure. Much of his piano music consists of a texture in which the left hand plays one of many different types of accompaniment figures, usually in arpeggiated or broken style, while the right hand plays a singing melodic line.

Preludes for the Piano, Op. 28

The variety of moods and emotions evoked in Chopin's piano music is phenomenal. Each movement, no matter how extended or how diminutive, is a world of its own; and because of this the term character piece is particularly appropriate. Nowhere is this more clearly illustrated than in the Twenty-four Preludes, Opus 28.

They were written, for the most part, during the years 1838–1839 although many of them are completed versions of fragments and sketches composed earlier. It was during this time that Chopin was carrying on his celebrated romance with the French authoress Aurore Dudevant, whose pen name was George Sand. The pair spent the winter of 1838 together at her retreat on the island of Majorca and it was there that much of the final polishing of the Preludes was done. Their affair persisted stormily until the year 1847.

Chopin was a devoted student of the music of J. S. Bach. He played the *Well-Tempered Clavier* frequently and his own Preludes were undoubtedly inspired by that great work. As in the *Well-Tempered Clavier,* there is one Prelude for each of the twenty-four major and minor keys and, with a few exceptions, each of the Chopin Preludes is restricted to a single mood throughout.

The majority of the Chopin Preludes are short vignettes, each evoking its own unique musical imagery. The first one, in C major, consists of nothing more than a single broad musical gesture. It is made of repetitions of a one-measure figure building up to a fortissimo just past the middle and then dying to a soft ending. Number two is sharply contrasting in character, more melodic, and with considerable ambiguity regarding its tonal center. Number three is somewhat longer although it too is restricted to a single mood—light and airy throughout. Number four in E minor is a miniature of indescribable beauty and is one of the most famous of the Preludes. A view of these first four begins to give some idea of the variety of pianistic imagery of which Chopin was capable. Each tiny piece is a microcosm, unique in mood and emotion.

Some of the Preludes are built on a somewhat broader scale. Numbers thirteen, fifteen, and twenty-one are quite substantial ABA forms, while number seventeen is organized on the same principles as a rondo form. None of the Preludes is conceived on a really large scale. They show the artist in his best light—unsurpassed as a composer of short piano pieces and a wizard of musical imagery.

ROBERT SCHUMANN (1810–1856)

Author, poet, critic, one-time student of law, the composer Robert Schumann personifies the multifaceted character of the romantic era. Though he studied piano as a child and made his first attempts at composition at an early age, he did not seriously turn to a career of music until he was nearly twenty. Then, in his eagerness to become a concert pianist, he sustained a permanent injury to his right hand, the result of using a mechanical gadget that he had invented as an aid to perfecting his piano technique. His aspirations as a pianist thus ended, he turned his interest enthusiastically to composing.

During the decade from 1830 to 1839 he composed almost exclusively for piano solo, and the foremost interpreter of these works was Clara Wieck, daughter of his former piano teacher, Friedrich Wieck. The works of this period include a vast number of short piano pieces, many of them grouped in collections such as *Papillons, Intermezzi, Kinderscenen* (Scenes from Childhood), *Novelletten,* and *Kreisleriana.* Many aspects of his piano style typify the piano idiom of the romantic era: rhythmic freedom (seen particularly in the use of accents that conflict with the bar line), sudden and surprising shifts of harmony, the use of new sonorities, and the fusing effect of the damper pedal. Although he was not inclined to relate "programs" to his music in the form of stories or poems, the programmatic influence is nevertheless apparent in the use of fanciful titles for piano pieces, most of which were added after the music was completed.

In 1840, the year of his marriage to Clara Wieck, he became vitally interested in composing lieder. His song cycles *Frauen-Liebe und Leben* (A Woman's Love and Life) and *Dichterliebe* (Poet's Love), both written in that year, rank along with the best of Schubert's art songs. Schumann's song style differs from Schubert's in that he used the piano more prominently in his fusion of instrument and voice. Extended sections for the piano alone are quite frequent. In accompanying passages, the piano lends great strength to the poetic images of the text, achieved primarily through a truly romantic treatment of harmony and texture. Chromaticism abounds in the songs, though there are extended diatonic passages as well. His imaginative use of piano texture is akin to that of Chopin. Schumann's lyrical genius found its finest expression in the art song, most eminently in his two great song cycles.

In his chamber music and symphonic works, Schumann is often criticized for inadequacy of orchestration, occasional inept instrumental writing, and a conception of form unsuited to large-scale instrumental works. There is some truth in these statements, but, on the whole, these generalizations are too severe. Indeed, a number of his instrumental works are marvelously conceived and are very highly regarded by musicians and concertgoers alike. Among these are the *Piano Quintet* (piano plus string quartet) and the *Piano Quartet* (violin, viola, cello, and piano), both in E flat major. The nineteenth century saw an increased use of the piano as a chamber music instrument and it is significant that Schumann's best chamber works include the piano. His three string quartets, though they contain marvelous moments, particularly in the slow movements, tend to sound as if they were conceived for the piano rather than for the unique idiom of the string quartet.

Schumann sought to preserve the classical heritage of Beethoven, and made noteworthy endeavors in all of the large instrumental forms. His piano concerto and a cello concerto, both in A minor, have become staples of the concert repertoire. His essentially lyrical way of thinking inhibited his efforts in the symphony. Mendelssohn, master of all things in the technical province, managed to combine romantic lyricism with classical structural techniques, but Schumann was unable to do this successfully. As a result, his symphonies have structural flaws that are not found in his shorter works. Nevertheless, his four symphonies have maintained lasting places in the concert repertoire. The fresh lyricism of the First and Fourth Symphonies evokes the true romantic spirit—the orchestration, although inept, is curiously appropriate.

Song Cycle: *Frauen-Liebe und Leben, Op. 42*

Schumann, a man of letters as well as a musician, had a natural affinity for the combining of words with music. His understanding of the art of poetry enabled him to select his texts with unerring good taste, drawing from the works of Byron, Goethe, Heine, and other outstanding poets of the time. The text of *Frauen-Liebe und Leben* (by Chamisso) depicts a woman's thoughts from the time she first sees her lover, through their courtship, marriage, and the birth of their child, closing with her thoughts upon the tragic death of her beloved. The imagery is typically romantic and Schumann was undoubtedly drawn to the poems because of his state of mind during his courtship and marriage to Clara Wieck. (Both *Dichterliebe* and *Frauen-Liebe und Leben* were written in 1840, the year of their marriage.)

The eight songs of the cycle show great variety of texture and mood: the choralelike effect of I, the repeated chords against a triadic melody in II, the quasimartial chordal effect of III, the flowing inner voice line of IV, the unison accompaniment figure at the opening of V, the recitativelike effect in VI, the arpeggiated accompaniment figure in VII, and the somber declamatory style of VIII. This rich contrast, however, did not prevent Schumann from producing a highly unified total work. To this end he used a number of cyclical devices, of which the most prominent is the return of the material of the first song at the end of the final movement, producing the effect of an epilogue that binds the beginning to the end.

An additional, and perhaps even more important effect of this final section for the piano alone is found in its relation to the text. Her lover's death becomes apparent at the beginning of the final song and, as the song progresses, the woman expresses a feeling of bitter emptiness and denial of the living world. Thus, the return of the material of the first song in the piano alone (after the singer is finished) dramatically reinforces the woman's silent withdrawal into the memories of her dead lover, particularly to her thoughts of their first meeting.

It is difficult to categorize the forms of the songs, mainly because Schumann often did not follow the clear-cut form of the text, but preferred to allow the music to fit the changing images of the poetry. No. I is clearly strophic in form. A comparison of the verses or strophes of the first song will reveal that the only changes made in the second were necessitated by slight differences in the rhythm of the words between the first and second verses. No. II is a kind of ABA form although the return of A is much abbreviated and modified harmonically. No. III, though it has some suggestion of a strophic form, is so free as to be more properly called through composed.

No. IV is like a miniature rondo form, with varying melodic material interpolated between the repetitions of *"Du Ring an meinem Finger"* (Figure 76).

Figure 76.

This melody demonstrates an important stylistic trait of Schumann, his very frequent use of melodies that are built out of triads.

No. V is a clear-cut ABA form, again with a shortened and modified return of A. The marchlike section added at the end is intended to depict a wedding march, revealing Schumann's strong programmatic tendencies. No. VI is an extended ABA, while No. VII is strophic in form. No. VIII is like a tragic declamation, essentially in through-composed recitative style, concluding with the extended epilogue mentioned earlier.

An art song is a sensitive musical setting of a fine piece of poetry, usually for solo voice and piano. Since the poem itself has artistic merit and since it was conceived in a specific language with its own peculiar rhythms of speech, it is extremely difficult to find satisfactory translations of art songs. Fine poetry is notoriously untranslatable and this is why an art song is most appropriately performed in its original language. An opera libretto, on the other hand, since it does not usually have great artistic value of its own, is most satisfactorily performed in the language of the audience, even if this necessitates translation. The text of an art song should, of course, be understood by the listener and for this reason it would be wise to listen to this cycle with a good literal translation in hand.

Schumann, in addition to some relatively unsuccessful dabbling in conducting and teaching, was one of the finest music critics of his time. He was one of the founders of the *Neue Zeitschrift für Musik* (New Journal for Music), serving as editor for a number of years. His penetrating and incisive criticism did much to raise the standards of the music of his time. His finest writings are forthright, full of insight, and exuberant. His finest compositions reveal the tremendous nobility, warmth, and enthusiasm of his spirit.

FRANZ LISZT (1811–1886)

Although Liszt composed in a variety of vocal and instrumental media and was recognized as the greatest piano virtuoso of his time, perhaps his greatest contribution to music is in the development of the symphonic poem. The programmatic aspects of romanticism touched him profoundly and he developed a new means of expressing extramusical ideas through the medium of the symphony orchestra—a technique that was essentially an extension of Berlioz' principle of the idée fixe. An important difference between the cyclical and programmatic techniques of Berlioz and Liszt is that Berlioz (as seen in our brief discussion of the *Symphonie Fantastique*) used a well-rounded theme of substantial length as the primary thematic element in a symphonic work, while Liszt used a short motive, transforming and modifying it according to the needs of the program. Liszt achieved unity by basing most of the thematic material upon this single short motive, while contrast was furnished by imaginative alteration of the motive. In the music dramas of Richard Wagner this technique led to the leitmotif principle, in which each character, mood, and occasionally even a stage prop was represented in the music by its own short theme or motive. Similar devices were later used by Richard Strauss.

Liszt began his career as a highly successful child prodigy, achieving international renown as a pianist at an early age. While living in Paris in his late teens and early twenties, he came under the influence of a number of excellent musicians, particularly Chopin, Berlioz, and Paganini. From Chopin he received the heritage of diverse and imaginative piano textures as well as a bent for harmonic experimentation. His typically romantic interest in giving musical expression to literary and poetical ideas was strengthened by his association with Berlioz. Paganini's incredible virtuosity inspired him to attempt to build a piano technique that paralleled the great violin virtuoso's command of his instrument.

Liszt's life is perhaps the most colorful among nineteenth century musicians. As an international figure of great renown, he lived life publicly, on a grand scale. His rather public love affairs and various other episodes have been immortalized by his many biographers. In addition to his activities as a piano virtuoso and composer, he was well known as a conductor, teacher, and as champion of several lesser known composers whose causes he chose to espouse. Another great service to music was found in the vast number of arrangements that he published based on the music of Bach, Beethoven, and other great composers of the past. In an era unblessed by electronic sound reproduction this was a very significant contribution, but one which is difficult for us to fully appreciate today.

Until about 1848 Liszt wrote predominantly for piano, bringing his remarkable mastery of the instrument to bear upon the art of composition. A number of these works, such as the *Hungarian Rhapsodies* (which demonstrate the nationalistic aspect of romanticism), the two piano concertos (particularly the E flat), and the *Transcendental Etudes* have established lasting places in the concert repertoire, although they are currently somewhat out of fashion. The influence of Chopin is clearly apparent in his piano music but, in addition, there is a certain brilliant lustre that belongs uniquely to the style of Liszt.

Les Préludes, Symphonic Poem, No. 3

In 1848 Liszt was appointed musical director of the court at Weimar. His fame and his avowed support of "progressive" music soon established the town as an important center for new music. It was here that Liszt turned his attention almost exclusively to orchestral composition and to the development of the single-movement programmatic symphony known as the symphonic poem. Of his twelve symphonic poems only the third, Les Préludes, is well known to today's audiences.

Its programmatic association is a rather loose one, for it is based not upon a narrative but upon a relatively short poem, Meditations Poetiques by the French poet Lamartine. The imagery of the writing is of a nature that lends itself well to free interpretation, not to detailed realism.

The work is in six sections, opening with an andante. Following two pizzicato notes, the basic motive of the entire work is played by the strings (Figure 77). The manner in which this three-note motive is treated in the course of the work is demonstrated by the examples in Figure 78.

Figure 77.

Liszt achieved great contrast of tempo, sonority, and timbre in his orchestral works. He was endowed with a natural gift for orchestration, and even in his piano music he seemed to be frequently thinking in terms of the coloristic possibilities of the symphony orchestra. The phenomenon of a romantic piano virtuoso who devoted much effort toward the orchestral medium resulted in a remarkable cross influence by which his piano music seems to be straining toward orchestral sonorities and his orchestral music seems to realize an imaginary ideal in piano sonority. From the microcosmic quality of lieder and the character piece to the earth-shaking sonorities of a great symphony, the piano exerted a telling influence upon all composition of the romantic era.

Figure 78.

Liszt, *Les Préludes*

The most significant younger composer to come under Liszt's wing at Weimar was Richard Wagner, who married Liszt's daughter Cosima. Wagner, the controversial composer who was to become the most influential figure in late nineteenth century music, profited much from the strong support of Franz Liszt.

SUGGESTED ASSIGNMENTS

1. Compare *Die Winterreise* to *Frauen-Liebe und Leben,* noting particularly the difference in the function of the piano.
2. Discuss the development of the romantic character piece in terms of the composers discussed in this chapter.
3. Listen to a number of Berlioz's works with the score in hand, attempting to relate the brilliantly expressive colors to the notated music. What did Berlioz do with instruments that Mozart did not?
4. For a special project write a paper comparing the Mendelssohn Violin Concerto to the Mozart D Minor Piano Concerto studied earlier.
5. List and describe the various types of left-hand accompaniment figures used in the Chopin Preludes. How did Chopin produce such variety of mood?
6. Read examples of Schumann's musical criticism. How closely do Schumann's evaluations of his contemporaries coincide with today's judgment of the same composers?

7. Compare Berlioz' use of the *idée fixe* in *Symphonie Fantastique* to Liszt's unifying motive in *Les Préludes*.
8. Find and summarize stylistic traits that are common to all of the composers discussed in this chapter. What does this reveal in regard to the general characteristics of romanticism in music?

THIRTEEN

WAGNER AND VERDI

One of the few similarities between Wagner and Verdi is that each devoted himself almost exclusively to works for the operatic stage. In almost every other way they are diametrically opposed, their works complementing each other in such a way as to illustrate many of the diverse facets of nineteenth century opera.

Verdi's operas represent the Italian tradition of singer's opera—the bel canto heritage and an emphasis on stage action. In Wagner, on the other hand, the singer is nearly eclipsed by the orchestra. Indeed, the progress of the drama takes place primarily in the action and interaction of Wagner's leitmotifs, woven into complex orchestral textures. Where Verdi typically set a lucid vocal solo against a relatively simple homophonic accompaniment, Wagner used complex polyphonic textures. Verdi's characterization is realistic and human (albeit melodramatic), while Wagner, with few exceptions, painted allegorical, even superhuman characters. The opposite poles of simplicity and complexity are ideally symbolized in the work of Verdi at the one extreme and Wagner at the other.

RICHARD WAGNER (1813–1883)

Wagner's entire career was characterized not only by a determination to succeed as a composer of opera but also by an intense craving to dominate the musical world. In spite of his limited formal training in music, he succeeded in these ambitions to an almost unbelievable degree. Today, although not recognized as the greatest composer of the romantic period, he is viewed as the most influential musician of his time, the one whose ideas have had the most impact upon the musical thought of today.

He was a tremendous egotist, a self-styled superman who believed not only in his supremacy as a composer but also in his abilities as a poet and philosopher. His achievements outside of music are open to some question, though it must be said that Wagner's gifts were, in a sense, universal in nature. He was capable of teaching himself whatever he needed and this ability was by no means limited to music.

Early in his career he became aware of the necessity of creating a new type of opera, a dramatic work that combined all of the arts into a magnificent and profoundly significant whole. Such a work would be called a *Gesamtkunstwerk* (universal art-work) and the principal points of Wagner's Gesamtkunstwerk theories are as follows: (1) Music had become excessively important in operas of the past and although Beethoven had shown the importance of *instrumental* music as a dramatic expression, it was necessary now for poetry to become more important in the drama. To put it metaphorically, the poetry should "fertilize" the music. (2) Legendary, allegorical, and historical material was more suitable to music drama than the realistic, melodramatic plots used in most other nineteenth century operas. (3) Feeling was more important than understanding, and to this end a new type of poetic verse needed to be developed which would stimulate the emotions. Wagner attempted to develop new poetic devices along these lines. (4) Operatic conventions such as stereotyped ensemble scenes had a false purpose that did not serve the drama. Above all, continuity was essential, with no break between arias and recitatives as are found between the "numbers" of traditional opera. Wagner attempted to maintain a continuous symphonic texture with his "endless melody" pervading the atmosphere. To this end he developed a type of vocal line called *Sprechgesang* (speech-song), in which the voice half sings, half declaims the text, a merging of recitative and aria that inclines toward the destruction of periodic phrase structure. (5) The orchestra should do much more than simply accompany the voice—it should express what voices and words cannot, and should powerfully and specifically reinforce word associations, particularly those of a sensuous or mystical nature.

In the four music dramas comprising the cycle entitled *Der Ring des Nibelungen* (1. *Das Rheingold,* 2. *Die Walküre,* 3. *Siegfried,* 4. *Götterdämmerung*) these theories were carried out quite consistently. The association of music to words was realized by means of the leitmotif principle, in which a vast number of short thematic fragments (leitmotifs) were woven into a continuous symphonic texture. Each of these represented a particular character, emotion, mood, or object and they recurred constantly throughout the drama in varying forms appropriate to the action. In addition to the motivic association with the drama, the orchestration was a powerful force in evoking the moods and emotions represented on the stage. Wagner professed to believe in a fusion of the arts in which poetry, music, design, and theater were welded together in a common dramatic purpose; but in actuality, by his emphasis on the orchestra, the music predominated. In general, this is a saving grace in Wagner's work, for his instinctive musicianship transcended the limitations of his elaborate theories. At his best he demonstrates a fine melodic gift, a daring harmonic expression, and a mastery of orchestration.

It was inevitable that a musician so self-centered and dictatorial would succumb to the lure of the conductor's baton. He was highly successful as a conductor, partly because of his keen perception of orchestral sound and color, and partly because of the strength of his dominating personality. Performances of Wagner's music dramas required an extremely competent symphony orchestra, for he made unprecedented demands upon the instrumentalists' technical skill; and as a conductor he was equally uncompromising. In order to bring his ideas of music drama to full realization, he secured financial backing to construct a special theater at Bayreuth, a center which is still used for festival performances of his works.

The twentieth century felt Wagner's influence most strongly in the area of harmony. Using the chromaticism of Liszt and Chopin as a jumping-off place, Wagner developed a harmonic style that relied upon chromatic dissonance, seventh and ninth chords, a continuous feeling of harmonic fusion and instability, and, above all, upon a deliberately vague and ambiguous tonal center. This is most apparent in his later works, particularly in *Tristan and Isolde,* a music drama based on Arthurian legend. Figure 79 shows a passage from the beginning of the prelude to *Tristan,* an excellent example of Wagner's revolutionary harmonic style. Passages such as this set the stage for the development of the twelve-tone technique used by Schoenberg, Berg, and Webern in the first half of the twentieth century,

Figure 79.

Langsam und schmachtend

which in turn led to present-day usage of the twelve-tone (serial) technique.

The course of late nineteenth century and twentieth century opera was profoundly affected by Wagner's work. His theories about opera, and their realization in his own music dramas resulted in an increased awareness of opera as a drama of significant content, more self-consciously an "art work" and less of an entertainment. His abandonment of clear-cut arias and other set pieces was perhaps just as influential, resulting in a strong deemphasis on phrase and period structure and an increase in the importance of the orchestra as a connective force. Gone was classical balance and symmetry, to be replaced by what might be called a musical "stream of consciousness." His most significant operas and music dramas are *Rienzi, The Flying Dutchman, Tannhäuser, Lohengrin,* the four operas of *The Ring of the Nibelungs, Tristan and Isolde, Die Meistersinger von Nürnberg,* and *Parsifal.* Of his few works in other media, the most well known is a single-movement work for small orchestra called *Siegfried Idyll.*

Finally, there are his voluminous writings in prose. It is typical of his egotistical nature that in most of his efforts he was almost completely self-taught, dabbling (in some cases, significantly) in playwriting, poetry, philosophy, and even in politics. As a result of the Wagner cult that sprang up toward the end of the nineteenth century, his prose works were published in ten volumes and translations subsequently appeared in several languages. The literature *about* Wagner is incredibly large. The late nineteenth and early twentieth century Wagnerites included such persons as Shaw, Hardy, Galsworthy, Swinburne, Baudelaire, Valéry, Mallarmé, Nietzsche, Whitman, and many others; all of whom wrote logically or illogically, pro or con, about Wagner and his art. The influence of this man, around whom so much controversy has centered, is still felt today; and, although the popularity of his music dramas may be on the wane, there remains a hard core of Wagner enthusiasts who will continue to keep the legend alive.

Die Meistersinger von Nürnberg, an Opera in Three Acts

The Mastersingers of Nuremburg was begun in 1845 but was not completed in its final form until 1867. The story is historically based upon the sixteenth century Mastersingers who formed guilds, held contests, and were guided in the composition and performance of their songs by a well-established set of traditions and customs. Wagner borrowed several actual names of real Mastersingers, paraphrased some of their poetry, and used a very small amount of their music. *Meistersinger* is less chromatic and, in general, composed with a lighter touch than any of Wagner's other operas. The nationalistic subject matter suggested the use of melodies somewhat folklike in nature, resulting in a less complex rhythmic structure and an essential simplicity of idiom. Comic scenes, very rare in Wagner's operas, are also found. All of these things combine to make this quite the most accessible of Wagner's works.

The libretto, as in all of Wagner's operas, was written by the composer himself. The primary issue presented is the age-old clash between tradition and the creative spirit in art. The Mastersingers' Guild represents tradition, while the character of Beckmesser satirizes the misuse of tradition, the blind adherence to rules without regard for esthetic considerations. Beckmesser was intended as a veiled representation of Eduard Hanslick, an excellent Viennese music critic who had written in opposition to Wagner's music.

The spirit of unrestrained innovation and artistic creativity is symbolized by Walther von Stolzing, a young knight newly arrived in Nürnberg who, in order to win the hand of Eva, must become a Mastersinger and win the song contest. The simple love story centers about the manner in which he does this, interspersed with scenes with the apprentices and comic scenes involving Beckmesser and his attempt to steal Walther's song for the contest. The character of Hans Sachs symbolizes the wise artist capable of resolving the conflict between tradition and impetuous creativity. He shows that neither tradition nor innovation is sufficient by itself, that there must be a constant flux between the old and the new, each learning from the other.

Wagner's operas are of great length and he thought of them as powerful dramas in symphonic form. Several of his operas are in an arch form, like a gigantic ABA, while others are cast in a form called bar form. Bar form is an ancient song form used in the Middle Ages, consisting of two more or less identical formal units (called *Stollen*) followed by a third and final contrasting unit (called the *Abgesang*). *Meistersinger* is in bar form, each of the three acts functioning as one of the three sections. Acts One and Two represent the two Stollen of a bar form of symphonic proportions, the action of Act Two being almost parallel to, and a kind of parody of, the action of Act One. Act Three is a gigantic Abgesang with an additional unifying factor found in the finale, which is essentially a return to the overture, presented in expanded and varied form.

The idea of the bar form becomes an essential part of the drama as well, for it is the traditional form of the songs composed by the Mastersingers and is the most prevalent form type in the opera. A very clear example is heard near the end of Act Two just after a love scene between Eva and Walther when Beckmesser demonstrates his art as a Mastersinger by performing a very square and excessively symmetrical song accompanied by Hans Sachs marking each error in the performance by a stroke of his hammer (*"Den Tag seh' ich erscheinen"*). In this instance the bar form is sung three times to form a song in three verses. It is given a deliberately pedantic realization appropriate to the character of Beckmesser. This is one of the finest comic scenes in the opera, for, as Sachs' hammer strikes with increasing frequency, Beckmesser sings louder and louder, waking the neighbors who add their vocal complaints—finally ending with a fugue. Other examples of the bar form are heard throughout the opera, particularly in Walther's trials before the Mastersingers, the most beautiful example of which is Walther's Prize Song, shown in Figure 80, which is also the love theme of the opera (excerpt, Figure 80).

Figure 80.

WALTHER

A - bend- lich   düm - mernd   um - schloss mich die— Nacht;   auf stei-lem Pfad war ich ge-

The beautiful Prelude to Act Three exemplifies Wagner's philosophy toward opera, namely, that every detail of the work must further the fundamental dramatic purpose by its direct relation to the action. Overtures of the eighteenth and early nineteenth centuries did not often do this. Frequently they did nothing more than set the general mood, were not directly related to the action, and in the worst instances were nothing more than a potpourri of themes to be heard in the opera. In *Meistersinger* the prelude to the third act carries on the inner action of the drama, particularly as it is related to the noble character of Hans Sachs.

Wagner was partial to the use of symbols and, although *Meistersinger,* unlike his other works, is not fraught with symbolism, it is quite possible that the character of Sachs combined with Walther symbolized Wagner's view of himself as the wise, mature artist who was also endowed with a passion for unbridled and revolutionary creativity. The opera as a whole is Wagner's protest against that portion of the musical world that did not pay him the homage he felt he deserved. Beckmesser and the other Mastersingers symbolize Wagner's critics and the prejudiced public. It is perhaps because of the composer's real identification with the characters of Walther and Sachs that these are the most sympathetic and lifelike characters in all of his works.

The overture, since it gives a synoptic view of the entire opera, serves admirably to demonstrate the composer's use of leitmotifs. It is such a finely wrought, self-contained piece of symphonic music that it is often performed separately in orchestral concerts. It opens with the Mastersingers motive shown in Figure 81. The ponderous, even pompous dignity of the theme serves well to depict the intractable conservatism of the Mas-

Figure 81.

tersingers. This is followed shortly by the motive of courtship which, because of its rhythmic freedom and unrestricted quality, might also be called the theme of artistic freedom (Figure 82). The return to conservatism comes with a theme that is closely related to the Mastersingers motif and

Figure 82.

serves in the opera as a march theme for the Mastersingers (Figure 83). The section which follows is built out of the theme shown in Figure 84 and may be called the art theme of the Mastersingers in that it represents the best aspects of the Mastersingers' art, the commendable qualities of artistic

Figure 83.

principles and ideals. This motive is also called the motive of the fraternity of art.

Figure 84.

Walther's yearning for a new ideal in art is represented by the motive shown in Figure 85 which, in the opera, is symbolized by his aspirations for the hand of Eva. The love theme (Walther's Prize Song, Figure 80) follows shortly and leads into one of the loveliest themes of the opera, the spring motive shown in Figure 86. This theme builds in a typically Wag-

Figure 85.

nerian manner and at the point of climax drops suddenly into the final section of the overture. This section is a masterpiece of contrapuntal writing, with all of the thematic material thus far presented woven into a complex but nevertheless expressive polyphonic fabric. The overture concludes tri-

Figure 86.

umphantly, its final chord coinciding with the entrance of the chorus on the stage. The overture admirably demonstrates Wagner's use of leitmotifs and, above all, the overpowering emotional and sensual impact of his music.

In Wagner is found the synthesis of romantic mysticism, spectacle, sensuality, fantasy, idealism, individuality, nationalism—in short, most of the general traits associated with the romantic movement, plus many of the more specifically musical ones. So great was his impact, not only upon the musical world, but also upon the world of ideas, that it is only in recent years that we have been able to view him objectively. In spite of his personal shortcomings of ruthless and tyrannical self-indulgence—characteristics which can be heard in his music—in spite of these traits, and to some extent because of them, he takes his place in history as one of the two or three most powerful and influential figures of the romantic era.

GIUSEPPE VERDI (1813–1901)

So dominating was Wagner's influence during the second half of the nineteenth century that only a man of Verdi's stature was able to maintain the Italian tradition of "singer's opera." That he was able to do this is partly accounted for by his strongly rooted nationalistic feelings. Not only was he reared in the traditions of Italian opera, he was also closely involved with the Italian nationalists who were working for a united Italian kingdom. So strong were his political commitments, that he was elected to the first National Parliament in 1860. A most humane individual, his involvement with Italy and its traditions touched many aspects of his life quite separate from his activities as a composer.

In contrast to Wagner, Verdi always kept the orchestra in a role subservient to the voices. His superb dramatic sense was manifest by treating the characters on the stage as living creatures, not as mythical or allegorical figures. His requirements for librettos were that they should contain no extraneous material, should be relatively brief and always to the point, and should be filled with human passion and emotion.

Verdi avoided the kind of lush polyphonic texture favored by Wagner. It was most natural for him to be direct and relatively simple in his means of communication. For the most part, he did not adopt the continuous texture used by Wagner but maintained the tradition of "number opera," that is, separation into self-contained arias, recitatives, ensembles, etc. Each act was a separate unit built out of these "numbers," and only rarely would themes recur significantly from one act to another. Because Verdi did not use the leitmotif principle or other cyclical devices, his music does not have the symphonic character and scope of development found in Wagner's music dramas. This was totally intentional, for Verdi viewed opera, above all, as theater—not as a symphonic form. There are no traces of Gesamtkunstwerk ideas or other theories about art. The orchestra functions primarily to support the action on the stage and, as a result, the music is not as self-sufficient as in Wagner. Verdi used a relatively large orchestra, and used it well, but he never allowed it to become the central, primary element as in Wagnerian opera.

In keeping with Verdi's emphasis on the stage action, his overtures, when they exist, are not designed to call attention to themselves but to set the stage for the action of the characters. Thus, few of them stand by themselves as orchestral pieces. He treated the orchestra masterfully, nevertheless; emphasizing the separate colors of solo instruments and frequently using the brass section as a group. Generally, his orchestration sounds clear and brilliant, like that of Berlioz, rather than thick and diffuse, as in Wagner. Verdi was well in touch with new orchestral developments and was quite willing to experiment for the sake of the right dramatic effect.

A highly gifted melodist, Verdi's attractive tunes are often combined with rhythmically clever orchestral accompaniments. A good example is found in *"La Donna e mobile"* from *Rigoletto*. Yet his melodies are more than just "catchy," they are also supremely expressive, particularly in his later works, in which the use of large leaps and a remarkably wide vocal range contributes much to their evocative qualities.

The emphasis upon the singer—upon the character on the stage —is intensified by his masterful dramatic characterization. The orchestra plays an important part in this; but does so without calling undue attention to itself. Color, harmony, rhythm, and strongly contrasting dynamics are used with tremendous dramatic effect. The vocal lines strikingly depict both the character and his particular mood or emotion of the moment. Individualizing of each singer's melodic line is particularly apparent in large ensembles, causing each character's unique qualities to stand out, even though several voices are singing at once. The famous quartet in *Rigoletto* is a good instance of this.

The librettos of Verdi's operas (with the exception of *Falstaff*) are essentially serious, utilizing intense dramatic contrast at a very fast pace. Much of it is typical romantic melodrama marked by situations of gloomy violence, pathos, and passion. None of the librettos were written by the composer although he often worked with his various librettists in the final polishing. The literary sources of the librettos are many and varied, including works of Shakespeare, Hugo, Schiller, Dumas, and Byron. The Italian poet Arrigo Boito wrote the librettos for Verdi's last two operas, *Otello* and *Falstaff*, both based upon works of Shakespeare. The fact that Boito was also an opera composer of considerable skill and reputation may account for these two librettos being so well-suited to Verdi's gifts. They contributed in no small part to the success of the operas.

Of Verdi's twenty-six operas, the best known are *La Traviata, Il Trovatore,* and *Rigoletto* (the culminating works of his early career); *Don Carlo, Un Ballo in Maschera* (A Masked Ball), and *La Forza del Destino* (The Force of Destiny), middle-period works which culminated in *Aida;*

and *Otello* and *Falstaff,* both written in the decade following the composer's seventieth year. These last two are unquestionably the best, *Falstaff* being particularly unique in that it is his only comic opera. Based on *Henry IV* and *The Merry Wives of Windsor, Falstaff* is notable for its wit and human warmth—and for the incredible fact that it was written by a man of eighty. Among Verdi's few nonoperatic works is his *Requiem* for chorus, orchestra, and soloists, an excellent work written in memory of the Italian novelist and patriot Alessandro Manzoni.

Otello, a Lyrical Drama in Four Acts

This opera appeared in 1887, sixteen years after *Aida,* the only intervening work being the Manzoni *Requiem.* To satisfy Verdi's demands for extremely fast pacing, the original Shakespearean play was cut from about 3500 lines to less than 800. Boito did a superb job of compressing the libretto; but obviously it was no longer Shakespeare's *Othello.* What is left is a fast-paced drama with essentially the same story, using many of Shakespeare's lines in near-literal poetic translation, Shakespeare's tremendous scope of conception being replaced by Verdi's music.

The story, as it appears in the opera, is condensed as follows: The Moore Otello, governor of Cyprus, returns from war with the Turks and is welcomed back by his bride Desdemona and the populace. His ensign Iago, jealous and bitter that Otello has promoted Cassio rather than himself, plots with Roderigo and arouses Otello's jealousy and suspicion of his wife and Cassio by telling him that Cassio has dreamed of Desdemona. He also says that he has seen Desdemona's wedding handkerchief in the hands of Cassio. Otello becomes convinced of his wife's guilt and his anger is aroused. He insults her in the presence of the Venetian ambassador. He later strangles her in her bed, only to learn from the horror-stricken Emilia (Iago's wife) that Desdemona is innocent. He stabs himself and dies at her side.

Unlike his other operas, *Otello* has an almost continuous musical texture. Within this texture, however, there remains a clear separation of set numbers so that this continuity is quite unlike that of Wagnerian opera. Often the feeling of separate numbers is created by the orchestra playing a few measures of the accompaniment figure prior to the beginning of the voice line. Set pieces in earlier Italian opera, in addition to being self-contained, tended to be rhythmically square and a bit lacking in melodic freedom. In his later operas Verdi does remarkable things within the

typical framework of the set piece, spinning long, imaginative melodic lines
of great rhythmic freedom.

Opening without an overture, Act One begins with the chorus (populace) on stage during a storm, awaiting the arrival of Otello's ship. The
storm music perfectly sets the mood for Otello's entrance with the words,
"Esultate! l'orgoglio musulmano sepolto è in mar." ("Hear glad tidings.
Our wars are done. The ocean has whelmed the Turk.") (see Figure 87).

Figure 87.

The plot unfolds quickly in this seaside scene and soon it becomes
apparent that, although outwardly devoted, the ensign Iago really hates
Otello because of the preferential treatment given to Cassio. There follows
a scene in which Iago purposely makes Cassio drunk and involves him in a
fight with Roderigo who is secretly in love with Desdemona. Iago sings a
drinking song in this scene that typifys the kind of set piece used in many
of Verdi's earlier operas (see Figure 88). The introductory accompaniment
figure used here sets off the drinking song as a separate number even though
the texture leading up to it contains no break. Otello arrives on the scene
in the midst of the brawl and imperiously dismisses Cassio from his service.
Act One concludes with a beautiful love duet between Desdemona and
Otello. Here the softer, more poetic side of Otello's personality is emphasized in such a way as to establish him as a character whom the audience
can view sympathetically throughout the opera, in spite of the depths of
jealousy and suspicion to which he ultimately sinks.

At the opening of Act Two, Iago cleverly advises Cassio to seek reinstatement as Otello's lieutenant by appealing to Desdemona. There follows
Iago's famous soliloquy known as the "credo of evil" ("I believe in a cruel
God, who has fashioned me in his own image, etc."). The lines of this aria
were added by Boito, virtually the only lines in the opera that were not
translated more or less directly from Shakespeare. Near the end of the aria
a chromatic line is presented in the vocal line to the words *"al verme
dell'avel"* ("to feed the worm of death"). In addition to its function as text
painting, the chromatic line serves as an identifying mark for Iago's char-

Figure 88.

acter later in the opera (see Figure 89). The remainder of Act Two deals mainly with Iago's devious and subtle means of arousing Otello's jealous suspicion. His temptation is musically realized in Iago's vocal lines by melodic passages that descend in a most suggestive manner, and by the use

Figure 89.

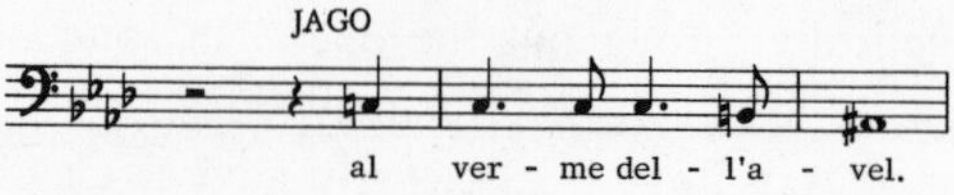

al   ver - me del - l'a - vel.

of chromaticism. The subtle fluidity and sinuous character of the melodic threads sung by Iago show Verdi's great skill as a dramatist as well as a composer—a tremendous achievement in musical and dramatic characterization.

In Act Three, Desdemona, unaware of Otello's suspicion, innocently pleads for Cassio's reinstatement. Otello, his jealousy thus further aroused, berates her with great irony and near hysteria. Protesting her constancy, she rushes from his presence. Otello's soliloquy follows. It is introspective and very much in the nature of a recitative and aria. Otello hides himself at

Iago's urging, and in the ensuing scene hears and sees more to add to his jealousy—all contrived by Iago.

The arrival of the Venetian ambassador and other dignitaries leads to Cassio's appointment as the new governor of Cyprus. Otello is ordered to return to Venice and, in the course of the action, strikes down Desdemona, precipitating an ensemble scene in which the whole company joins her in a plea for mercy. In the intensity of his rage and emotion, Otello orders everyone from the hall and falls in a swoon. The ironic final scene of Act Three finds Iago at the height of his evil triumph. To the accompaniment of the populace outside the window who are lauding Otello, thinking that he has been recalled to Venice for new honors, Iago points with horrible pride to the motionless body of Otello, saying, *"Ecco il Leone!"* ("See here the Lion!") (Figure 90).

Figure 90.

Act Four opens with a deeply expressive orchestral introduction leading into a short dialogue between Emilia and Desdemona. Desdemona then sings the famous "Willow Song," a beautiful example of the simple side of Verdi's melodic gift. Its heartrending pathos concludes with Emilia's exit and Desdemona's prophetic cry, *"Ah! Emilia, Emilia, Addio!"* Desdemona then kneels and intones the *Ave Maria* which begins and ends in a pathetic monotone, emulating the style of a liturgical chant. Otello enters hesitantly, kisses her three times, vainly tries to elicit a confession from her, and then strangles her in her bed.

The murder thus committed, Emilia returns and in horror confronts Otello with the falsity of his accusations against Desdemona. The final scene moves quickly to avoid anticlimax, uncovering Iago's plot and concluding with Otello's suicide. In his final utterances Otello regains some of the nobility of the beginning of the opera. The music of the final scene recaptures some of the qualities of the ending of the Shakespearean drama.

Viewing Wagner and Verdi comparatively, it is interesting to note that Wagner's greatest contribution is found not in his operas and music dramas per se, but in the musical ideas and philosophies expressed in them. It is because of this that his influence is felt so strongly in the twentieth century. Verdi was not without influence upon later composers of opera. Indeed, the "verismo" movement in opera—which emphasized realism in plots of contemporary situations, often in sordid detail—owes much to Verdi's kind of realism. (Bizet and Puccini are among the important composers of this movement.) Verdi's greatest contribution, however, lies not in his influence upon later composers but upon the *intrinsic* value of his operas themselves. They retain their popularity today because of their genuine humanity and their ability to speak directly to the heart.

Although a detailed discussion of nineteenth century opera is beyond the scope of this book, two other developments in opera during the latter half of the nineteenth century should be mentioned here. One is the French lyrical drama, represented most prominently by the works of Charles Gounod, particularly by his opera *Faust;* and the other is the Russian national opera, of which Moussorgsky's great opera *Boris Godunov* is the most distinguished example. The Russian opera movement emphasized nationalistic materials such as folk song, folk legend, and Russian history. *Boris Godunov* is a masterful tragic opera of the historical type, based upon the story of a Tsar and his people. Many of its scenes achieve a depth of passionate realism that is unsurpassed in operatic literature.

Suggested Assignments

1. In summary form, draw a comparison of the salient features of the works of Wagner and Verdi, using supplementary resource material if necessary.
2. Develop your listening abilities through repeated hearings of *Die Meistersinger,* attempting to follow the progress of the leitmotifs. Catalogs of the leitmotifs in all of Wagner's works are available in published form.
3. Review Chapter Eleven, noting the characteristics of the romantic movement that are represented in Wagner.
4. Expand your knowledge of Verdi's operas by listening to representative works from his early and middle periods. *La Traviata* and *Aida* would be good works to begin with. If possible, see them in live productions, studying the libretto in some detail prior to the performances.

FOURTEEN

JOHANNES BRAHMS
(*1833–1897*)

In contrast to the colorful innovations of Berlioz, Liszt, and Wagner, Brahms stands out as a champion of the established instrumental forms, and of classical reserve. He represents the continuation of the classical trend within romanticism. His music can be called abstract in the sense that it is not representational or programmatic; but in a purely musical way it is supremely expressive, for he infused his sonatas, chamber music, symphonies, and concertos with real warmth and emotion. Far from being austere, his music evokes the true romantic spirit in a language that reveals his remarkable intelligence, strength, and idealism.

The classical characteristics to be found in Brahms' music fall, for the most part, under the general heading of form. Many of his instrumental works are in four movements and in almost every instance the first movement is a sonata form. He handled the sonata form with the understanding of a classicist, recognizing that its essence was the conflict and interplay of contrasting musical ideas. In his development sections this dramatic conflict is presented in a manner that is both classical and romantic in nature—classical, in that the ideas to be developed are often relatively short, fragmentary ideas that are rhythmically worked and reworked in varying textures; and romantic, in that his melodic style and harmonic idiom are clearly of the late nineteenth century.

His frequent use of variation forms is another manifestation of the classical influence. Among his first major orchestral works was the *Variations on a Theme of Joseph Haydn;* and other sets of variations appear as movements in many of his works, both chamber and orchestral. Many scherzos are found as movements among his chamber works, as well as isolated examples of the minuet. The rondo form also retains its place among Brahms' chamber works, frequently being used as the finale of a four-movement work.

In some respects his veneration for the past extends back further than the classical period. This is manifest in the use of baroque forms such as the passacaglia, the most notable examples being the ending of *Variations on a Theme of Joseph Haydn,* and the finale of his Fourth Symphony. Fugatos, or passages in fugal style, also appear frequently, along with contrapuntal devices such as augmentation, inversion, and diminution. Occasionally there is an archaic quality in both melodic and harmonic passages that can be attributed to the use of modes, possibly influenced by the vocal music of the Renaissance. A beautiful example of this is found in the second movement of his Fourth Symphony, opening with a unison melody of marked Phrygian flavor played by the woodwinds and horns. This antique quality is continued in the harmonic passages that follow (Figure 91).

Figure 91.

Brahms' use of the element of rhythm stands out as one of the most significant aspects of his style. His phrase lengths are often irregular, although symmetrical phrases are found as well. At times the rhythm of the melody may not coincide with the apparent rhythm of the bar line, resulting in interesting cross rhythms. The use of rhythms that do not fit the bar line are particularly prevalent in development sections and in intricate contrapuntal passages. Recurrences of a melody will often be cast in a changed relationship to the bar line or accompaniment figure, resulting in a rhythmic stress that differs from its earlier presentations. The imaginative use of rhythm adds much to the vitality and fascination of his music.

Brahms' orchestration is in the tradition of the romantic period, though conservatively so. He used a large symphony orchestra but did not aspire to the far reaches of coloristic possibilities explored by the programmatic composers of his time. The most typically romantic trait in his orchestration is found in the frequent use of what might be called the "German nature sound," the kind of orchestral sound heard in Mendelssohn's *Hebrides Overture,* studied earlier. It emphasizes the dark colors of the orchestra, particularly horns, clarinets, and violas; and uses the strings as a body to achieve a rich, full quality. Percussion is used sparingly. Brahms, unlike Berlioz and other programmatic composers, did not call attention to the uniquely expressive qualities of timbre itself, but used orchestral color primarily as a vehicle to serve the other elements of the music.

The romantic side of Brahms is found in its purest form in his songs. As a lieder composer he is in the direct line of succession to Schubert and Schumann. His more than two hundred songs, along with those of Hugo Wolf, represent the most significant contribution to art song literature during the late nineteenth century. Here, as in Schumann, we find the true romantic sentiment expressed in melodies that are often of ravishing beauty, supported by piano accompaniments that are always appropriate to the text. The influence of folk song is clearly apparent in Brahms' lieder as it is in much of his instrumental music, showing the nationalistic side of his character.

Brahms was born into a musical family of very moderate means, and as a boy was required to work as a tavern pianist. His humble origins may have been a factor in a certain elemental quality that is apparent in much of his music, endowing it with a universal kind of attraction. The folklike quality of many of his melodies gives them a strength and beauty that speaks to all social and intellectual levels. When Brahms was in his twentieth year his talents were discovered by Schumann, who wrote an article in the *Neue Zeitschrift für Musik* describing the "young eagle" as the most significant new composer on the horizon—an important event in Brahms' early career. The young composer became a close friend of Clara and Robert Schumann and, after Robert's death in 1856, maintained a devotion to Clara that nearly led to their marriage.

The painstaking care with which Brahms worked resulted in a total output which, though not remarkably large, is notable for its overall excellence. He suppressed many of his earlier works, discarding numerous compositions that a lesser composer would have been happy to claim. The bulk of his work is instrumental, including the four symphonies, which stand out as monuments in the orchestral repertoire. Of his two piano concertos, the D Minor is an excellent early work while the B Flat Major is a mature composition of great depth and beauty. His single Violin Concerto is among the best of its kind, equaled only by the Beethoven Violin Concerto. The unique *Double Concerto,* a work for solo violin, solo cello, and orchestra inspired by the baroque concerto grosso, is particularly popular with today's audiences. The two concert overtures, the *Academic*

Festival Overture and the *Tragic Overture,* complete the list of Brahms' major orchestral works.

It is safe to say that Brahms was the most successful chamber music composer of the late nineteenth century. Chamber music, by its very nature, is abstract in the sense that its values and meanings are almost entirely musical. This does not mean that chamber music should not evoke images of a nonmusical nature. But its emotional meaning and other evocative qualities are achieved primarily through musical means, not by deliberate extramusical devices. Thus, in chamber music perhaps even more than in symphonic media, developmental technique is a factor of prime importance. So great were the problems of accommodating romantic concepts of melody and harmony to the classical ideals of development, that few late nineteenth century composers wrote first-rate chamber music. Indeed, most programmatic composers didn't attempt it. Brahms alone, with painstaking self-criticism, produced a group of chamber works in the best tradition of Haydn, Mozart, Beethoven, and Schubert.

His chamber works are uniformly good and include three string quartets, two string sextets, two string quintets, a piano quintet (piano plus string quartet), a clarinet quintet (clarinet plus string quartet), three sonatas for violin and piano, two sonatas for cello and piano, two sonatas for clarinet and piano, and several trios and quartets involving the piano. Of these, the string quartets, the sonatas for violin, and those for cello are perhaps the best known; but the overall quality of his chamber music is so even that the other works are frequently heard as well. In the sonatas for piano and a solo instrument, as well as in the other chamber works with piano, the piano part is on an equal basis with the other instruments and, for this reason, the piano part should not be viewed as an accompaniment.

It is interesting to note that about two thirds of Brahms' chamber music includes the piano, while in the chamber works of Haydn, Mozart, and Beethoven, works with piano are definitely in the minority. This illustrates the romantic attitude toward the piano as well as Brahms' own particular inclinations. Some of his finest piano writing appears in the chamber works. He wrote extremely well for the instrument and often made startling demands upon the abilities of the pianist. His works for solo piano do not quite attain the luminous poetic qualities of Chopin, perhaps because he tended toward thicker textures and seemed to be striving, at times, toward an orchestral type of sound. Nevertheless, several of his works for piano are fine pieces, particularly the *Variations and Fugue on a Theme of Handel* and the Intermezzi. Also among his piano works are several other sets of variations, three early piano sonatas, and several sets of character pieces.

Brahms' finest choral work is the *German Requiem* for chorus, orchestra, and soloists, the texts selected by himself from the Bible. In addition to a few other works for chorus and orchestra, he composed several shorter works for various choral combinations, including a number of folk song arrangements and the *Liebeslieder Waltzes.*

Symphony No. 2, in D Major, Op. 73

The Second Symphony was written in 1877, the year after the completion of the First. The two symphonies are the fruit of the composer's early maturity, the First having required twenty years of intermittent work. The Third and Fourth Symphonies were written in the decade of 1877 to 1887. All of them use a four-movement pattern, in this and other ways manifesting the classical heritage. A devout admirer of Beethoven, Brahms strove to imbue his symphonies with the same kind of intensity and dramatic conflict found in Beethoven's nine symphonies. This becomes particularly apparent in the developments, which are often the central, dominating sections of the movements. In popularity as well as in quality, the Brahms symphonies are paralleled only by those of Haydn, Mozart, and Beethoven.

The Second Symphony is bright and lyrical in character, somewhat less intense than the other three. As in all of his symphonies, the first movement is in sonata form. It opens immediately with the thematic material of the first tonal group, a triadic melody played by the French horn, prefaced by a three-note motive played by the basses and cellos (see Figure 92). On the first hearing, these first three notes may sound quite unimportant, ap-

Figure 92.

parently functioning only to set the stage for the melody which follows. Actually this motive is the most important building block of the entire symphony. It is the source of much thematic material of the first movement and is also used significantly in the subsequent movements as a cyclical device. Figure 93 shows several of the places where the motive is prominently used in the first movement, often in expansion, inversion, or rhythmic alteration.

Figure 93.

Brahms, *Symphony No. 2*

The second tonal group (shown in Figure 94) is presented in the key of the dominant, demonstrating the classical key relationship. This passage is very typical of Brahms, first, because of its songlike character, and second, because of its motion in parallel thirds (two moving voices of identical rhythm consistently separated by the interval of a third). Brahms so frequently harmonized passages in this way (in thirds or sixths) that this be-

Figure 94.

came a distinguishable feature of his style. Most typically, the thirds or sixths are found between the two upper voices of the harmonic texture. The use of songlike melodies—often with folk song qualities—is most frequently found in the melodic material of his second tonal groups. The exposition ends quietly with reiterations of the three-note motive in its original form. In following the score, it is interesting to note that the double bar repeat sign invariably used in the classical sonata form (a vestige of the baroque binary form) is found also at the end of the exposition of this work.

The development section is somewhat shorter than is usual for Brahms; and it begins in the classical manner with material from the first tonal group. Much of the excitement of the development section is furnished by the contrast of the lyrical first tonal group material to the vital and intense figurations in shorter note values, all realized with great economy of means. Near the end of the development is heard a flowing theme that was first presented by the violins as a part of the first tonal group. This use of the theme prepares for its return at the start of the recapitulation, played by the violas against the oboes' presentation of the main opening theme. This carryover of the themes achieves a smooth transition from the development to the recapitulation. The second tonal group, when it returns, is back in the home tonality of D major, played in parallel thirds by the oboes and bassoons. Developmental activity continues throughout the rest of the movement as it proceeds to a serene ending.

The second movement presents a key contrast that should not, at this point, appear as a startling innovation. It is the third relation, seen so often in the works of Schubert and also in Beethoven. The movement is in the key of B major, furnishing a fresh key feeling after the predominant D major key of the first movement. It opens with an intensely passionate melody played by the cellos in the rich middle register accompanied by the low instruments of the orchestra. The movement is basically a large ABA form with the climax occurring near the end of the middle section in preparation for the return. The use of melodic fragments in a contrapuntal texture is especially notable.

We proceed from the second movement's key of B major to the key of G major in the third movement, once again using the descending third relation. It is a quiet movement, somewhat in the pattern of a scherzo and trio. An inverted form of the three-note motive from the first movement appears at the outset. Its metamorphosis is illustrated in Figure 95. In the faster

Figure 95.

middle section this material is then varied further, using exactly the same pitches as at the beginning, but ornamented by means of repeated notes (see Figure 96). Another form of the three-note motive appears in the 3/8 section found near the end of the movement. Here it is altered not by

Figure 96.

inversion, but by changing the interval of the half step to a whole step (see Figure 97). The movement concludes with a return to the mood of its opening.

The finale also presents the cyclical device, clearly apparent in the first

Figure 97.

three notes of the opening unison passage. This swift, sotto voce melody is the main thematic material of the first tonal group of the sonata form (Figure 98). After some development, and after a transitional theme

Figure 98.

evolves, the theme of the second tonal group appears, marked Largamente (Figure 99). Its deep richness of sonority is achieved by placing it in the low register of the violins, chiefly on the G string. This melody, also, presents the three-note motive, this time inverted. The course of the movement is formally quite conventional, particularly in regard to the key relationships. The pastoral mood that has pervaded the entire work is

Figure 99.

Largamente
Violins
arco

mp

especially apparent in this development section. After a conventional re-capitulation, the movement concludes in a brilliant coda.

The uses of the three-note motive mentioned here are only those which stand out most significantly. The motive is heard so often throughout the total work that there have been attempts to show that the work draws almost all of its material from this generating fragment. Cyclical devices became very prevalent in symphonic works of the late nineteenth century. Perhaps the most famous example is the César Franck *Symphony in D Minor,* a work which draws virtually all of its material from a three-note motive heard at the very beginning.

Trio for Piano, Cello, and Clarinet, in A Minor, Op. 114

Chamber works involving the clarinet are relatively few in number, the most significant compositions before Brahms being the Mozart Clarinet Quintet and the Beethoven Clarinet Trio.[1] Brahms' attraction to this instrument is shown by his use of it in four major chamber works, all of them of his late period (Op. 114, 115, Op. 120, No. 1, and Op. 120, No. 2). They were written for Mühlfeld, a distinguished clarinetist of the Meiningen orchestra. His playing had apparently made a tremendous impression upon the composer, for all of the works have a special quality that seems to be brought out by particular attention to the unique idiomatic capabilities of the clarinet.

The Op. 114 Clarinet Trio utilizes the same combination of instruments that Beethoven had used in his chamber work for clarinet. The Brahms work, however, is more mature and of greater scope than its predecessor. The first movement opens with the cello alone playing a melody which, like so many of Brahms', is based upon the tones of a triad rather than upon the steps of the scale. As the movement gains momentum, triplet figures, a dotted rhythm, and rapid scale passages appear against this melodic mate-

---

[1] The Beethoven Septet and the Schubert Octet both use clarinet but in combination with strings and other wind instruments. Thus, the clarinet part is not as significant in the total effect as in the above-mentioned works.

rial. The first tonal group concludes with material built out of the melodic fragment shown in Figure 100, first presented in the cello. The second tonal group (in C major) begins in the cello with a melody that is very similar in style and general mood to the opening theme (see Figure 101).

Figure 100.

As the cello completes its statement of this melody, it is taken up by the clarinet and answered one measure later by the cello, the cello playing the melody in inversion. This use of a canon in which the second voice is an inversion of the first shows Brahms' interest in contrapuntal devices of past centuries.

Figure 101.

Although the development begins with the cello playing the opening theme in E minor, the section is built primarily out of other material from the first tonal group—the rapid scale passages and, above all, the melody shown in Figure 100. The opening theme doesn't return at all, not even in the recapitulation. For this reason the recapitulation is defined primarily in terms of the clear-cut return to the key of A minor which occurs after a series of ascending and descending scale passages, rather than by means of the thematic material. The material that does return at this point is the same as that shown in Figure 100, played by the cello in double stops.

The second tonal group material (Figure 101) appears this time in the clarinet and then in the cello, with the piano imitating the cello in inversion—the same canonic device that appeared in the exposition. Next a new theme is introduced by the cello (Figure 102) which becomes the basis of the next section, closing with further development of the material shown in Figure 100. The movement closes with a brief coda, also based on the material of Figure 100 combined with ascending and descending scales and arpeggios.

Figure 102.

The form of this movement is quite remarkable. The absence of a clear-cut recapitulation and the fact that the development begins in the key of the dominant suggests a kind of nineteenth century version of the baroque binary form. The most striking feature of the movement, however, is its wealth of delicious thematic material. Many of these lyrical passages contain wide leaps, undoubtedly suggested by the fact that the clarinet can easily negotiate fast leaps throughout its range. Such passages also work well on the cello with the result that much of the melodic material is quite out of the ordinary, and uniquely expressive.

The second movement is an adagio of surpassing beauty and romantic sentiment. Its captivating effect is achieved primarily by emphasizing the intimate qualities of the instruments, each instrument at various times being cast in a role that causes it to stand out as a soloist above the other two. The clarinet dominates the opening phrase, next the cello playing the same material, contrast being furnished by the change in register and timbre. The clarinet then presents a second theme which again is taken up by the cello. These two melodies furnish most of the material for the movement.

The form is quite free, utilizing variation techniques rather than developmental treatment. It is basically in three sections, the first being the presentation of the two main themes, the middle section consisting primarily of variation of the material, and a third section which begins with a clear-cut return of the first theme. This return, played by the cello, is notable for its being in the subdominant rather than in the tonic. In terms of tonality this gives a fresher sound to the return and furnishes a key contrast that causes the coda and ending in D major to sound more convincing. The coda is characterized by the use of short melodic fragments tossed back and forth between the cello and clarinet.

The third movement is a scherzo that sounds very much like a waltz. The basic key is D major with a trio in D major. Folk elements are emphasized here, but it is by no means an unsophisticated movement. The final section is greatly truncated, being less than half as long as its initial presentation. It is an attractively tuneful movement with the wind instrument in a dominating role, the bucolic clarinet timbre adding to the folklike effect.

All of the first three movements have quiet endings, a fact that contributes to the dynamic and vital effect of the fourth movement. It is a sonata-rondo form with an intense and angular rondo theme that furnishes great contrast to the gently flowing quality of the B section (Figure 103). The

Figure 103.

ABACABA pattern is marked by very free returns of the A section; but these returns are always in the tonic key. On its first presentation, the B section is in the key of the dominant and on its return, in the tonic—the classical key pattern for the sonata-rondo. The C section is developmental in style, particularly characterized by fragmented intervals of the descending third. The movement is concise and forceful with an emphatic conclusion that is in direct contrast to the endings of the earlier movements.

It was Schumann's hope in championing the young Brahms, that he would become an exponent of the Germanic "music of the future" movement—the cause supported by Liszt and Wagner. In this he was wrong, for Brahms drew more upon the past than the future to establish his unique means of expression. After a few painful experiences in controversy with the Liszt-Wagner camp, Brahms retired from the scene of battle and remained aloof. Shy and reserved in manner, this great musician left a heritage of masterworks that breathe the true spirit of romanticism and, at the same time, reflect his veneration of the art of earlier centuries.

SUGGESTED ASSIGNMENTS

1. Make a list of stylistic traits of Brahms' music in terms of the works studied in this chapter. Try to decide which of these traits show the influence of the

past and which are in line with practices that are unique to the romantic period.

2. Find features of Brahms' music that show the influence of Beethoven.
3. Expand your knowledge of Brahms' orchestral music by listening to works not studied in this chapter. The Second Piano Concerto would be a good work with which to begin.
4. Do the same with the chamber music, perhaps starting with a string quartet or a violin sonata.

FIFTEEN

THE LATE ROMANTIC PERIOD

PETER ILYICH TCHAIKOVSKY (1840–1893)

Nationalism flourished during the late nineteenth century, the strongest single movement in this direction occurring in Russia. A serious musical culture developed there later than in the European countries and, as a result, Russia remained relatively untouched by European romanticism. During the early nineteenth century two significant composers had emerged in Russia, Michael Glinka (1804–1857) and Alexander Dargomijsky (1813–1869). Both were known chiefly for their operas—Glinka's *Russlan and Ludmilla* and Dargomijsky's *The Stone Guest*. Both works are based on subjects of Pushkin (known as the first great Russian poet) and both have a Russian quality that is unmistakable. These works marked the beginning of the Russian nationalist movement in music.

The Italian, Germanic, and particularly the Wagnerian influences were actively resisted by many late nineteenth century Russian composers. Five of these men, informally drawn together by common feelings of musical intent and motivation, began to be viewed as a group. A Russian critic named Stassov dubbed them "The Five." Mily Balakirev (1837–1910) was the unofficial leader of the group which also included César Cui (1835–1918), Borodin, Moussorgsky, and Rimsky-Korsakov. Opera was their most characteristic medium and, by using Russian history, legend, folk song, and folk dance, they filled their music with a unique and typically Russian flavor. The works of Balakirev and Cui are seldom heard outside of Russia, but certain works of the other three are well loved by today's audiences.

Tchaikovsky, though not one of "The Five," to some extent shared their nationalistic attitude. His nationalism, however, did not need to be self-consciously "applied." It seems to have been a natural and intrinsic part of his style, apparent in the frequent use of certain characteristic melodic intervals as well as in the general mood of his music. His music also draws much from the European traditions, for his treatment of the orchestra shows the influence of Berlioz and Liszt, while, from the standpoint of sheer technique, he owes much to Brahms. Of his six symphonies, the last three are mature masterpieces filled with melodic passages of rich romantic sentiment, intense contrast, and spectacular climaxes. Examination of his scores will reveal the extremes of dynamics to which he resorted, ranging from *fffff* to *ppppp*. He used an orchestra somewhat larger than that of Brahms, and contributed to the general expansion of orchestral resources taking place during the late nineteenth century.

Perhaps the most popular of all his works are the concertos—the famous First Piano Concerto in B Flat Minor and the Violin Concerto. His *Rococo Variations,* a virtuoso work for cello and orchestra, is also well known. In his symphonies and concertos he assimilated the European tradition in a unique way. The influence of classical form is certainly apparent, but his violent and colorful outbursts seem to be typically Russian. His rhythms are vital and inventive, with frequent passages of reiterated syncopations. Bold masterful orchestration worked well with his programmatic inclinations. This is vividly seen in his Sixth Symphony, the *Pathétique,* which was frankly intended as a programmatic work.

In his other orchestral works the programmatic tendency is given free rein. His most important works in this area are the overture-fantasy *Romeo and Juliet,* the symphony-fantasy *Francesca da Rimini,* and the *Caprice Italien.* His ballets *Swan Lake, Sleeping Beauty,* and *Nutcracker* are widely performed in the concert hall as well as on the ballet stage. Of his eight operas, *Eugene Onegin* and *Pique Dame* are often performed in Russia and are occasionally heard in this country.

Overture-Fantasy: *Romeo and Juliet*

This is one of Tchaikovsky's earlier works and is dedicated to the mentor of the "Russian Five," Mily Balakirev. It draws on the spirit of the Shakespeare play but is not intended as a depiction of the complete drama. The specific images that the composer purported to deal with are (1) Friar Laurence, (2) the feud between the Montagues and the Capulets, (3) the meeting of the lovers, and (4) the death of Romeo and Juliet. The first and fourth of these are found in the prologue and epilogue.

The slow moving harmonies at the opening create a medieval, even monastic feeling that serves well to depict Friar Laurence. This is achieved by the use of a simple triadic harmony that avoids the progression of dominant to tonic. All of the sonorities in the first four measures, in fact, are minor triads. The adjective "modal" is conventionally applied to passages of this sort, although the harmonic technique is different from the modality of the Middle Ages and the Renaissance. The four-part texture of bassoons and clarinets further contributes to the archaic quality. The strings, harp, and other winds are added as the music softly begins to gain momentum.

A gradual acceleration leads into the rapid second section which is marked by jagged syncopations and significant use of rests. The love theme (shown in Figure 104) is heard in the third section, introduced by the violas

Figure 104.

and English horn. The oboes and flutes are used in the second presentation of this glowing theme, attended by a "sigh figure" played by the French horn. This figure is closely related to the theme itself, being derived from the two notes at the beginning of the third measure (see Figure 104). This and other characteristic aspects of Tchaikovsky's music were destined to exert a strong influence upon later composers, particularly the Finnish composer, Jan Sibelius.

There follows a section of development that is based primarily upon the material of the second section. The second section is then recapitulated, more or less in its original form, followed by a return of the love theme. All of this contributes to a general shape that can be likened to a rather free sonata form.

The final section is slow like the opening and uses portions of the love theme. The repeated notes in the timpani and pizzicato double basses add an ominous tone to this section. After a suggestion of the opening material, the work concludes with tragic intensity. The repeated chords in the final four measures of the work vividly show Tchaikovsky's imaginative use of rhythm. They are placed in such a way that their relationship to the symmetrical pulse of the bar line is obscured. Yet there is an inner logic to this rhythm that beautifully depicts the tragic finality of the lovers' deaths.

ANTONÍN DVOŘÁK (1841–1904)

The nationalistic movement in Bohemia (Czechoslovakia) was centered primarily in the music of Bedřich Smetana (1824–1886) and Antonín Dvořák. The Bohemian composers had much to draw on in their native land, for their folk heritage was large and diverse. Their folk melodies are marked by unique rhythms (probably originating with the accents of the language) and a pervasive melancholy, offset at times with striking contrasts. Their folk dances, such as the *dumka* and *furiant,* contain a wealth of fascinating rhythms.

Smetana's music is not as widely known as that of Dvořák, although some of his works—notably *The Moldau* from the symphonic cycle *Ma Vlast,* and the opera *The Bartered Bride*—have established well-deserved and lasting places for themselves. In his own country Smetana is considered the father of the Bohemian musical tradition.

Although Dvořák wrote many songs and choral works, today he is best known as an instrumental composer. Of his five symphonies,[1] the Fourth and particularly the Fifth (the famous *New World Symphony*) are frequently performed. The Second, in D minor, is often played; and his violin concerto and cello concerto are also well known. Dvořák composed numerous string quartets, trios, and other chamber works for various combinations. His chamber music is not as deftly wrought as that of Brahms but it is motivated by the same intent to fuse the classical forms with romantic expression.

Dvořák spent a number of years as a hard-working professional violinist and violist while striving to further himself as a composer. International fame came gradually, and only after considerable effort, along with some help from Brahms, who recognized Dvořák's talents. When, at the age of forty, he found himself in a relatively well-established position, he devoted much effort to furthering the cause of Bohemian music and encouraging the younger composers of his country. In 1892 he came to America to become the director of the newly established National Conservatory in New York. Here he composed some of his finest works, including his *Concerto for Cello and Orchestra in B Minor* (inspired by the cellist-composer Victor Herbert), the *American Quartet,* and the Fifth Symphony. He did much to encourage American composers to draw on their own national heritage rather than continue to be dominated by the European tradition. No immediate effects resulted from these efforts but they have borne consid-

[1] He actually wrote nine, though the usual numbering includes only the last five.

erable fruit in this century. He returned to Bohemia in 1895 where he remained for the rest of his life, becoming director of the Prague Conservatory in 1901.

Symphony No. 4 in G Major, Op. 88

Written in 1889, this work shows the clarity and honesty of Dvořák's musical thought. It is cast in the classical four-movement pattern and is filled with the delightful Bohemian-flavored melodies for which Dvořák is famous. The influence of Brahms is seen in the manner of development and in the general approach to symphonic structure.

The first movement opens with a plaintive melody played by the cellos in the rich upper register doubled by the woodwinds. Although the symphony as a whole is in G major, this opening section is clearly in the parallel minor key (G minor). This contrast of major and minor keys remains an important characteristic throughout the movement. The primary thematic material to be developed comes not from this opening theme but from the short melodic passage played by the flute just after the cello melody (Figure 105). The rhythm of the second measure of this theme is heard throughout and in the recapitulation the entire theme is elaborated in

Figure 105.

various ways. The closely knit rhythmic treatment heard in this movement is typical of Dvořák.

The second movement is an adagio in C minor, concluding in C major, with much exchange between the major and minor feeling. It opens with the strings alone in a passage that is built primarily out of the fragment shown in Figure 106. The first four notes of this fragment are heard in varying forms throughout the movement.

Figure 106.

The flute theme heard just after the strings' opening presentation (Figure 107) bears a resemblance to the first movement theme shown in Figure 105 and quite possibly is a consciously applied cyclical device. The two themes (Figures 105 and 107) have the repeated descending intervals in

Figure 107.

common and their initial presentation is in about the same location within their respective movements.

The shift to C major begins softly with rapidly descending scale passages in the violins above which the woodwinds present thematic material generated from the fragment shown in Figure 106. These scale passages are briefly interrupted by a violin solo but resume immediately after to build toward the climax of the movement, firmly in the bright key of C major. The movement continues with alternation and some development of the ideas already presented and concludes quietly. The overall form of the movement gives the impression of a large arch, a feeling that is heightened by the dynamic and rhythmic intensity at the center of the movement.

The third movement is dancelike in quality and contains many delightful folklike melodies. It is not unlike the type of movement Brahms often used in place of the scherzo—quite free in form—and could be termed an intermezzo. Its triple meter continues to the coda with frequent shifts between G minor and G major. At the coda there is a change to duple meter resulting in a striking change as the movement concludes in the mood of a rousing polka.

After an introductory fanfare dominated by the trumpets, the finale begins with the cellos' presentation of the main theme of the movement (Figure 108). A comparison of the first three notes of this theme with the first-movement theme shown in Figure 105 will reveal once again the use of a cyclical device. The movement possesses a clear structure, pre-

Figure 108.

dominantly in the sunny key of G major, with contrasting sections of C minor and C major. Most of the thematic material is drawn from the opening fanfare and from the cello theme.

Dvořák, even more than Tchaikovsky, fused his nationalism with classical structure and technique. He was influential in emphasizing the value of folk material and stimulated much fruitful scholarship in this area. Never really happy outside of the boundaries of nineteenth century Bohemia, his music sings of the rich and colorful heritage of that delightful land.

NICHOLAS RIMSKY-KORSAKOV (1844–1908)

The man who is often described as the most skillful and imaginative orchestrator of the nineteenth century and who was the only teacher of the most distinguished composer living today, began by regarding music as a sideline. Rimsky-Korsakov, teacher of Stravinsky, was a career officer in the Russian navy until he was nearly thirty. His first success as a composer resulted from his First Symphony, a work composed on an extended cruise during his last years in the navy. Its performance in Russia was sufficiently impressive to secure him an appointment as teacher of composition and orchestration at the St. Petersburg Conservatory. The work is practically unknown in this country.

It is probable that his world travels during his tour of duty in the navy contributed to the exoticism in his music, to his interest in evoking images of faraway places. Certainly he saw instruments that were not used in the European orchestra and the effect upon his orchestration is apparent. His use of a wide variety of percussion sounds is particularly notable. He combined instruments in such a way as to bring out their unique soloistic qualities or blended them to produce new and refreshing tone colors. He also strove to find ways to produce new sounds upon the instruments in order to increase the coloristic possibilities of the orchestra. This has been a major influence in experimentation with instruments during the twentieth century.

He had a profound knowledge of the technical and musical possibilities of all of the instruments. The result was that his instrumental parts are very playable and rewarding, though often quite difficult. In contrast to the dark, homogeneous textures of many of his German contemporaries, his music sounds strikingly clear and colorful.

Rimsky-Korsakov was primarily an opera composer but, oddly enough, his operas are almost totally unknown in the United States. His reputation in the West rests primarily upon his orchestral suite *Scheherezade,* the *Capriccio Espagnol,* and a few other pieces. Of his fifteen operas, works which continue to delight his countrymen, we know only excerpts.

Along with the rest of the "Russian Five," he had a nationalistic interest in things indigenous to his homeland. In spite of his late commitment to a musical career, he acquired a phenomenal technical mastery and, though not blest with Moussorgsky's profound imagination, he became the most accomplished composer among the "Five."

Capriccio Espagnol, Op. 34

From the standpoint of sheer sound the impact of this work is tremendous. It vividly illustrates the virtuoso use of orchestral timbre as an intrinsic part of musical meaning, for much of its effect relies upon its orchestral setting. To learn more about how such colorful orchestral sounds are achieved, it would be well to listen to this work with the score in hand. First performed in 1887, it typifies the late romantic period in its emphasis upon local color, nationalistic elements (in this case, Spanish), and exotic imagery.

The first of its five movements is entitled *"Alborada,"* a morning song of greeting. It opens at full tilt in a boisterous passage that uses nearly every instrument of the orchestra. The triangle, tambourine, cymbals, and bass drum add much to the color of this opening tutti. Based essentially upon one thematic idea, contrast is achieved with dynamics, and by the use of the violin and clarinet in solo passages.

The second movement is a set of variations in slow triple meter. The theme is first stated by the horns in four-part harmony supported by the low strings. The five variations which follow maintain the contour and general character of the original theme but vary it by means of the orchestration. In variation I, the cellos take the melody with the strings, including the violins, used in the texture below them. This shifting of the normal roles among the strings gives a uniquely rich sound to this passage.

Variation II employs the English horn with tremolando [1] accompaniment in the strings. The English horn's passages are alternated with triadic "horn calls" played by the French horn. Each alternating horn call is colored by a French horn technique called "stopped horn," which is achieved by placing

---

[1] A characteristic string technique consisting of very rapid unmeasured repetitions of a single tone, usually soft.

the hand in the bell. It produces a muffled faraway sound that is much different from the full noble timbre of the open horn.

Variation III uses rich double stops in the strings with the woodwinds carrying the melody. Variation IV finds the cellos once again with the melody with an accompaniment texture that includes pizzicato notes in the violins. In the first part of variation V the melody is given to the first violins in their highest register doubled by the woodwinds. In the second half of the variation, the violins carry the melody down to a low register while above this the flute plays ascending and descending chromatic scales, serenely concluding the movement. All of the variations are continuous with no pause between.

The third movement is a return of the opening Alborada in a new key and with the solo parts for violin and clarinet now exchanged. The harp makes its initial appearance in this movement to add color to the harmonic accompaniment against the brilliant virtuoso passages of the solo instruments.

Without pause the fourth movement, called "Scene and Gypsy Song," is announced by a loud snare drum roll. The "Scene," comprised of a series of cadenzas, serves as an introduction to the impassioned "Gypsy Song." The first cadenza is for the entire brass section in a free fanfarelike passage. Next is a cadenza for the solo violin followed by a concerted cadenza for percussion, woodwinds, and violins. Then in succession are heard the flute, clarinet, and harp in solo cadenzas accompanied by various percussion instruments. The "Gypsy Song" is based on material already presented in the "Scene" and includes prominent passages for the solo cello and the woodwinds. Of particular interest are the guitarlike effects near the end produced by the pizzicato strings with a rapid back and forth strumming motion.

The fifth movement, *"Fandango Asturiano"* begins fortissimo without pause. After the brilliant opening the solo violin is again used in prominent virtuoso passages along with similar passages in the woodwinds. The movement ends with an extended coda based upon the Alborada. The material of the Alborada serves as a unifying element throughout the work, being heard in the first and third movements as well as in the final coda.

JAN SIBELIUS (1865–1957)

The name of Sibelius is inextricably linked with his native Finland. He represents the greatest musical achievement in the history of countries north of Germany, and the reverence held for him in his native land is perhaps greater than that of any other nation for its favorite son. His personal musical expression is felt to be so intrinsically linked with Finnish nationalism that for many listeners his music seems to sing of the rugged Finnish countryside, of brooding lakes and deep forests. His music bears the stamp of his homeland but does so without the use of folk tunes or even folklike melodies.

A specific source of nationalistic material for Sibelius was literary, not musical—the Finnish national epic, the Kalevala. Most of his early orchestral works are symphonic tone poems based upon this and other Finnish sources. The appeal of these works to the Finnish people during the last years of the nineteenth century was heightened by their struggle for independence from Tsarist Russia, and Sibelius was raised to the eminence of a national hero. So strong was this feeling that in 1897 the Finnish government freed him from economic concerns by granting him a lifelong stipend to allow him to devote his efforts entirely to composition.

Among his works in the overt nationalistic vein are four *Legends* based on the Kalevala (*Lemminkäinen and the Maidens, Lemminkäinen in Tuonela, The Swan of Tuonela,* and *The Return of Lemminkäinen*), *En Saga,* and *Finlandia,* all composed before 1900. Other tone poems and incidental orchestral works followed but his achievement as a serious composer centers primarily upon his seven symphonies (1899–1924) and his Violin Concerto (1905). Although he composed in small forms for various combinations of piano, strings, and voices, his greatest strength lies in the area of symphonic music.

Sibelius' music is rather conventional in view of the musical upheavals taking place during the first quarter of the twentieth century, and he has enjoyed great popularity with audiences in England and the United States who find that his music speaks a language that is meaningful to the twentieth century, but not so modern as to cause bewilderment or confusion in the minds of conservative listeners. His style is based essentially upon nineteenth century techniques. The pulsating accompaniment figures are similar to those of Tchaikovsky, and so is his penchant for striking contrasts and jagged syncopated rhythms. His orchestration, often quite lush, departs in some ways from nineteenth century practices. He preferred the somber colors of the lower instruments and often used the instruments in families—all of the double reeds by themselves, the strings alone, or all of the brasses at once. His string writing is marked by frequent use of repeated notes, tremolandos, and arpeggios in thick harmonic textures. In line with the general expansion of orchestral resources taking place at the end of the nineteenth century, he sometimes divided the strings into eight or more parts and used additional instruments in the wind sections.

Perhaps his greatest originality lies in his concept of musical structure. In his symphonies he appears to be striving for a cohesive organization without sacrificing the feeling of freedom and flux. Classical sonata forms—those of Haydn, for example—often present themes in the exposition from which motivic fragments can be extracted, the fragments, not the themes, being used as the basis for the development section. The reverse process is typical of Sibelius' approach to form. Fragmentary ideas are frequently presented near the beginning and it is only after they start to multiply and take on clear-cut relationships to each other that they begin to form longer themes. In many of Sibelius' symphonic movements a singing romantic theme is heard at the climax, the product of the evolution of fragments and motives heard earlier. A tendency toward cyclical techniques and the erasing of divisions between movements is seen in many of his symphonies, culminating in the Seventh, which is a single-movement work.

Symphony No. 7, Op. 105

This symphony, subtitled "in one movement," is regarded as Sibelius' most mature work. Its structure renders pointless any discussion in terms of conventional symphonic form. It is neither a series of symphonic movements linked together for continuity, nor is it simply a symphonic sonata form of large proportions. Rather, it is a host of minutely chiseled details, all related and all finally uniting to form a totality of ingenious design. The term arch form can be applied, as is illustrated in Figure 109.

Figure 109.

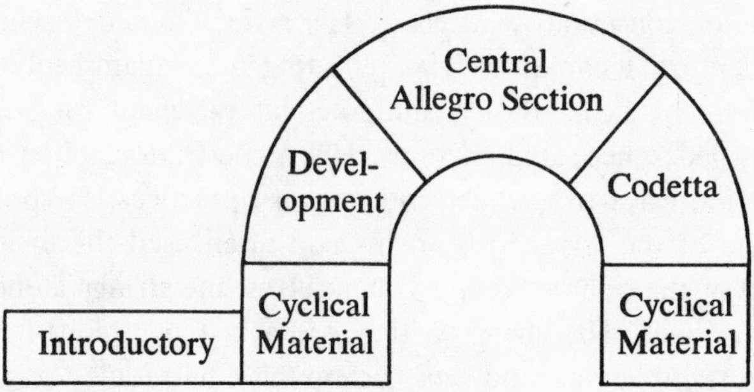

The introductory section is considered separately from the arch itself, in that it is clearly in the nature of a preface and because it contains most of the material of the entire work in fragmentary form. In many of his works the pervading mood is established at the outset, along with the initial presentation of the thematic germs of the composition.

Each of the two cyclical sections—the sides or corners of the arch, as it were—begins with the first trombone playing the theme shown in Figure 110. Although these two sections are relatively short in terms of time, they are the most important unifying factors in the symphony, lending added significance to the material heard between them, and, in general, supporting the whole structure.

Figure 110.

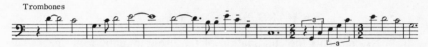

The central allegro section, the keystone of the arch, is actually heard somewhat past the middle of the work in terms of time. It nevertheless has the feeling of being the center because of its climactic qualities and because the material heard earlier has prepared the way for it. One hears it as an important point of arrival. This central section opens with a theme not previously heard (Figure 111) and gradually accumulates speed and excitement until it arrives at a presto tempo. The codetta section allows

Figure 111.

some relief in preparation for the cyclical trombone theme. The work concludes in a short epilogue that is deceptively calm until the final cadence, where it explodes to a fortissimo.

It is interesting to note that the arch is not symmetrical, either in terms of time durations or thematic relationships. Yet it gives the effect of musical symmetry because of the relative importance of the various sections to the total form, regardless of their time durations. The result is a work in which much of the beauty lies in the rare combination of a finely wrought organic structure and freedom of form.

In spite of the chronological fact that Sibelius lived most of his life in the twentieth century, he is best viewed as a composer of the romantic era. He grew in stature, and extended the framework of his own means of musical expression, but was unable to assimilate the new developments of the twentieth century—a fact that may account for his apparent nonproductivity during the last thirty years of his life. The human sincerity and idealism of his music gives it a universal appeal and assures him a unique place in the history of music.

RICHARD STRAUSS (1864–1949)

Strauss represents the culmination of the programmatic trend in romantic music and is in the direct line of succession with Berlioz, Liszt, and Wagner. As a child he received excellent and rigorous musical training, composing competently at a remarkably early age. His early works—somewhat in the style of Brahms—show a mastery of the classical forms. With his first tone poem, *Aus Italien* (1887), he turned from the abstract vein toward depictive music and there followed a series of tone poems that, with his operas, brought him international recognition as the foremost German composer of the early twentieth century.

He was also renowned as a conductor and in many ways this aspect of his career paralleled his activities as a composer. He possessed the professional conductor's knowledge of the symphony orchestra and among romantic composers his orchestrational talents are rivaled only by Rimsky-Korsakov and Berlioz. Strauss, however, demanded more of the instruments than either of these composers and expanded the resources of the orchestra to an unprecedented degree. Soaring melodic lines and virtuoso passages involving wide leaps and rapid arpeggios are characteristic of his instrumental writing. So demanding are many of his instrumental parts that orchestra players often find it necessary to practice them as they would a concerto. Such passages in Strauss' tone poems are a real test of the performer's abilities and are often used by professional orchestras as audition material in employing new members.

Chapter Five, in the discussion of the use and meaning of programmatic techniques, dealt with several specific examples of programmatic devices in

Strauss' tone poems. Essentially they fall into two categories, (1) the literal depiction or imitation of extramusical phenomena and (2) the more general evocation of a mood or emotion—related to a situation but not depicting it specifically. Examples in the first category are the use of flutter-tongue by the wind instruments to imitate the sound of baaing sheep in *Don Quixote,* and the use of an irregular rhythm in repeated chords to depict the breathing of a dying man at the beginning of *Death and Transfiguration.* Examples in the second category are, in *Don Juan,* the spacious and heroic horn melody beginning with the ascending octave leap, intended to portray Don Juan's passionate feelings toward Donna Anna (possibly this passage evokes a more literal image as well); and, in *Thus Spake Zarathustra,* the mood of philosophical contemplation established in the opening. In all such examples the listener is likely to associate the musical device with its intended extramusical meaning only if he is aware of the program and knows what the device is supposed to mean. Good program music is like all other music in that it has a musical meaning of its own separate from the extramusical association; and program music is best judged by the validity of this purely musical meaning. It is necessary, then, for the composer to have great skill in bringing his programmatic devices in line with sound musical principles.

With few exceptions, Strauss' phenomenal technique was equal to the task of being simultaneously depictive and musically meaningful. Along with frequent use of leitmotif techniques, his style is marked by complex but lucid multivoiced contrapuntal textures, diverse rhythms, and extremes in dynamics. His harmonic usages, based primarily upon nineteenth century practices, in a few instances show traces of twentieth century trends by the use of polytonality, extreme chromaticism, and daring dissonances. His unique ability to adapt to the musical requirements of each different libretto or program makes it difficult to speak of his style in general terms. In a sense, each tone poem has its own unique style and structure, which accounts for the great diversity in Strauss' music. His most remarkable general feature is his ability to invent appropriate orchestral sounds, harmonies, themes, and motives for the purpose of characterizing ideas, events, and persons.

In addition to those mentioned earlier, his tone poems include *Till Eulenspiegel, Macbeth, Ein Heldenleben, Sinfonia Domestica,* and *Alpine Symphony.* Of his fifteen operas, the best known are *Salome, Elektra,* and *Der Rosenkavalier.* He composed a number of concertos for various instruments, some chamber music, and a few piano pieces—mostly early works. He also was an excellent lieder composer, though only a few of his songs are widely known today.

As an internationally acclaimed composer and conductor, Strauss traveled widely. He nevertheless remained spiritually rooted to his native Germany. His unfortunate involvement and apparent sympathy with the Nazi regime resulted, at the end of World War II, in the confiscation of most of his royalties that had accumulated outside of Germany during the war years. In straitened circumstances, he continued to compose until 1948. Known as a fiery musical rebel during his early career, the twentieth century viewed him as a conservative in contrast to such men as Stravinsky, Bartók, and Hindemith. Like Sibelius, he was unable to assimilate the ideas of his younger contemporaries.

One may criticize Strauss for the excesses in his music, or for his self-indulgent sensuality, but never for purely technical reasons. He is unquestionably one of the most accomplished composers of all time and the orchestral repertoire is distinctly enriched by his contributions to it.

Ein Heldenleben (A Hero's Life), Op. 40

Graphically illustrating the expanded orchestral resources of the late romantic period, the instrumentation page of the score of *Ein Heldenleben* lists 108 instruments, including eight French horns, five trumpets, two harps, four bassoons, two tubas, seven percussion instruments, a large string section, etc. Such imposing forces are quite appropriate for the musical biography of a romantic hero and, in this case, the hero is the composer himself. Completed in 1898, it shows the composer at the height of his powers and tells us much about the man.

Its form is essentially that of a gigantic sonata movement subdivided into six main sections. Strauss gave revealing titles to these sections but later withdrew them. Part I, opening with the theme shown in Figure 112, was called simply "The Hero." The variety of rhythms and motives in this theme may be presumed to depict various phases of the hero's personality, his gentler inner self being heard later in the section.

Part II was called "The Hero's Enemies" and begins with the chattering

Figure 112.

theme shown in Figure 113. It is a satirical view of Strauss' enemies, presumably his critics. The hero theme enters here and gradually rises above the antagonists. In the midst of the tumult the "Hero's Mate" ap-

Figure 113.

pears, portrayed by the solo violin with the theme shown in Figure 114. This is Part III of the tone poem, a real tour de force for the solo violin. Again, as in Part I, the various aspects of the character's personality are revealed by means of a diversity of rhythmic and melodic inflections. As the

Figure 114.

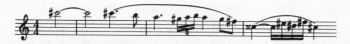

tumult of battle subsides, the themes of the hero and his mate intermingle, rising to a warmly suggestive climax. The section concludes with faint echoes of the antagonists in the background.

Viewing the work as a large sonata form, Parts I, II, and III together form the exposition, while Part IV, "The Hero's Battlefield," begins the development section. Heralded by offstage trumpets, Part IV furnishes the most intense conflict of the drama as the antagonists theme, presented in augmentation, once more hurls itself against the theme of the hero. The theme of the hero's mate is heard briefly above the frightful din, high in the violins. At length, with the musical effect of a recapitulation, the victorious hero emerges with a triumphant statement and lengthy elaboration of his theme.

Part V, "The Hero's Deeds of Peace," beginning with the theme shown in Figure 115, may be viewed as a kind of reprise of much of Strauss' work up to that time, for many themes of earlier compositions are cleverly

Figure 115.

woven into the fabric. Most notable are themes from *Don Juan, Death and Transfiguration,* and *Don Quixote,* although numerous themes from his operas and other tone poems are heard as well. Part VI, "The Hero's Retreat From the World and Fulfillment," functions as a coda to the entire work. Depicting the hero's memories upon meeting death—again with thematic references to earlier works—it ends on a note of calm assurance.

The overblown and sometimes bombastic style apparent in *Ein Heldenleben* and other works of Strauss typifies the end of the romantic era in Germany. German composers such as Gustav Mahler, Anton Bruckner, and Hugo Wolf, all influenced by Wagner, strove, like Strauss, toward a strongly emotional musical expression that, at times, bordered on the pretentious. Their works contain a wealth of fine music, yet much of it is marred by a feeling of striving toward the unattainable.

As might be expected, this extravagant expansion of musical and emotional resources was met by a violent reaction in the opposite direction, particularly in France. To many musicians during the last decades of the nineteenth century, the time when romantic expressiveness seemed to be bursting the seams of the symphony orchestra, it became obvious that the romantic era was dying of its own excesses. Thus, Strauss and his German contemporaries are, in reality, post-romantic composers. Their activities extended well into the twentieth century but were paralleled by events that ushered in the new musical ideals of the twentieth century. The first strong reaction in a new direction was the late nineteenth century movement known as impressionism, to be discussed later.

Suggested Assignments

1. Through the examination of orchestral scores, trace the gradual expansion of the symphony orchestra from 1750 to 1900. Cite specific ways in which it grew.
2. Investigate nationalism in late nineteenth century music, naming specific works and the traits that make them nationalistic. Use additional resource material recommended by the instructor.
3. Trace the evolution of formal structure in works written for symphony orchestra from 1750 to 1900, noting such things as the number of movements, types of movements and their placement in the total work, methods of expansion and development, etc.

4. Examine the score of Rimsky-Korsakov's *Capriccio Espagnol,* making a list of unique orchestral devices found in the work.
5. As a special project trace the history of the use of programmatic devices in music. Use reference material recommended by the instructor.
6. Expand your knowledge of the music of the composers discussed in this chapter. Listen also to works by other members of the "Russian Five," particularly Borodin and Moussorgsky.

PART FOUR

MUSIC OF EARLIER PERIODS

SIXTEEN

RENAISSANCE MUSIC

The period from 1450 to 1600, the arbitrary dates for the Renaissance in music, embraced a wide variety of significant musical achievements, including the development of choral polyphony, the establishment of an art of secular music, the beginnings of a new instrumental style, and the development of music printing. Josquin des Prez (c. 1440–1521), often referred to as the first great renaissance composer, established in his choral music, both sacred and secular, the foundations of the renaissance tradition of vocal polyphony. Born in the lowlands north of France, he was among the first of the French-Netherland composers whose musical influences spread to other European countries, particularly to Italy. The best known of these French-Netherland or Flemish composers was Orlando di Lasso (Lassus), an international figure who wrote in all of the musical styles of the time. Other significant events occurred in Germany, where the new style of Protestant church music led to the development of the Lutheran chorale; while in Rome, Palestrina and other composers developed a supremely refined style of polyphonic church music.

Music was touched by many of the same influences brought to bear upon the art, literature, science, and philosophy of the period, for the fifteenth century was a turning point in cultural history, a time of changing attitudes and reevaluation of human activity, much of which focused in the broad movement known as Humanism. Humanism stressed the significance of earthly human activity for its intrinsic value as opposed to the medieval attitude of viewing human activity as an expression of religion. Most of man's activities during the Middle Ages was directed toward the glorification of God, not toward giving joy to man; and the renunciation of earthly pleasures for the sake of the hereafter had been an important aspect of human behavior. This is seen in the fact that the most significant and highly organized musical culture of the Middle Ages was centered in music

237

for the church service; and most of the significant works of art of that time were on religious subjects. Religious subjects continued to be used in the art of the Renaissance, along with secular subjects, but throughout there began to appear a subjective and often sensual surface, an emphasis on beauty per se and the expression of nonreligious values not often found in medieval art. The face of a madonna by a renaissance painter such as Leonardo da Vinci is not likely to be fraught with sublime sorrow in the medieval manner but may bear an expression of delightful contemplation; while the Venuses of Botticelli appear to be quite worldly young ladies, not at all like immortal goddesses. The human form began to be viewed as a thing of beauty, not simply a temporal casement for the immortal soul. This is manifest in the sculpture and painting of such an artist as Michelangelo, who devoted an attention to anatomical accuracy not seen since the time of the ancient Greeks and Romans.

Indeed, a reverence for the culture of classical antiquity was a guiding force in renaissance thought. Scholars began to revive the ancient Greek and Latin languages and architects emulated the gracious proportions of Hellenic structures. The seeds sown in ancient times by men such as Plato, Aristotle, Galen, and Sophocles began to bear fruit in the work of many renaissance figures including Erasmus, Galileo, Vesalius, and Shakespeare, to mention only a few.

Thus, to the fifteenth and sixteenth centuries, rebirth or renaissance meant a return to the ideals of ancient classical culture, and had its most impressive beginnings in Italy, the center of the ancient Roman civilization. In the twentieth century the Renaissance is viewed as the beginning of modern history, for the ideals of rationalism, idealism, and humanity embodied in the humanistic movement continue to exert their influence to the present day.

GIOVANNI PIERLUIGI DA PALESTRINA (ca. 1525–1594)

Nearly all of Palestrina's music was written for the church and manifests the general renaissance characteristic of surface beauty seen in its smooth lines, balance, and symmetry. The dominating mood is one of reserve and contemplation, but within this framework there is also a profoundly emotional feeling, and the human voice is revealed as an instrument of deeply sensuous beauty. He composed primarily in a choral texture of four to eight voice parts, occasionally in as many as twelve parts. He did not compose instrumental accompaniments for his works, though it is assumed that in sixteenth century performances the organ, or perhaps other instruments, frequently played along with the voices, probably substituting for a voice when necessary. Because of the absence of written instrumental parts, renaissance choral music is traditionally performed without accompaniment, or *a cappella*. Literally, a cappella means *in church style,* but it has come to imply simply *unaccompanied,* applied specifically to choral music (usually sacred), not to other musical media.

Palestrina served as musical director at various churches and cathedrals, including St. Peter's in Rome, and was one of several composers who attempted in their music to comply with the precepts of the Council of Trent (1545–1563), an august body of Roman Catholic clergymen who met to consider reforms in church policy. The story that he was asked by certain members of the council to "save" polyphonic music for the church, though interesting, is untrue. He composed more than a hundred settings of the Mass, over 250 motets (short polyphonic choral works using a sacred text other than the Mass), a vast number of miscellaneous sacred choral works, and a few secular compositions.

Palestrina's musical style is extremely consistent, the inevitable result being the extraction of rules and principles of counterpoint which are today commonly used as the basis for the study of sixteenth century counterpoint—frequently a required course in university music curricula. It should be remembered, however, that his is only one of several polyphonic styles and that there are significant differences among the practices of sixteenth century choral composers.

Renaissance polyphony is based upon the church modes, discussed briefly in Chapter Two, and upon the diatonic scale. Palestrina's most characteristic texture is imitative, the various voices weaving their way through the fabric in a predominantly stepwise melodic style. It is the stepwise character of his melodic style that causes it to sound so smooth and eminently well suited to the human voice. The natural rhythm of the text influences the rhythm of the music, stressed syllables usually being set to longer note values. Imitative choral music, with the various voices singing the words at different times, produces a fascinating counterpoint of rhythm and words, and, since bar lines did not come into common use until the seventeenth century, the rhythm of each individual voice line in relation to all of the other voices results in a delightful rhythmic freedom untrammeled by the restrictions of a regular metrical beat. This feeling of free yet highly organized rhythm is one of the great beauties of renaissance music.

Many renaissance composers, particularly those noted as madrigal composers, used a great deal of dissonance as a text painting device and to heighten the emotional intensity. The expressive use of dissonance within a polyphonic texture is an important feature of renaissance music but is very carefully and sparingly used in Palestrina's music. His use of dissonance may be described as being predominantly diatonic as opposed to the chromaticism practiced by certain madrigal composers. This means that, for the most part, his dissonances consisted of harmonic intervals of seconds, fourths, and sevenths within the mode, using chromatic alterations very sparingly. The careful placement of these dissonances in relation to the rhythm of the music is an important aspect of his style.

Missa Papae Marcelli

The *Pope Marcellus Mass,* named after a member of the Council of Trent who later reigned briefly as Pope, is the composition around which grew the legend of Palestrina as the "saviour" of polyphonic church music. Included in the deliberations of the council was a consideration of church music, for some held that it had become so complex that the texts were unintelligible and, among other things, a ban on imitative polyphony was proposed. Fortunately, such drastic measures did not come to pass, but it is possible that the council influenced many composers toward a simpler kind of polyphony. The *Pope Marcellus Mass,* though it contains much polyphony, has numerous passages in which several voices sing the same words at the same time, resulting in frequent homophonic textures in which the words can be clearly understood.

As in most musical settings of the Mass, this work deals only with the portion of the text called the Ordinary of the Mass and some of its sections are subdivided. In addition to the natural divisions of the text within each of the five sections (see Chapter Ten), the *Sanctus* is very clearly separated from the *Benedictus,* and there are two complete settings of the *Agnus Dei.* The work is written for a basic chorus of six parts: soprano, alto, two tenor parts, and two bass parts. Certain sections, however, are written in only four parts, while the second *Agnus Dei* uses a texture of seven voices.

Canonic imitation, one of the most important technical resources of the renaissance composer, is heard very clearly at the opening of this work as each of four voices enters in turn, as shown in Figure 116. The cadence arrives when the words *"Kyrie eleison"* have been stated once by four voices to complete the first phrase, and at this point the other two voices enter the texture to begin a section of free counterpoint.[1] The manner in which the new section is connected with the first phrase typifies sixteenth century practice and is achieved by arranging for the entrance of the new voices to coincide with the ending of the first phrase. In some instances the

Figure 116.

Opening of the Pope Marcellus Mass. *Bar lines are added in most modern editions of renaissance choral music.*

new voices may enter with a new idea just before the actual cadence point of the preceding phrase, creating an even stronger feeling of continuity from phrase to phrase. Obviously, not all of the phrases are linked in this way, for there are times when a more complete feeling of repose is desired, and in such instances the phrases are not overlapped. Normally there is a

[1] Free counterpoint is a term denoting a texture in which the voices do not adhere to strict canonic imitation, but move according to the wishes of the composer without the restrictions of canonic (or fugal) devices. Lengthy passages in strict canonic imitation are rare in sixteenth century music; usually an imitative passage remains strict for only a short time at the beginning of a phrase.

cadence at the end of each line or phrase of text and the degree of partial or complete repose is determined not only by the amount of continuity furnished by overlapping of phrases (the rhythmic factor), but also by the harmonic implications of each cadence in terms of the overall tonal center (the harmonic or tonal factor).

The *Kyrie,* with C as a tonal center, is built in three sections corresponding to the three parts of the text: (1) *"Kyrie eleison"* (2) *"Christe eleison"* (3) *"Kyrie eleison."* There is a complete cadence (sustained final sonority without overlapping) at the end of each of these sections, the first ending on C, the second on G, and the third on C. Although sixteenth century composers were still consciously using the modal system, there are obvious indications of tonic and dominant relationship within this movement. Actually, the fifth relation is quite prevalent in sixteenth century music, presaging the firm establishment of the tonic-dominant concept as the basis of tonal structure in later periods. The tonal structure of this movement, then, is not unlike that of music written in more recent times; for the final chord of the first section sounds very much like a tonic, that of the second sounds like a dominant with its attendant lack of finality, and that of the final section sounds like a tonic. The implication of an ABA form, with tonal contrast furnished in the B section by emphasis on a secondary tonal center of G, complies with the pattern of the text.

The *Gloria* opens with a line of Gregorian chant sung by a solo voice to the words *"Gloria in excelsis Deo,"* followed by the chorus with the words *"Et in terra pax"* in homophonic texture. In length the text of the *Gloria* is second only to the *Credo,* so that it becomes a very substantial movement in musical settings of the Mass. In view of the attitude of the Council of Trent toward the treatment of the text of the Mass, it is interesting to note that the more complex sections of the text (*Gloria* and *Credo*) are given a predominantly homophonic treatment so that they may be clearly understood, while the short, simple texts (*Kyrie, Sanctus, Agnus Dei*) are in a more complex polyphonic texture with more repetition of words than in the longer texts. Rhythmic freedom, generated by a faithful but imaginative treatment of the words in terms of natural speech rhythm, is particularly apparent in both the *Gloria* and the *Credo.*

The *Credo* also opens with a line of Gregorian chant sung by a solo voice. Because of the several separate theological concepts expressed in the text, the *Credo* is quite sectional in form. The first section extends through the words *"Et homo factus est,"* the second, beginning with the word *"Crucifixus,"* is in four-part texture, while the third and final section, beginning with the words *"Et in Spiritum Sanctum,"* returns to six parts. In addition, several shorter segments are found as subdivisions of these larger sections. Of particular interest in the *Credo* is the abundance of subtle text painting and musical symbolism heard throughout on such phrases as *"descendit de coelis," "Crucifixus," "secundum Scripturas,"* and *"ascendit in coelum."*

The serenely beautiful *Sanctus,* with its concluding section, *"Hosanna in excelsis,"* encloses the *Benedictus* by means of the following sectional pattern: (1) basic text of the *Sanctus* concluding with (2) *"Hosanna in excelsis,"* (3) *Benedictus,* (4) exact repetition of *"Hosanna in excelsis."* The smooth, freely imitative texture heard at the opening establishes a mood of deep calm, with contrast achieved later with the words *"Pleni sunt coeli"* treated with repeated notes and wide leaps. The *Hosanna* section provides a short, jubilant high point to the movement and is sung twice with the meditative *Benedictus* (bass parts omitted) placed between the two statements.

The first *Agnus Dei* opens with an imitative section in which the melodic material and texture are very similar to the opening *Kyrie,* providing an element of thematic unity within the Mass as a whole. The polyphonic fabric continues without break in both *Agnus Dei's* with the individual voice parts clearly delineating the rhythm and mood of each line of text, and with contrast furnished by subtle changes in texture. The seven voice parts heard in the second *Agnus Dei* furnish the richest and strongest web of sound heard up to this point in the Mass, concluding the work on a note of confident affirmation.

Palestrina's music is most admirable as an example of great music inspired by profound religious faith, and perhaps it incarnates the ideal of pure vocal polyphony. As the finest representative of the sixteenth century Roman school of church music, it nevertheless represents only one of several musical currents moving in the Renaissance.

ELIZABETHAN MUSIC

The reign of Queen Elizabeth I (1558–1603), musically the richest era in England's history, was graced by a host of distinguished English composers including William Byrd, Thomas Morley, John Bull, Thomas Weelkes, John Wilbye, Orlando Gibbons, John Dowland, and many other composers of madrigals, church music, and instrumental pieces. It is impossible here to discuss all of the significant musical trends of this golden age of English music, and for this reason we will restrict our study to a few

of the more remarkable aspects of the time, of which one of the most striking is the Elizabethan madrigal.

The sixteenth century madrigal is a short, secular work for several solo
voices (typically five) with a poetic text that is generally rather light in
nature, though frequently it used the subject of unrequited love or pointed
a moral. It had reached a point of near perfection in Italy during the late
sixteenth century in the works of Willaert, Lassus, de Monte, Marenzio,
Verdelot, and others. Madrigals by many of these composers were circu-
lated in England and appeared in English translation in two publications in
the years 1588 and 1590, wielding a strong influence upon English
madrigalists, who followed the Italian models in their use of imaginative
text painting and musical symbolism, but were somewhat less inclined than
the Italians toward polyphonic and chromatic complexity.

Usually performed with a single voice to a part, they were published in
"part books," that is, a separate book for each of the four or five voice
parts, each book containing only the part for one singer. Present-day editions are published in full score. According to the writings of the time,
madrigals were often performed as entertainments by amateurs, which
suggests that the ability to sing a vocal part at sight was a fairly common
talent. Undoubtedly the more difficult polyphonic madrigals were beyond
the reach of most amateurs, but it is certain that musical activity was a
vital part of many Elizabethan households.

Elizabethan madrigals can be divided into two general categories, (1)
light homophonic pieces of the "fa-la" variety, often strophic in form,
sometimes called "ballets," and (2) madrigals with more serious secular
texts and textures tending to be more polyphonic. Those of the first type
were very popular, then as now, and were written in great abundance by,
among others, Thomas Morley (1557–1603), a composer known also for
his book on music theory and sight-singing entitled *A Plaine and Easie
Introduction to Practicall Musicke*. In most of these short pieces each verse
concludes with a fa-la refrain, two of the most typical pieces being "Now is
the Month of Maying" and "Sing we and Chant it," both by Morley. Easily
performed by amateur singers, they represent the lightest and freshest side
of Elizabethan music.

For an example of the second more sophisticated type of madrigal, let us
turn to a work by Orlando Gibbons (1583–1625), a composer who is also
well known for his fine Anglican church music and his instrumental works.
Figure 117 shows an excerpt from his five-part madrigal "The Silver
Swan." Typifying the more serious madrigal, the text points a moral and is

realized in a polyphonic texture. Its simple form can be diagrammed as ABB, the A extending through the word "throat," the first B starting with the word "Leaning," and the final section beginning with the word "Farewell." A poignant bit of text painting is found on the word "death" (top

Figure 117.

voice, Figure 117), the five parts forming at this point an augmented triad, a sonority that evokes a sinister mood, all the more because of its rarity in sixteenth century music.

Another form of secular vocal music gaining popularity at the very end of the sixteenth century was the air or "ayre," a simple song for solo voice with instrumental accompaniment. Songs of this type became so popular during the first quarter of the seventeenth century that they began to supersede the madrigal as a form of music for entertainment. Among many others, John Dowland (1563–1626) is noted as a composer of ayres. The typical example shown in Figure 118 is the first phrase of a Dowland song with lute [2] accompaniment entitled "My Thoughts Are Wing'd With Hope." Its clear-cut phrase structure typifies the style with most of the four-bar phrases ending with a feeling of repose, usually on the tonic or dominant.

Books of English lute songs or lute ayres were frequently published in two versions and placed on facing pages, the version on the left being a

---

[2] A stringed instrument popular during the sixteenth and seventeenth centuries with a pear-shaped body and eleven strings, plucked in the manner of the guitar.

Figure 118.

My thoughts are wing'd with hopes, my hopes with love,

polyphonic transcription of the lute version, realized in several voice parts so that it could be performed by a vocal or instrumental ensemble. Thus, four different versions were possible and it is likely that any of them might have been used according to the performance practices of the time: (1) the solo song with lute accompaniment, (2) a solo voice accompanied by instruments such as viols reading from the transcribed version, (3) voices without instruments reading from the transcribed version like a madrigal, and (4) instruments alone reading from the transcribed version.

The fourth of these methods of performance illustrates one of the ways in which instrumental ensemble music had developed during the Renaissance. As mentioned in Chapter Three, sixteenth century Italian pieces for groups of instruments were originally nothing more than polyphonic vocal pieces performed by instruments. The ricercar was originally a transcription of the motet, while the canzone was an instrumental version of the French polyphonic chanson—a secular form similar to the madrigal. To further illustrate this point, the Dowland song discussed above appears as an instrumental piece in his *Lachrimae, or Seaven Teares Figured in Seaven Passionate Pavans* for viols or violins, and also is found as a lute solo.

The Elizabethan counterpart of the ricercar was the fantasia, or "fancy," ensemble pieces for viols or recorders (or both) usually in six parts. These were written in great number by Dowland, Byrd, Morley, Bull, Gibbons, and many others. Keyboard music also flourished, the most popular keyboard instrument being a small harpsichord known as the virginal. The *Fitzwilliam Virginal Book,* a fine collection of keyboard music by various Elizabethan composers published around 1600, contains nearly three hundred pieces including dances, sets of variations, and pieces with descriptive titles.

William Byrd (1540–1623), mentioned several times earlier and probably the greatest composer of Elizabethan England, composed in all the forms and media of his time. He produced music for the Church of England, which was established in 1563, yet some of his finest works are those written for the Catholic church including three Masses and a number of motets. Byrd was a most prolific madrigal composer and composed secular music of other kinds as well. His madrigals were published in three sets (1588, 1589, and 1611) and uniformly demonstrate a prime characteristic of all of his vocal music, the ability to maintain melodic beauty in each individual voice line while skillfully weaving a complex web of polyphony. His rhythmic treatment is freely imaginative; and he often used dissonance expressively and with considerable daring. All of Byrd's madrigals bring great delight to listener and performer alike, but one which is of particular interest for its inspired unconventionality is No. 19 of the set of 1611, "Come Woeful Orpheus."

Many of the great composers of the Renaissance have necessarily been passed over in this chapter; for so vast are the musical treasures of this time that a comprehensive survey would be impossible here. The profoundly beautiful choral works for the church are no less impressive than the abundance of fine secular music and instrumental works. The tremendous diversity of this great cultural revival is just as apparent in the architecture, literature, painting, and sculpture of the time, vividly illustrating a renewed emphasis on the value of human endeavor.

As the sixteenth century drew to a close, instrumental music increased in importance, and more and more music was written with specified instrumentation. Typical sixteenth century practice had been to leave the choice of instruments to the discretion of the performers without detailed indications as to which instruments should be assigned to the various parts; and in choral works, separate accompaniments were seldom written. Certain composers, however, such as Giovanni Gabrieli and other composers centered at St. Mark's in Venice, began to include separate instrumental parts in vocal works, often with lengthy sections for instruments alone. Such works were designated with the term *concerto* or *concertato* and represent an important step in the development of the instrumental styles of the Baroque. At the same time, many aspects of renaissance practices continued well into the new century. Thus, the date 1600 as the end of the Renaissance in music is indeed arbitrary, for some of the seeds of baroque musical thought had been planted long before and were already beginning to flower.

Suggested Assignments

1. Listen to examples of sacred choral music by sixteenth century composers such as Lassus, Byrd, Willaert, and Giovanni Gabrieli, noting the differences in the general sound of their music as well as similarities.
2. As a special project examine the history of musical settings of the Mass.
3. Listen to examples of Gregorian chant, noting its general similarity to the melodic style of Palestrina. Discuss reasons for this being so.
4. Examine a copy of Morley's *Plaine and Easie Introduction to Practicall Musicke* and discuss its implications regarding music's place in Elizabethan England.
5. Attempt in class to perform a simple Elizabethan madrigal.
6. Using additional reference material, make a list of sixteenth century musical instruments and compare them to their modern counterparts, noting differences in timbre, construction, and performing technique.
7. Expand your knowledge of renaissance music by listening to the works of Josquin, Lassus, Gabrieli, Jannequin, and others.

SEVENTEEN

CORELLI AND VIVALDI

In our previous discussion of the beginnings of the baroque period (Chapter Six) it was mentioned that the early seventeenth century style of accompanied monody represented a striking change from the polyphonic practices of the Renaissance. The new vertical, homophonic concept of harmony made possible the development of figured bass and continuo practices which were essential to the evolution of the bel canto style in baroque opera and oratorio. The growth of idiomatic instrumental music also relied heavily upon this changed harmonic concept, and a vast amount of purely instrumental music was written in which continuo and stringed instruments played an indispensable role.

Although viols continued to be used during the Baroque, they gradually were supplanted by the instruments of the violin family, the first examples of which were built around 1600. The most important center of violin making during the seventeenth and eighteenth centuries was Cremona, Italy, where Niccolò Amati, Antonio Stradivari, Giuseppe Guarneri "del Gesù," and other fine craftsmen produced a tremendous quantity of fine violins, violas, and cellos. Many of these great instruments have survived two or three centuries of use and continue to be played and treasured by today's performers. It is no coincidence that some of the greatest contributions to violin literature and technique originated in Italy during the time of these renowned violin makers. For the presence of the finest violins went hand-in-hand with the development of chamber and orchestral music; and many of the most accomplished violinists of the time were also eminent composers.

ARCANGELO CORELLI (1653–1713)

In the latter half of the seventeenth century the most significant developments in chamber music occurred in Bologna where Maurizio Cazzati, G. B. and Tommaso Vitali, and other violinist-composers produced solo

249

violin sonatas (with continuo accompaniment) and trio sonatas in great abundance. The style of these Bolognese composers was fully assimilated by Arcangelo Corelli whose trio sonatas and violin sonatas represent the culmination of this aspect of baroque chamber music. As a performer he laid the foundations of modern violin technique and, through his students, passed on a concept of violin pedagogy that has influenced string players to the present day.

Most of his life was spent quietly in the city of Rome, although he lived for a time in Germany in addition to four years of study in Bologna. Of his forty-eight trio sonatas, half (twelve in Op. 1, twelve in Op. 3) are church sonatas (da chiesa)—most of them four-movement works with the tempos alternating in a slow-fast-slow-fast pattern; while the other half (twelve in Op. 2, twelve in Op. 4) are chamber sonatas (da camera)—lighter works in four to six movements utilizing dance rhythms. Although the two types are clearly distinguishable, they are often mixed, with dance movements being found in the church sonatas, and non-dance movements occurring as first movements in the chamber sonatas. Binary form is the most typical formal pattern for the movements of both types along with occasional sets of variations (chaconnes or passacaglias).

Of his twelve violin sonatas (Op. 5), six are chamber sonatas and six are church sonatas; and the set also includes the famous variations on the *Folia* theme, a typical eight-bar, triple-meter melody used by a number of seventeenth century composers as the basis for passacaglias and chaconnes.

All of these are beautifully polished and finely balanced works, exemplifying seventeenth century chamber music at its very best. Corelli's smooth, homogeneous style uses clear homophonic textures (the keyboard parts were originally written in figured bass without realization), moderate use of imitation which at times includes the bass line (played by a cello), and serenely contemplative slow movements. Because of the improvisatory practices of the baroque period, it is probable that these slow movements, particularly in the violin sonatas, did not sound quite so serene in baroque performances as they do today. It appears that these melodic lines were deliberately left in a state of unadorned simplicity in order to allow the violinist to demonstrate his ingenuity in improvisation. Yet present-day violinists seldom attempt to add to the music in this way, usually preferring to play the slow movements exactly as notated, without improvised embellishments.

Particularly noticeable in Corelli's music is the consistency of mood preserved throughout each movement. This is a trait of the baroque period in general, having to do with the "doctrine of affections." "Affection" is used here in an archaic sense to mean a passion or emotion, and was manifest in baroque choral works by the use of elaborate text painting and musical symbolism, particularly apparent in the accompanying instruments. The elements of rhythm, harmony, and melody were put to the task of expressing emotions and even specific concepts in highly stylized ways. The single "affection" was carefully preserved in its purest state throughout a movement so that the specific emotional and musical mood remained consistent. An example of this was seen in the second movement of the *Brandenburg Concerto No. 2* discussed in Chapter Six, where the sigh figure plays an important part in establishing and preserving the emotional climate. Bach developed a kind of musical symbolism as a means of expressing certain feelings; in choral works jubilation was characteristically created by the use of triplet rhythms, the power of death by an ostinato bass line; many similar examples appear throughout his works. The unflagging rhythms of fast movements in baroque music also illustrate this phenomenon, with a pulsating rhythmic figure continuing relentlessly throughout a movement to evoke its own particular musical mood.

Concerto Grosso Op. 6, No. 1

Corelli composed only for instruments and the only works not mentioned so far are his twelve concerti grossi of Op. 6, published in 1712 but perhaps composed as early as 1682. The first eight are in the form of the church concerto (concerto da chiesa) which does not necessarily mean that they are in the usual four-movement pattern of the sonata da chiesa but that they are serious in nature, intended for church performance. The last four are chamber concertos utilizing dance rhythms. The best known is No. 8, intended for performance on Christmas Eve and popularly known as the "Christmas Concerto." All of them use a concertino that consists of the trio sonata group (two violins, cello, and continuo) and a string orchestra consisting of the usual two violin sections, violas, cellos, and basses (the cellos and basses reading the same part).

The sectional pattern found in the first movement of Op. 6, No. 1 typifies Corelli's concerto grosso style, for he frequently utilized short adagio sections between extended fast passages. So often does this occur that the four-movement da chiesa pattern is frequently obscured.

The opening adagio section presents the complete tutti, the concertino playing the same parts as the ripieno. It cadences on the dominant, and in the fast section which follows, the solo instruments are heard by themselves briefly and then with the orchestra, followed by a very short adagio section. This pattern—an allegro followed by a brief adagio—is played twice more on different tonal levels with the solo instruments continuing in the same roles.

The extended largo which follows (still part of the first movement) clearly demonstrates the concertato style, as the solo instruments and tutti alternate throughout the section. The movement concludes with an extended fast section in which the concertino and ripieno play identical parts.

The slow second movement, rather short and in the key of the relative minor, demonstrates the following stylistic traits of Corelli: (1) the use of the two violin solo parts as a pair, the cello being relegated to a supportive role, (2) the use of poignant dissonances, particularly between the two solo violins, all of which resolve in the proper linear manner, and (3) preservation of a consistent mood and homogeneous texture throughout. In the final tutti the series of dissonances in a descending scale passage (chain suspensions in the first violin part) particularly characterizes Corelli's contrapuntal style.

The third movement is a vigorous four-voice fugue beginning with the solo instruments, but with the tutti definitely predominating. Listen for statements of the short fugal subject and for fugal devices such as augmentation and *stretto* (causing the voice entries in an entry group within a fugue to occur more frequently—at shorter time intervals—than they did in the initial exposition). The final statement appears in the bass part in the key of the dominant. Numerous fugal movements are found among the first eight concertos of Op. 6.

Almost all of the solo passages in the brilliant final movement emphasize the two solo violins with the solo cello functioning simply as a member of the orchestra, again demonstrating the relatively greater importance given to the two upper parts of the concertino. Typical of Corelli's style in non-fugal fast movements is the use of sturdy rhythmic figures of arpeggios and repeated notes in a predominantly homophonic texture. The preeminence of the first violin is apparent here, forecasting the development of the solo violin concerto.

Undoubtedly Corelli's greatest contribution to the art of music was the development of the concerto grosso style; for it led not only to the solo violin concerto of the eighteenth century, but also, in the nineteenth and twentieth centuries, to numerous distinguished works for various combinations of solo instruments and orchestra. Quite aside from its historical significance, his music stands as an ideal model for purity of style, economy of means, and nobility of expression.

ANTONIO VIVALDI (1678–1741)

Vivaldi, even more than J. S. Bach, is a composer who fell into obscurity shortly after his death; for his works were not brought to light and fully appreciated until nearly a century and a half later. Indeed, even then they might not have been unearthed had it not been for Bach's admiration of his music; for the initial interest in Vivaldi was generated by finding some of his music among Bach's possessions, and by Bach's transcriptions of some of Vivaldi's concertos. Vivaldi brought the concerto grosso to its height, developed the solo concerto, and established the three-movement form (fast-slow-fast) imitated by Bach and many subsequent composers.

He was born in Venice, received his musical training there, and became a priest in 1703. Nicknamed the "Red Priest" because of the color of his hair, he was employed by the Ospedale della Pietà in 1704, became its musical director in 1716, and remained in that post until 1740. The Ospedale was an orphanage for girls, one of several similar institutions in the city of Venice which had schools of various kinds attached to them. The conservatory of the Ospedale was famous for the musical accomplishments of its young ladies, and Vivaldi had ample opportunity for composing and supervising performances in all vocal and instrumental media. That most of his music involved orchestra attests to the excellence of the instrumentalists at the Ospedale; its orchestra was known throughout Europe.

Vivaldi traveled extensively, was a familiar name in European musical centers, and was one of the most prolific composers of his time. Although many of his compositions may be permanently lost, his surviving works include over four hundred concertos for various solo instruments and orchestra, about fifty concerti grossi, dozens of trio sonatas and solo sonatas, a sizable quantity of church music, and nearly fifty operas. With so vast an output one might expect to find numerous works of mediocre quality, or a repetitive sameness among his compositions. Actually, though his music has been criticized for these very things, its quality is surprisingly even and there is abundant variety of form, media, and content.

His style is not unlike that of Corelli, although the fast movements of the concertos seem to dominate the form and they are not broken up with short slow sections as in Corelli; nor did he incline toward fugal writing as much as Corelli. Parts for solo instruments, particularly the violin, are brilliant and virtuosic to an unprecedented degree, manifesting Vivaldi's abilities as a violinist and leading toward the development of the classical concerto style. In comparison to earlier concertos the solo passages were more extended and the number of rondolike alternations of the tutti (ritornello) and solo were increased. Typical of the mature three-movement concerto grosso style is the use of three heavy chords like hammer strokes at the beginning of the first movement, rapid scale passages, strong rhythms remaining consistent within each movement, and frequent unison passages.

The Seasons, Op. 8

Opus 8 is a set of twelve concertos entitled "The Trial of Harmony and Invention," and the first four of these are *The Seasons,* concertos for solo violin and orchestra based upon four sonnets presumably written by Vivaldi himself. Each of the concertos depicts its sonnet in a charmingly literal manner, typifying the baroque composer's delight in programmatic devices. All four are three-movement concertos in the fast-slow-fast pattern, with a solo violin part that approaches the scope and brilliance of the classical and romantic violin concertos. A translation of the four sonnets [1] is given below:

SPRING

Spring has come, and the birds greet it with happy songs, and at the same time the streams run softly murmuring to the breathing of the gentle breezes.

Then, the sky being cloaked in black, thunder and lightning come and have their say; after the storm has quieted, the little birds turn again to their harmonious song.

Here in a pleasant flowery meadow, the leaves sweetly rustling, the goatherd sleeps, his faithful dog at his side.

Nymphs and shepherds dance to the festive sound of the pastoral *musette* under the bright sky that they love.

SUMMER

In the season made harsh by the burning sun the men and the herds languish; even the evergreens are hot. The cuckoo unlocks his voice and soon the songs of the turtledove and the goldfinch are heard.

[1] Marc Pincherle, *Vivaldi,* Translated by Christopher Hatch (New York: W. W. Norton & Co., Inc., 1957), pp. 187–188.

Soft breezes breathe, but unexpectedly the north wind from its quarter seeks out a quarrel, and the shepherd weeps because he is overwhelmed by fear of the gusts and of his fate.

Fear of the flashing lightning and of the fierce thunder denies his tired body any rest while his furious troop is on the move.

How justifiable is his fear! The sky lights up, the awe-inspiring thunder brings down the fruit and the proud grain.

FALL

With songs and dances the peasants celebrate the happiness of a fine harvest, and after being greatly kindled by bacchic spirits, their rejoicing ends with sleep.

Thus everyone quits both his singing and his dancing. The air is pleasant and moderate, and the season invites everyone to the agreeableness of a sweet sleep.

At the break of day the hunter goes to the hunt with guns, dogs, and horns; he puts the wild beast to flight and tracks him down.

Tired and terrified by the loud noise of the guns and dogs, the beast, now in danger of being wounded, longs for escape, but is overcome and dies.

WINTER

To tremble frozen in the icy snow; to be buffeted by the wild wind; to stamp one's frozen feet; to have excessive cold set one's teeth to chattering;

To pass to a fireside of quiet and contentment, while outside the downpour bathes all; to walk carefully on ice, going slowly in fear of falling;

To slip and fall sharply to the ground, start out again on the ice, and run until the ice breaks apart;

To hear the south wind, the north wind, and all the other winds unloosed in battle: such is winter, these are joys it brings.

It is possible to find literal musical depictions of almost every line of the text, and it is great fun to listen to the four concertos from this point of view. Yet the sonnets do not dictate the form, for Vivaldi followed his usual formal pattern, even while cleverly handling the programmatic element. Such things as buzzing insects, bird calls, a flowing brook, slipping on the ice (and many others) are vividly and unmistakably illustrated by the music. The unabashed simplicity of this kind of musical depiction has a peculiar charm not found in the lofty and self-conscious programmatic expression of the nineteenth century.

Corelli has long been recognized as a master of the Italian baroque instrumental style, but it is only recently that this distinction has also been accorded to Vivaldi. Today he is recognized as a great innovator and a composer of distinction, a truly versatile musician worthy to stand among the giants of his art.

Suggested Assignments

1. Review Chapter Six.
2. Having studied several concertos of Bach, Handel, Corelli, and Vivaldi, would you describe the concerto grosso as a form, a style, or a medium? Discuss in class.
3. Listen to a sonata da chiesa and a sonata da camera of Corelli (trio sonatas or violin sonatas), comparing them to his concerto style in terms of division of sections and movements, use of continuo, and other stylistic traits.
4. Expand your knowledge of baroque music by listening to a choral work or opera of Vivaldi.

EIGHTEEN

HENRY PURCELL
(*1659–1695*)

Purcell, a native English composer, holds one of the most honored places in the history of the music of his country. A view of the status of musical art in several periods of England's history will show why this is so. The earliest English composer of international distinction was John Dunstable (d. 1453), a much-admired early renaissance vocal composer. He was, however, an isolated and unique figure, for there was no English musician to equal him until the time of Elizabeth I. Then the Elizabethan composers led English music to a position of international prestige, for such an aggregation of distinguished native musicians had never before been seen in England. Indeed, no period in English music history can match the Elizabethan era, and it is for this reason that it is called the "Golden Age of English Music."

During the eighteenth and nineteenth centuries much musical art was imported from the continent—by Handel's adoption of England as a homeland, and through extended visits from such figures as Haydn and Mendelssohn. It was not until the late nineteenth and early twentieth centuries that a few native English composers of stature began once again to appear on the scene, notably, Edward Elgar (1857–1934), Ralph Vaughan Williams (1872–1958), and Benjamin Britten (1913–   ).

Thus, to the English, Purcell represents the most significant native musical achievement from the seventeenth century to the twentieth. In addition to being the only distinguished composer of the English Baroque, he stands in direct line of succession to the great Elizabethan composers, carrying on the fine tradition of English choral music and also excelling as an instrumental composer.

Perhaps the most striking feature of Purcell's vocal style is its superb prosody, his ability to create unique and arresting rhythms while preserving

257

the natural inflections of the English language and beautifully expressing the text through the music. As Dr. Charles Burney stated in his *General History of Music* [1] (1789), "yet in the accent, passion, and expression of *English words,* the vocal music of Purcell is, sometimes to my feelings, as superior to Handel's as an original poem to a translation."—high praise indeed, during a time when Handel was considered by the English to be the greatest composer of all time. Elsewhere Burney describes Purcell as being, "as much the pride of an Englishman in Music, as Shakespeare in productions for the stage, Milton in epic poetry, Locke in metaphysics, or Sir Isaac Newton in Philosophy and mathematics."

Like the Elizabethan composers, Purcell was strongly influenced by musical trends on the Continent, particularly by Italian and French music. From this and his heritage of sixteenth and seventeenth century English music he developed a uniquely personal yet characteristically English style. He used free and original forms as well as such established patterns as the French overture and the da capo aria. Harmonically, his music is bold and frequently dissonant, often with massive contrapuntal effects that presage the dramatic choral style of Handel.

His church music includes three services for the Anglican church, a number of religious songs and hymns, and more than fifty anthems, most of which are of the type known as the "verse anthem." Verse anthems are choral works with instrumental accompaniments utilizing concertato effects between a small group of solo voices and the full chorus. Many of Purcell's verse anthems include a French overture and extended passages for the instruments alone. The verse sections of the anthems are sung by the small group of soloists and are often very demanding for the voices, with coloratura passages, wide skips, and dotted rhythms. The dramatic and expressive effect is heightened by the use of imaginative text painting and evocative harmonies. The chorus sections are in various styles, usually contrasting to the verse sections. One of the most famous of Purcell's verse anthems is one known as the "Bell Anthem" to the text "Rejoice in the Lord alway."

Purcell composed numerous incidental secular vocal works of varying quality among which are a number of lengthy works with arias and ensemble movements for chorus, soloists, and orchestra called "Odes." These were composed for special occasions for the nobility with texts filled with

---

[1] The first comprehensive history of music in English, it was originally in four volumes and is one of the earliest examples of a methodical approach to musicology.

extravagant and mannered flattery. The *Three Odes for Queen Mary's Birthday* are typical examples. Excerpts from his Odes as well as separate solo songs are collected in *Orpheus Britannicus,* published in 1698 by his widow.

Purcell's instrumental music includes keyboard music for harpsichord and organ and a quantity of works for various combinations of stringed instruments. Many of the latter are in the tradition of the Elizabethan fancy or fantasia, in three to seven parts without continuo, and constructed sectionally. Others are of the sonata da chiesa variety, manifesting the Italian influence with the standard trio sonata medium and continuo.

Some of his finest works are among his incidental music for masques and plays, the masques being amateur theatricals presented as entertainments by the nobility. Although the texts were set as arias, recitatives, choruses, and other typical operatic forms, their organization and the prevalence of spoken dialogue make it impossible to view them as full-fledged operas, the only real opera by Purcell being *Dido and Aeneas,* discussed below. The overtures, music for between the acts (entr'actes or act tunes), and dance music have been extracted from these theatrical presentations to form instrumental suites. Some of the best known of the plays set by Purcell are *Dioclesian* and *King Arthur* (texts by Dryden), *The Fairy Queen* (an adaptation of *A Midsummer Night's Dream*), and *The Tempest.*

Dido and Aeneas, an Opera

A kind of musical drama had begun in England during the Commonwealth period (1649–1660), not because of any great delight that the English had in opera, but because theatrical presentations were prohibited during this time (until the Restoration) and it was possible for an opera to masquerade as a concert, thus providing the English with something close to theater. Most such presentations were very thinly disguised dramas in which the music played only an incidental part, but in about 1682 John Blow composed the first true English opera (at least the first surviving one), entitled *Venus and Adonis.* Purcell's *Dido and Aeneas* was soon to follow, written some time before 1689.

It was written for a girl's school near London to a libretto by Nahum Tate, one of the less distinguished Poet Laureates of England. Based on Virgil's *Aeneid,* it is the love story of Dido, Queen of Carthage, and the Prince Aeneas. The score calls for a standard string orchestra with continuo, and the cast includes ten solo voices and four-part chorus, the chorus playing much the same part that it does in the later Handelian oratorio, commenting on the action and occasionally playing a part in the plot.

The opera consists of three short acts plus a prologue and utilizes a multiplicity of forms and styles including binary form, ABA, rondo, da capo, motet style, recitative, aria, canon, and a number of ground bass movements of which "Dido's Lament" (mentioned in Chapter Five) is the most famous example. The mood of tragedy is created immediately after the spoken prologue by a very short and concise French overture. The curtain rises to reveal Dido surrounded by her court and attended by Belinda, her lady-in-waiting, who addresses the Queen with the words, "Shake the cloud from off your brow," echoed by the chorus with the words, "banish sorrow." A text painting device is used on the very first word of Belinda's solo with the word "Shake" set to a rhythm that strongly suggests the meaning of the word and evokes the appropriate musical mood as well. Each time that "shake" occurs in the ensuing passages it receives a similar treatment. Purcell's vocal music is filled with depictive devices of this sort, some of them more subtle or profound than this one but all of them a great delight to the listener. The second movement, an aria sung by Dido, is based on a four-measure ground bass figure. Its text foreshadows the sorrow to come later and, with great dignity, establishes the character of the tragic Queen. The dialogue between Dido and Belinda in the recitative which follows typifies Purcell's remarkable gift for compressing the most intense emotions into a few bars, and shows his skill in dramatic character-ization. A choral set piece follows without break and in the next recitative we begin to see that the dotted rhythm (seen also on the word "shake" in Belinda's short aria) is a trademark of Purcell's style, in part resulting from the natural rhythms of the English language.

It has become apparent that Dido loves Aeneas and, as Act One con-tinues, Aeneas enters to declare his suit. Dido responds coldly, fearing the shadow of coming tragedy, but Aeneas prevails and Dido's acceptance of the Prince is celebrated in a joyous chorus and dance. The scene suddenly shifts to the cave of a sorceress who conjures up a chorus of witches and exhorts them to assist in the downfall of Dido. A demoniac chorus, a duet in canon between two witches, an echo chorus ("In our deep vaulted cell"), and a dance of furies conclude Act One on a most ominous note.

Act Two opens with a short instrumental prelude as Dido, Aeneas, Belinda, and their train are found pausing in a grove during the hunt. Belinda, in a short aria with chorus, sings of the wild spot in which they find themselves, suggesting that Diana, Goddess of the hunt, might frequent the place. One of the attending women then sings an aria (No. 24) based on a bustling four-measure ground in which she asserts that Diana does indeed come to the spot, and that here also the hunter Actaeon met his fate, torn to shreds by his own hounds. Trophies of the hunt are then brought out, when suddenly the party is interrupted by threatening sounds of thunder. Belinda and the chorus sing "Haste, haste to town," and the idyllic scene is ended. But as they depart Aeneas is detained by the mysterious appearance of the spirit of Mercury, in reality an underling of the Sorceress in disguise. The evil plot to drive Aeneas from the shores of Carthage unfolds as the spirit tells him that Jove has commanded him to return to Troy. With deep sorrow, Aeneas reluctantly agrees to leave his beloved Dido and weigh anchor that very night. The poignant beauty of this concluding scene of Act Two shows Purcell at his height in effectively combining the dramatic situation with a deeply moving musical expression.

Act Three presents the harbor of Carthage with the Trojan fleet in the background and an opening scene with the sailors and chorus in a farewell song and dance. Lines such as "Take a bowsey short leave of your nymphs on the shore, and silence their mourning with vows of returning, tho' never intending to visit them more," establish a mood of flippant farewell that in no way aids Aeneas when he later attempts to explain to Dido the reason for his sudden departure. The Sorceress and witches enter gloating over the success of their plot and break into peals of highly organized demoniac laughter followed by a furious dance (Nos. 30–32).

The final scene begins with the entrance of Dido bemoaning her fate and Belinda attempting to comfort her. Aeneas enters and there follows a dialogue in recitative between the two lovers in which Aeneas says that he will stay in spite of Jove's commands. Dido will have none of this, saying, "For 'tis enough, whate'er you now decree, that you had once a thought of leaving me." He insists on staying, though he knows he cannot, and the ensemble number ends on an impassioned note as Aeneas sings "I'll stay and love obey!" while Dido sings "To death I'll fly if longer you delay; away, away!" Aeneas exits and in the short recitative that follows Dido says that "Death must come when he is gone." At this point the function of the chorus is not unlike that of the chorus in Greek drama as it comments with the words, "Great minds against themselves conspire, and shun the cure they most desire." (No. 35)

As Aeneas and the Trojan fleet depart, Dido sings a short recitative in which she welcomes death and then begins her final aria "When I am laid in earth." This is the famous "Lament" discussed in Chapter Five (see Figure 34, p. 83) built on a chromatic, five-measure ground bass. The incredible beauty of this aria transcends the fact that it is a set of harmonic variations on a ground; and, indeed, it is pointless to dwell on such technical matters when captured by the spell of this music. Purcell's musical and dramatic genius is further demonstrated by the manner in which he concludes the opera. The deeply emotional mood established in the "Lament" is preserved by linking Dido's aria to the final chorus without a pause between; and the rhythm, tempo, harmony, and general mood of this chorus are exactly right to furnish a convincing conclusion to the opera without detracting from the wondrous feeling of tragedy.

Purcell was endowed with a superb dramatic sense and an ability to handle both the meaning and the cadence of the words in a manner that is deeply imaginative as well as musically expressive. These qualities are seen in all of his vocal works, both choral and solo; and it is music's loss that he lived to compose only one true opera. Many vocal composers acknowledge their debt to him and one can only speculate as to what other operatic masterworks he might have produced had conditions been different, or if he had lived a longer life.

SUGGESTED ASSIGNMENTS

1. Using supplementary reference material, trace the history of English music from John Dunstable to Benjamin Britten, noting persistent trends such as favored media, forms, and styles.
2. Compare *Dido and Aeneas* to Handel's *Judas Maccabaeus,* noting ways in which Purcell's vocal style influenced that of Handel.
3. Examine Burney's *General History of Music,* looking up references to Purcell.
4. Expand your knowledge of Purcell's music by listening to several of the works mentioned in this chapter.
5. Make a list of specific examples of the influence of Italian and French music upon Purcell's style.

PART FIVE

MUSIC OF THE
TWENTIETH CENTURY

NINETEEN

IMPRESSIONISM

Impressionism in music draws its name from the movement in painting led by Monet, Renoir, Degas, Manet, and other French painters active during the two final decades of the nineteenth century. The most striking characteristic of the impressionist painters is their use of light and color in revolutionary new ways. Finding new techniques to replace academic formulas, they strove to capture the lights and shadows of the world around them through their subjective impressions of the sky, clouds, water, landscapes, people in casual attitudes, and still lifes of everyday objects. The hazy outlines and shimmering textures of some of their paintings seem to be closely related to the French music of the time, for painters and composers were motivated by the same desire to free themselves from the traditions of the romantic century, from practices and philosophies that were, to them, no longer valid.

Even more significant than painting as an artistic counterpart of impressionistic music is the symbolist movement in poetry. Poets such as Verlaine, Mallarmé, and Rimbaud attempted to endow words with music's ability to deal with general truths rather than actualities, to suggest rather than state specifically—in short, to express the unutterable. Emotions impossible to represent concretely were conveyed by using words as symbols, and the rhythms and sounds of spoken language were used for their evocative qualities, quite separate from literal meanings. Mallarmé's conception of Symbolism was "to evoke in a deliberate shadow an unmentioned object through allusion," and he believed that "to name the object is to sacrifice three-fourths of the pleasure in it." Swayed by Wagner's writings on the fusion of music and poetry, Mallarmé and his contemporaries were guided by their belief in the kinship of the two arts. The communicative abilities of subtle allusion and understatement demonstrated in their poetry wielded a significant influence upon French music of the time.

265

Musical impressionism began in Paris as a reaction against the domination of late nineteenth century German music, yet in many ways it was an extension of romanticism. In fact, Debussy admired Wagner's music, though this admiration was tempered by a hearty dislike of his romantic excesses. The large romantic orchestra of Strauss and Wagner is similar in size, complexity, and instrumentation to that of the impressionists, and the romantic trend toward the programmatic is also found as a vital feature of impressionism. There are many characteristic harmonies common to both, and the blurring of phrase structure is as prevalent in Wagner's music as in Debussy's. The similarities are there, yet the impressionistic musical language differs sharply from that of the German romantic tradition.

The French may say that these differences derive largely from the dissimilarity between the French and German temperaments—French understatement against ponderous German rhetoric, matter-of-fact realism versus lofty German idealism, subtle French sensibility against German emotionalism, and French nonchalance against German system and methodology. Slanted though they may be, these comparisons do pertain to certain specific musical traits of impressionism, some of them easier to identify in actual sound than to discuss in technical terms. Thematic organization and development, so important to the German romanticists, are handled quite casually in most impressionistic works, and it is often impossible to fit the works of Debussy and Ravel into conventional preconceived formal patterns. Most impressionistic music is, in a sense, programmatic, but devices such as the leitmotif or idée fixe are seldom found and the extramusical element is usually no more than an allusion to a descriptive title, not a musical narration as in most romantic program music. Melodies are often short and improvisatory in character, modal in flavor, or based upon artificial scales. The prevalence of free and obscure rhythms produces effects of nonchalance or vague mystery and linked with this is the deliberate blurring of phrase outlines, traits that are clearly related to impressionistic painting and symbolist poetry. On the other hand, there are occasional examples of clear pulsating rhythms that are almost primitive in their regularity.

The unique orchestration of impressionistic music is significant in defining the style. The orchestra is a large one, abounding in percussion instruments, but seldom does it produce an extremely loud sound. Rather, its vast instrumental resources are heard in various subtle combinations producing magical effects of color and texture—the solo flute in its low register against the muted strings, the English horn and other low woodwinds in unique blends, the brass playing pianissimo, often with mutes, two harps coloring the sound of a large many-voiced (divisi) string section, exotic percussion sounds, and many more shifting colors that evoke enchanted images of distant and unreal places.

The harmonic element in impressionism is perhaps its most important single factor. Actually, nearly all of the sonorities used by the impressionists are common in earlier nineteenth century music, but it is the manner in which the sonorities are used that creates the impressionistic harmonic style, not the presence of new or unusual sonorities. Most impressionistic music is quite tonal. One has the feeling of beginning and ending in a key but no longer is this key feeling achieved primarily by means of the fifth relation. The dominant-tonic concept, which slowly lost ground during the nineteenth century, begins to be superceded by (1) parallel motion or "planing" of chords, with all of the voices moving equal distances in the same direction (Figure 119), (2) passages based in part

Figure 119.

Debussy, *Sarabande*

upon the whole tone scale, (3) "modal" progressions which contain major and minor triads but which avoid the progression of dominant to tonic (Figure 120), and (4) passages or chords separated by intervals such as the third and tritone [1] rather than perfect fourths and fifths.

Figure 120.

Debussy, *Passepied*

[1] Common synonym for the augmented fourth, a dissonant interval a half step larger than the perfect fourth and a half step smaller than the perfect fifth.

The triad continued to be the basic sonority but notes added to triads often occur to furnish an element of dissonance. Frequently such dissonances do not resolve in the traditional manner but are simply placed in the sonority for additional color. Also, the projection of thirds (upon which triads are based) frequently extends beyond the simple triad or seventh chord to form five, six, or seven-tone sonorities called ninth, eleventh, or thirteenth chords (Figure 121).

The luminous and transparent textures created by wide spacing between voices and abundant use of arpeggio figures add much to the effect of all of these harmonic devices in piano music as well as the orchestral works.

Figure 121.

Ravel, *Valses nobles et sentimentales*

Fusion of harmonies, seen earlier in Chopin's piano works, is also found, one splashy arpeggio shifting to another to achieve a momentary blend of two sonorities. Such effects led to the polychordal practices of certain twentieth century composers who built lengthy passages by superimposing one series of chords upon another. In this and many other ways the impressionists paved the way for the harmonic developments of today.

A few composers outside of France were moving in these directions around the turn of the century. Among these is the Italian composer Ottorino Respighi whose two descriptive orchestral works *The Pines of Rome* and *The Fountains of Rome* show many impressionistic traits, particularly in orchestration. In America Charles Martin Loeffler and Charles Griffes were composing in styles similar to that of Debussy, and the music of the English composer Frederick Delius also shows characteristics of impressionism. The movement, however, is primarily French and centers in the works of Debussy and Ravel.

CLAUDE DEBUSSY (1862–1918)

Debussy may be considered the father of musical impressionism, yet his style is the result of many varied influences, including that of the French poets and painters of his time. He was also interested in Far Eastern art, particularly in Javanese music, somewhat paralleling Gauguin's and other French painters' fascination with the primitive and exotic subjects of the South Seas. Many harmonic traits of Debussy's music are anticipated in the works of nineteenth century Russian composers such as Moussorgsky. Debussy had visited Russia in 1882 and it is likely that his knowledge of Russian music was a formative influence upon his harmonic style.

Some similarity to Chopin is seen in his piano textures, and the influence of Wagner is also apparent—not in esthetic ideals but in such technical matters as orchestration, the frequent use of certain sonorities, and the blurring of phrase outlines in favor of a more or less continuous texture. Indeed, the young Debussy admired Wagner's music, though a visit to Bayreuth in 1889 turned him into an outspoken anti-Wagnerian, and he soon espoused the cause supported by such French composers as Gabriel Fauré (1845–1924) and Erik Satie (1866–1925) that French music should be truly French, not derivative of other national styles. By "truly French" these men were speaking of a tradition nourished by the Gallic temperament and begun in renaissance music by composers such as Jannequin, continued in later times by Couperin, Rameau, and Lully, and preserved in the romantic era by Charles Gounod. Though separated by centuries, the works of these composers possess certain common traits that produce a typically French kind of effervescent classicism, a purity of style in which beauty of sound and intrinsic musicality are more important than impassioned emotional expression. That Debussy was, by temperament and inclination, led in the same direction is affirmed by the proud title with which he signed many of his last works: Claude Debussy, *Musicien français.*

He was born in the small town of St. Germain-en-Laye near Paris and entered the famous Paris Conservatory at the age of eleven. His teachers and fellow students soon learned that he was not to be bound by rules and conventions. He progressed rapidly as a composer and pianist and at the age of twenty-two he won the Prix de Rome, highest honor of the Conservatory, with his cantata *L'Enfant prodigue* (The Prodigal Son). The prize, offered annually in France and other countries, including the United States, consists of a period of residence in Rome along with the financial support necessary to afford time for composition. The most important work composed during his sojourn in Rome is *La Damoiselle élue* (The Blessed Damozel), a secular cantata based on the poem by Dante Gabriel Rossetti.

Upon his return to Paris his career was established with the first of his mature orchestral works, a long rhapsodic movement entitled *L'Après-midi d'un faune* (1894) based on an idyllic poem of Mallarmé. His other major orchestral works are *Nocturnes* (1899), *La Mer* (1905), and *Images* (1912), each in three movements, and each a staple of today's orchestral repertoire. It is pointless to attempt to describe the fantastic orchestral colors and subtle half shades achieved in these works. Percussion is used freely and imaginatively and many instruments, particularly the woodwinds, are heard in unusual registers. For the most part, these works are endowed with their own unique kind of musical logic. They are not musical narratives like the romantic tone poems, and only rarely did the composer resort to traditional forms.

The use of traditional preconceived formal patterns is a bit more prevalent in his chamber music, which includes the *String Quartet* (1893), *Sonata for Cello and Piano* (1915), *Sonata for Flute, Harp, and Viola* (1915), and *Sonata for Violin and Piano* (1917). Descriptive titles are not used in these works, yet they can hardly be appreciated in the same way as a Haydn or Beethoven chamber work. The epithet "absolute music" does not apply to them. In fact, one is tempted to call them programmatic works, for magical flickering images are conjured, and at various times one senses the presence of subtle satire or ironic pathos; all achieved with great economy of means by unique treatment of the instruments, fluctuating tempos, and an endless array of brief melodic ideas related and linked to each other with a minimum of formal thematic development. These pieces, particularly the sonatas, are among his greatest works.

Debussy's piano works include several suites, two volumes of *Preludes,* the *Etudes,* and a number of miscellaneous works. Their filigreed textures, abundant use of pedal, fusion of sonorities, and wide spacing demand a formidable piano technique capable of suggesting the variety of subtle colors heard in the composer's orchestral works. Well suited to the instrument, they form an essential part of the modern piano repertoire.

Debussy wrote over fifty art songs to texts of Baudelaire, Mallarmé, Verlaine, and others. The intimate quality of the poetry and the exquisite inflections of the language resulted in a style far different from that of German lieder. His songs live in a rarefied, perfumed atmosphere that lacks the earthy immediacy of, for example, the songs of Schumann. Instead, a lyrical French elegance fills the air contrasted at times with moments of pagan abandon or voluptuousness. The short cycle *Chansons de Bilitis,* to the decadent poetry of Pierre Louÿs, is perhaps his most popular work in this medium.

His lyric drama *Pelléas and Mélisande* is based on a play by the Belgian Symbolist Maurice Maeterlinck, and there is no other opera quite like it. Everything is seen as if in a dream and all things are understated, if mentioned at all. The characters take on a mystical, symbolic significance, and never does an operatic set piece intrude to break the spell. Rather, the voices sing in a free declamatory style, for the most part at a low dynamic level, within a continuous texture. The instruments are used sparingly yet the orchestra achieves tremendous suggestive power. The recurrence of a few motives in varying forms produces a loose structural unity in a form as free and intangible as the drama itself.

La Mer (The Sea), *"Three Symphonic Sketches"*

This, the largest in dimension of Debussy's orchestral works, marks an important stage in the development of the composer's concept of form. Earlier works such as *L'Après-midi d'un faune* or the *Nocturnes* were, for the most part, deliberately vague and amorphous in structure. Sharp formal outlines were avoided in much the same manner as in symbolist poetry or the pointillistic paintings of Seurat. These earlier works demonstrate the typical qualities of musical impressionism, but with *La Mer* Debussy showed an interest in an original but nevertheless classical approach to form, a concept of design that culminated in the three sonatas of his last years.

The first movement, "From Dawn til Noon at Sea," is based on three thematic ideas presented in a manner that suggests the arrangement of ideas in a classical sonata form. The sequence of keys of the three ideas is D flat major, B flat major, and D flat major, the first and most important theme being presented shortly after the opening by the English horn and trumpet in unison. Even without the descriptive title, the gradually increasing animation of rhythm and growing intensity of orchestration conjures images of the coming of dawn and the progress of day upon the watery wastes of a vast ocean.

The second movement, "Play of the Waves," is lighter in mood and in the form of a free rondo. The rondo theme, heard at the outset, appears in varying forms throughout but is overshadowed by the action and thematic development of the episodes. The frequent use of the solo violin typifies Debussy's delight in the pure color of a single instrument against a background of blended timbres.

The form of the final movement, "Dialogue of the Wind and the Sea," cannot be clearly related to a preexisting formal pattern but, unlike his earlier works, makes use of considerable thematic development. To round out the form, two themes from the first movement are presented. This is the most complex of the three movements and the one most difficult to discuss because of its fantasylike freedom of form. It does much more than furnish a musical realization of a descriptive title. It also speaks in a purely musical language of things impossible to translate into words, and with a meaning that must vary according to the imagination of each listener.

Debussy's music can be heard on several levels and it is quite easy to go no further than the attractive esthetic surface of the music. In fact, the rich and often soothing colors of Debussy's orchestration may lull the listener into a condition so passive as to discourage a deeper understanding and appreciation of his music. Certainly Debussy's music is eminently enjoyable in a way that manifests the Gallic temperament and the composer's instinctive approach to composition. His music tries to please, but beyond this, there is a working out of ideas that is even more rewarding, and it is this level that the listener must penetrate in order to fully reap the fruits of this composer's art. A great challenge to the listener is found in the variety and the originality of the structural plans in Debussy's music; and in appreciating his music at this level, the listener is prepared for an understanding of the less accessible aspects of later twentieth century music. In the words of Debussy, "rules are established *by* works of art, not *for* works of art."

MAURICE RAVEL (1875–1937)

Ravel's music added elements of clarity and order to the impressionistic movement. Indeed, the inclination toward classical structure, seen in only a few of Debussy's works, became a hallmark of Ravel's style. The two composers had much in common. Both were repelled by the impassioned excesses of late German romanticism, and both were influenced by the Parisian environment of impressionistic painters and symbolist poets. Exotic elements such as Spanish rhythms held great attractions for both composers, and both used descriptive titles, though neither could be called a programmatic composer in the late romantic sense. Above all, both were

Gallic in temperament and sensibility—French musicians who believed that the primary purpose of art was to delight the senses.

In spite of their similarities, both men established unique and highly personal styles, and by no means did Ravel work in Debussy's shadow. Ravel, though brilliantly imaginative, was not as intuitive a composer as Debussy. His compositions show precise workmanship and a conscious mastery of his craft. Phrase structure, harmonic motion, counterpoint, dissonance, orchestration—all are handled with the utmost lucidity, manifesting the classical spirit to such a degree that he is viewed as one of the foremost figures in the early twentieth century movement known as neoclassicism.

Ravel differed from Debussy in that he preferred functional diatonic harmonies to vague nebulous sonorities used for their color, such as those based upon the whole-tone scale. In general Ravel's harmonies are less chromatic than Debussy's, for many of his scores contain extended passages with no accidentals beyond those in the key signature. Ninth, eleventh, and thirteenth chords are found in Ravel's music, but these are typically in a context of horizontal linear motion, the result of contrapuntal activity among several clear voice lines rather than occurring as diffuse masses of rich sound as they do in Debussy's music.

Similar comparisons can be made regarding the orchestration of these two impressionists. Ravel was more consciously aware of what would work in the orchestra and, though he used many of the same orchestral devices as Debussy, Ravel's scores are easier to prepare in rehearsal and are more immediately rewarding to the performers. At times, Ravel's scores are more complex than Debussy's, but his timbres are more clearly etched; and his knowledge of the idiomatic capabilities of the instruments, singly or in combination, rivals that of Rimsky-Korsakov. Some of his orchestral works originated as piano pieces, chief among these being *Alborado del Grazioso* and *Le Tombeau de Couperin,* in addition to his orchestral version of Moussorgsky's *Pictures at an Exhibition* discussed in Chapter One.

Ravel was a significant composer of piano music, and many of his piano works were just as important as Debussy's in expanding the horizons of piano techniques. These include *Jeux d'eau* (Fountains), the *Sonatina,* and several collections of piano pieces such as *Gaspard de la nuit* and *Valses nobles et sentimentales.* He also composed much vocal music, including a song cycle for voice and orchestra entitled *Scheherezade,* two operas (*L'Heure espagnol* and *L'Enfant et les sortilèges*), and a quantity of songs for voice and piano. His classical orientation is most apparent in his chamber music, which includes a string quartet, a piano trio, and two sonatas, one for violin and cello and one for violin and piano. He also wrote several chamber works combining a solo voice with a small group of instruments. His major orchestral works are *Rhapsodie espagnol,* two orchestral suites from the ballet *Daphnis and Chloé, La Valse,* two piano concertos (one of which has a solo piano part for left hand only), and the famous *Bolero.*

La Valse, "A Choreographic Poem"

This work, along with many of Ravel's best-known scores, was intended for the ballet. Ravel had begun work on it as early as 1906 but its premier performance did not take place until 1920 in a concert presentation in Paris. *La Valse* was commissioned by the famous ballet impresario Serge de Diaghilev, although he did not subsequently stage the work.

Ravel described it as "a sort of apotheosis of the Viennese waltz linked with an impression of a fantastic whirl of destiny." A note appearing at the front of the score describes a vague program that is essentially a fluctuating tableau rather than a narrative: "At first the scene is dimmed by a kind of swirling mist through which one discerns, vaguely and intermittently, the waltzing couples. Little by little the vapors begin to disperse, and the illumination grows brighter, revealing an immense ballroom filled with dancers. The blaze of the chandeliers comes to full splendor. An imperial ball about 1855."

La Valse begins with a low vibration in the depths of the orchestra (double basses) along with percussion sounds suggesting the 3/4 rhythm. Then, in a characteristic Viennese waltz figure, the bassoons are heard with the first thematic material, beginning slowly to evoke the spirit of the popular Viennese composer, Johann Strauss. From here on the music unfurls in a long chain of waltzes gradually building and reflecting the moods of genteel nineteenth century Vienna. During this lengthy crescendo the vague, misty quality gradually disappears. Then it seems that the ballroom is clearly revealed; and the strings and harp emerge with all of the verve, nobility, and sensuous charm of a full-blown Viennese waltz, no longer obscured by mysterious clouds. The solo oboe figures prominently in the section which follows and, as the tempo increases, the brass and percussion lend support to furious waltz rhythms. The extreme contrast in mood in this first section is achieved partly by fluctuating rhythms and partly by the great variety of instrumental colors.

The work can be divided conveniently into two parts, the second section beginning in the same way as the first, with the bassoons playing the same fragmentary waltzlike figure. This section is much more developmental than the first but follows the same pattern of a gradual crescendo to a climactic ending. Fragments of melodies heard earlier are tossed and mixed and crashed together in a finely wrought but almost brutal working out of the thematic material. So intense and rhythmically complex is this second section that the listener is whirled into a feverish dizziness, a frightening but compelling mood that seems to be the antithesis of the first section. The work ends with a percussion flourish on a note of near tragedy.

Ravel's consummate mastery of the craft of musical composition placed him in the forefront of twentieth century composers. In addition to sparking the neoclassical movement, which will be discussed later, he established an ideal in his handling of instrumental timbres that has inspired many younger composers. Debussy and Ravel together represent one of the most important periods in French music. Their music effected a transition from the nineteenth century to the twentieth and they have significantly affected the course of music in our time. But more important than their historical position is the fact that they left a heritage of music in all media that will continue to delight generation after generation of listeners.

SUGGESTED ASSIGNMENTS

1. Examine reproductions of paintings by Monet, Manet, Pissarro, Renoir, Sisley, Degas, and other impressionist painters, attempting to draw parallels between musical impressionism and impressionistic painting.
2. Read the poetry of Mallarmé or Verlaine in translation or, if possible, in the original French. Note the imprecise nature of the language but try to see how it attempts to evoke images in much the same way that music does —through rhythms and sonorities.
3. Summarize the general stylistic traits of musical impressionism.
4. Listen to representative works of Rameau, Couperin, Lully, Gounod, Fauré, and Satie. Attempt to describe the distinctly French characteristics that these works have in common. Find examples of these traits in the music of Debussy and Ravel.
5. Expand your knowledge of the music of Debussy and Ravel by listening to examples from their works in media other than orchestra.
6. Expand your knowledge of the contemporaries of Debussy and Ravel outside of France by listening to some of the works of Respighi, Delius, Griffes, or Scriabin.

TWENTY

IGOR STRAVINSKY
(*1882–*   )

Stravinsky's musical output, spanning more than sixty years, represents most of the important trends of muscial composition in this century. Undoubtedly the most renowned, perhaps the greatest living composer, he has always been several jumps ahead of current musical thought. On the occasions when he has adopted the musical practices of his contemporaries (such as his use of serial techniques since 1952, or his use of jazz elements in the post-World War I period) he has turned things to his distinct advantage, endowing the preexisting technique with renewed meaning, and branding it with his own unique and powerful expression.

He was born in Russia near the city that is now called Leningrad (then St. Petersburg) and was raised in a decidedly musical environment that afforded ample opportunity to become acquainted with Russian orchestral and operatic literature. His father was the leading bass at the Imperial Opera and the young Stravinsky was encouraged in the study of music, though not toward a musical career. His parents preferred that he study law and he was enrolled in the University of St. Petersburg law school. Shortly after leaving the university he became acquainted with Rimsky-Korsakov and subsequently studied with him for a period of three years (1903–1906). This was Stravinsky's only period of formal study with a composer and in his autobiography he describes Rimsky-Korsakov as a "great teacher." The influence of Rimsky-Korsakov is seen in the works of the pre-World War I period in the use of native Russian materials and, above all, by the colorful orchestration.

During the period from 1909 to 1913 Stravinsky composed the three ballets that mark the beginning of his remarkable career and which, even today, are counted among his most popular orchestral scores. They are *The Firebird* (1909–1910), *Petrouchka* (1910–1911), and *The Rite of Spring*

276

(1911–1913), all written for Diaghilev and all three produced by him in Paris. All but the third achieved a successful premier performance. *The Rite of Spring,* however, at its first performance touched off an audience reaction that is unparalleled in the history of music. To many members of that Parisian audience the work seemed to have severed all ties with previous forms of musical expression and, in scandalized puzzlement, they expressed their confusion in the form of a riot. The shouting, slapping, hooting, and stamping of that eventful spring evening in 1913 vividly reflected a tremendous explosion taking place in the world of art.

In the visual arts it was the time of fauvism, cubism, and expressionism. Artists such as Matisse and Picasso seemed, like Stravinsky, to be breaking ties with previous styles and techniques. In literature and poetry such figures as James Joyce, T. S. Eliot, Jean Cocteau, Kafka, and Gertrude Stein were gaining eminence. It is interesting to note that many early twentieth century works by figures such as these, though they may be much in vogue, even today are not fully understood. So much of the art of that time seems so different from what had gone before that it is not difficult to make the mistake of assuming that it had no precursors. Actually, all of the persons mentioned above have strong links with their respective traditions, for seldom, if ever, can a valid work of art be produced without relying in part upon an existing style or mode of expression. Much of the art of the early twentieth century strove to break ties with the nineteenth century, to deal the death blow to romanticism. Because romanticism is the strongest tradition inherited by this century, it appeared to some that in denying this tradition the creative artist was denying all tradition.

In the case of Stravinsky, though traditional elements may be found in all of his music, they are seen most vividly in certain works that were frankly based upon earlier styles or upon the actual music of earlier composers. The ballet *Pulcinella* (based on the music of Pergolesi), the *Symphony in C* (based on the classical symphonic style), *The Rake's Progress* (based on Mozart's opera buffa style), and the ballet *Le Baiser de la fée* (after Tchaikovsky) are all cases in point. Such frank appropriations are by no means unique in the history of music. J. S. Bach was happy to utilize the music of Vivaldi for his purposes; Mozart and Haydn carried on a most congenial exchange of ideas; and Handel was willing to use anything he could lay his hands on. In cases such as these the end result was often more distinguished than the model, but this convention has also been the source of vast quantities of undistinguished and facile works by lesser composers who used the models as crutches to support their own feeble inventions.

In listening to those works of Stravinsky that are clearly based upon pre-existing models, one becomes aware of an important general trait of his music: his preoccupation with the contrast of the idioms of earlier periods with those of his own music. This is perhaps best seen in the ballet *Pulcinella* which has also been arranged by the composer as an orchestral suite. Much of the music is quoted exactly from various works by Pergolesi but here and there the material is adroitly and often comically reworked in such a way as to express something totally new. Stravinsky, like Haydn (see the discussion of Haydn's *Symphony No. 104,* Chapter 8), capitalizes upon the expectations of his audience so that within the framework of the charming but predictable style of Pergolesi, Stravinsky's personal interjections come as sharp flashes of bright light, surprising and captivating in their effect.

The effects and purposes of musical surprise merit some discussion at this point. Certainly it is true that Haydn intended the unfulfilled upbeats in the minuet of his *Symphony No. 104* to come as surprises; Berlioz' flamboyant orchestral colors were at times intended to shock; and the harmonic progressions in much of Wagner's music are intentionally suspensive and unpredictable. But the listener may ask, "Can such devices continue to have the intended effect of surprise or suspense after repeated hearings? Can audiences, in spite of knowing what is about to happen, somehow experience the sensation of hearing something new?" The logical answer might appear to be no. But just as in seeing *Hamlet* for the third or fourth time we are caught up in the drama and wait breathlessly for the next turn of events, so in listening to a familiar piece of music we become so intent upon what is happening *now* that seemingly we forget that we know what is about to happen, and certain occurrences in the music may affect us almost as they did on the first hearing. More sophisticated listeners may even be able to place themselves in historical perspective so that, for example, the first chord of Beethoven's First Symphony can sound unconventional in terms of the time when it was written, even though there are later symphonies that open in more strikingly unconventional ways.

The effect of surprise under such circumstances is perhaps not so marked as on the first hearing, but it is there nevertheless and contributes significantly to the esthetic effect. Surprise, after all, is not very important in itself. It may, however, be extremely significant for its effect of contrast in the overall pattern of a composition; and, under these conditions, devices of surprise can be most eloquent, even after repeated hearings.

During the World War I period, Stravinsky, living with his wife and children in Switzerland, turned from composing works for large orchestra toward more easily and economically performed works for smaller groups. The austerity necessitated by wartime may have partly accounted for the new style that he developed during this time, and out of it came an important twentieth century movement known as neoclassicism. Neoclassicism, in itself, cannot be called a style for it has taken many forms among various of Stravinsky's works as well as among the many composers who have subscribed to its philosophies. In general terms it rejects descriptive music, the large romantic orchestra, and over-emotionalism in favor of formal clarity, polished contrapuntal textures, precise but often unsymmetrical rhythms, and harmonies characterized by clean biting dissonances rather than lush sonorities. Bach, Handel, Haydn, and Mozart were the models for neoclassical composers such as Honegger, Milhaud, and Poulenc (the three most significant members of the "French Six"), as well as Bartók, Hindemith, Roussel, and a number of others. Although their works manifest the eighteenth century spirit, they are realized in the dissonant harmonies, varied instrumental colors, and striking rhythms of this century.

Among Stravinsky's earlier works which lean toward neoclassicism are *L'Histoire du soldat* (The Soldier's Story), *Pulcinella,* and several works influenced by ragtime and jazz. In 1920 he established residence in Paris and the works composed from 1920 to 1925 more fully manifest the neoclassical spirit, including the *Symphonies of Wind Instruments,* the *Concerto for Piano and Wind Orchestra,* and the *Octet for Winds.* From this time until early in the 1950's he continued, for the most part, in a neoclassical vein but in a variety of styles and media.

His apparent resolution never to repeat himself has resulted in a continuous evolution of style so that at no point has it been possible to categorize him as belonging to this or that school of composition. Some of the most important works of the period to 1952 are the opera-oratorio *Oedipus Rex* (1927, revised 1948), the ballet *Apollon Musagète* (1928), *Symphony of Psalms* (1930, revised 1948), the *Concerto in D* for violin and orchestra (1931), the *Symphony in C* (1940), the *Symphony in Three Movements* (1945), and the opera *The Rake's Progress* (1951).

In 1939 Stravinsky came to the United States to deliver a series of lectures at Harvard University. With the outbreak of World War II he decided to remain in this country and in 1945 established United States citizenship. From 1952 to the present he has used the techniques of the twelve-tone (also called dodecaphonic or serial) school of composition, to be discussed in some detail in the next chapter. He has used these techniques to develop an intricate contrapuntal style, more abstract than his earlier works and less accessible to the large mass of listeners. His earlier works such as *Le Sacre, Pulcinella, Symphony of Psalms, Firebird,* and *Petrouchka* continue to be more popular than those of his most recent period.

In the twenties and thirties Stravinsky had been opposed to the twelve-tone technique and in thus reversing himself he pointed the way for many younger composers who, guided by his example, had hitherto avoided serialism. Today the vast majority of serious composers have in one way or another incorporated aspects of the twelve-tone technique into their styles. Stravinsky's most important works composed since 1952 are the Cantata of 1952 (the first of his works to fully utilize serial techniques), *In Memoriam Dylan Thomas* (1954) for tenor and eight instruments, a large choral work entitled *Canticum Sacrum* (1956), *Threni* (1958) to the text of the Lamentations of Jeremiah, *Movements* (1959) for piano and orchestra, and *The Flood* (1962), a television ballet written for narrator, chorus, soloists, and orchestra.

Rhythm—vital, inventive, unsymmetrical, pulsating rhythm—has always been the most important and striking aspect of Stravinsky's style. Phrases of uneven length, sudden unpredictable accents, many changes of meter, rhythmic patterns that seldom turn out as expected—all of these abound in Stravinsky's music. His harmonic and contrapuntal style is almost as unique as his rhythmic practices, for he has consistently refused to be satisfied with outworn sonorities and textures, searching always for something that will sound fresh and new, even in terms of his own music. Something of his attitude toward innovation, and an answer to certain of his detractors who had accused him of opportunistically changing his style, is found in the last paragraph of his autobiography, written in 1936:

> Their attitude certainly cannot make me deviate from my path. I shall assuredly not sacrifice my predilections and my aspirations to the demands of those who, in their blindness, do not realize that they are simply asking me to go backwards. It should be obvious that what they wish for has become obsolete for me, and that I could not follow them without doing violence to myself. But, on the other hand, it would be a great mistake to regard me as an adherent of Zukunftsmusik—the music of the future. Nothing could be more ridiculous. I live neither in the

past nor in the future. I am in the present. I cannot know what tomorrow will bring forth. I can only know what the truth is for me today. That is what I am called upon to serve, and I serve it in all lucidity.[1]

Le Sacre du printemps (The Rite of Spring)

The subtitle of this work, "Scenes of Pagan Russia," points to the strong Russian influences found in Stravinsky's earlier works, such as the use of a large colorful orchestra (even larger than that of Rimsky-Korsakov) and the use of primitive folklike melodies that seem to stem from the Russian soil. In this as in many of his scores, both early and late, Stravinsky makes abundant use of polytonality, the simultaneous use of two or more tonal centers. The result is a dissonant and antiromantic harmonic language that is further colored with such devices as triads with both a major and a minor third and sonorities that are not triadic at all, such as quartal sonorities (chords built of vertical projections of fourths and fifths). The new tonal vocabulary was so different from that of the eighteenth and nineteenth centuries that even today it is not difficult to see why its early performances elicited such violent reactions. The work turned the corner on a new era and profoundly affected the course of music in this century, for many composers from 1913 to the present were strongly swayed in their writing by the styles and techniques seen in this and other Stravinsky scores.

Even more striking than the tonal language is the element of rhythm in Le Sacre. Unusual meter signatures such as 1/4, 5/16, and 11/4 are found throughout to create a constantly shifting rhythmic pulse. Nevertheless, the beat is there, with an impact both primitive and ominous. At times the pulse becomes so insistent that it creates a rhythmic ostinato, often in an irregular pattern. The ostinato device is found in so much of Stravinsky's music that it can be counted as an important stylistic trait.

Yet another aspect of Stravinsky's innovative personality is seen in the daring use of instrumental color in this work. A favorite device is the use of an instrument in its very highest or lowest register to produce an uncharacteristic sound. An example is heard at the beginning of this work in the opening solo for bassoon in its highest register. Unique composite tone colors achieved by unusual instrumental combinations appear in the score; and instruments rarely used in the symphony orchestra also are heard.

[1] Igor Stravinsky, An Autobiography, New York, Norton, 1962, p. 176. Used by permission of M. J. Steuer.

Among these are the guiro (a South American folk instrument made of a serrated gourd which is scraped with a stick), the bass trumpet, and the alto flute.

The primitivism evoked by the impelling rhythms, bizarre timbres, and powerful sonorities of *The Rite of Spring* finds its counterpart in early twentieth century paintings by Matisse, Picasso, and Rouault. Vestiges of this sophisticated primitivism are found in many of Stravinsky's later works and become an indefinable aspect of his style. Important passages from the various sections of *Le Sacre* are indicated in Figure 122. The ballet centers around the primitive ceremonies of an ancient pagan tribe and culminates in the ritual dance of a young maiden chosen to be sacrificed in order to ensure the fertility of the earth.

Symphony of Psalms

After the three ballets of the pre-World War I period, Stravinsky frequently departed from traditional instrumental combinations and *Symphony of Psalms* is a case in point. It is scored for an orchestra of reduced size using no violins, violas, or clarinets, plus the standard mixed chorus. The composer indicates that children's voices should be used in the alto and soprano parts, if available. There are no solo voices.

The work is in three parts (or movements) to be played without pause. The Latin text, taken from the Vulgate, consists of two verses of Psalm 38 for the first part, three verses of Psalm 39 for the second, and the complete Psalm 150 for the final part. The spirit of baroque sacred choral music is clearly apparent, not only in the seriousness and austerity of the work, but also in Stravinsky's use of a number of baroque techniques, particularly in the second movement.

The first movement is in a free ABA form and opens with an arpeggiated ostinato figure in the woodwinds punctuated at several points by a single accented E minor triad. The altos of the chorus then enter with a melody built entirely out of the tones E and F over a new ostinato figure in the orchestra. This half step melody is the dominating thematic material of the first and third sections of the movement and also appears as a cyclical element in the final movement. In the middle section, which begins with the altos and basses on the word *"Quoniam,"* contrast is furnished by another orchestral ostinato figure containing a series of repeated notes. The full chorus dominates this section as it builds a crescendo to a fortissimo on the word *"mei"* to end the middle section and mark the beginning of the final section. The movement is completed with the chorus intoning the two-note

Figure 122.

PART I. "The Fertility of the Earth"

A. Introduction

B. Dance of the Youths and Maidens

C. Dance of Abduction

D. Spring Rounds

E. Games of the Rival Towns

F. Entrance of the Celebrant

G. The Kiss to the Earth

H. Dance to the Earth

PART II. "The Sacrifice"

A. Introduction (The Pagan Night)

B. Mystic Circle of the Adolescents

C. Dance to the Glorified One

D. Evocation of Ancestors

E. Ritual Performance of the Ancestors

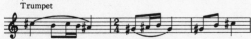

F. Sacrificial Dance

283

melody in four-part texture. The use of the Phrygian mode in much of the choral writing of this movement contributes to the pervading mood of archaic solemnity.

The second movement is a double fugue very much in the baroque style. It is built out of two fugue subjects, each with its own complete exposition and episodes, so that essentially the movement consists of two fugues proceeding concurrently to the end, one played by the orchestra, the other by the chorus. To emphasize the tonal nature of this movement as well as the next, the key signature for C minor is used. The first fugue subject, shown in Figure 123, is presented in a symmetrical exposition with the extrances of the four voices (in the flutes and oboes) alternating between

Figure 123.

the tonic and dominant tonal centers exactly as in a baroque fugue. After a short episode, the choral parts enter one by one with an exposition based on the fugue subject shown in Figure 124. This exposition also maintains the tonal relationships typical of the baroque style as both instruments and voices weave their way in an intricate contrapuntal texture. Fugal devices such as stretto and diminution are used, and near the end of the movement the inevitable ostinato appears, built out of the first four notes of the first subject. The movement ends quietly with the chorus chanting in unison against the ostinato figure in the bass instruments.

Figure 124.

The finale follows an ABCBDA pattern and is the longest movement of the three. The A section begins with a four-voice setting of the word *"Alleluia,"* after which the germinating motive of the section is presented (Figure 125). The harmony alternates between C major and C minor, at times with both tonic triads occurring simultaneously. The first B section, scored for the instruments alone, is characterized by repetitions of a repeated note figure on a major triad. The stepwise character of the short C section furnishes a moment of contrast between the two B sections. The thematic material of the C section is based on the two-note theme of the first movement (this time with a whole step instead of a half step), furnishing an element of unity in the total work.

Figure 125.

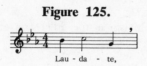

Lau - da - te,

In the second presentation of the B section the material is worked out more fully and the chorus assists with the development of the repeated note motive on the words *"Laudate Dominum."* In the first part of the D section the theme shown in Figure 126 is treated canonically. Then on the

Figure 126.

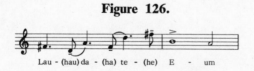

Lau - (hau) da - (ha) te - (he) E - um

words *"Laudate Eum in cymbalis"* a smooth, homophonic, four-part texture is established which continues to the end of the section. The work concludes quietly with a much abbreviated presentation of the A material.

Symphony of Psalms is one of the finest and most representative compositions of Stravinsky's middle period. It possesses a nobility of expression rarely seen in sacred music of this century, and is endowed with the same strength and incisive objectivity that have characterized so many of this composer's works during a fruitful career spanning more than sixty years.

SUGGESTED ASSIGNMENTS

1. Summarize the most apparent stylistic traits seen in the two works discussed in this chapter.
2. Begin to expand your knowledge of Stravinsky's music by listening to other works mentioned in this chapter.
3. Read excerpts from Stravinsky's autobiography and from his *Poetics of Music*.
4. Summarize the traits that the neoclassical style has in common with the music of the baroque and classical periods. How does neoclassicism differ from the earlier periods?
5. Find examples of primitivism in the other arts of the early twentieth century.

TWENTY-ONE

TWELVE-TONE MUSIC

ARNOLD SCHOENBERG (1874–1951)

The term "esoteric" can be aptly applied to the music of the composers in this chapter, for all three of them were consciously addressing themselves, in their day, to an audience limited to only the most knowledgeable and understanding of listeners. Even today, nearly fifty years after the first twelve-tone compositions were written, many in our concert audiences find most of the works of Schoenberg, Berg, and Webern to be hard going. Yet Schoenberg's twelve-tone system is now almost universally recognized as the most significant single development in music theory in this century. Virtually every contemporary composer has felt its impact and, though relatively few adhere strictly to its precepts, a great many of our most gifted composers utilize it with some freedom and have found it to be a most useful tool.

One reason for its great importance to musical composition during the first half of this century is that it furnished a means of organizing tones at a time when every existing traditional technique was being questioned and when it was becoming apparent that the tonal system in use for 250 years was losing its validity. The nineteenth century had seen a gradual departure from the tonal system in which the key center was determined by the seven notes of the diatonic scale. Composers of the seventeenth and eighteenth centuries had, of course, departed from these seven tones in order to make use of the harmonic contrast and color furnished by the other five, but they did so within a stable tonal framework, for the harmony was always focused upon the key center furnished by the diatonic scale.

When a piece of music makes frequent use of the tones outside of the diatonic scale, the music is said to be chromatic. During the nineteenth century the use of chromaticism increased to the point where, in certain

287

instances, all twelve tones of the tempered scale were heard so frequently within a relatively short time span that the traditional conception of tonality began to disappear. Chromatic harmony within a diatonic framework had been an important aspect of the styles of such composers as Bach, Mozart, Schubert, Beethoven, Chopin, Liszt, and many others; but in the works of such late romantic composers as Wagner, Gustav Mahler, and Anton Bruckner it took an extreme form that led toward the establishment of a new harmonic language. It must be added that the diatonic scale has by no means disappeared from use. Almost every serious contemporary composer still finds some use for it; and within the framework of contemporary harmonic devices it remains one of the most important materials of musical composition.

Schoenberg, a native Viennese, was very much aware of his link with German late romanticism, particularly with Wagner, whose music he used to demonstrate the validity of his new system. Works of his earliest period, such as the string sextet *Transfigured Night* and the orchestral song cycle *Gurrelieder,* show the influence of the post-Wagnerian environment of his youth, and it was quite logical for him to move from the extreme chromaticism of this period toward the gradual abandonment of the old tonal concept.

In the absence of a diatonic key center, the works that Schoenberg composed during the pre-World War I period (known as his second period) were, for the most part, short pieces and songs, compositions small enough not to require the form and unity furnished by a diatonic key center. In works of this period, such as the *Three Piano Pieces,* Op. 11, the *Five Orchestral Pieces,* Op. 16, and *Pierrot Lunaire,* Op. 21, tonality is replaced by a free use of chromaticism. They represent the movement in music known as expressionism. Like impressionism, the word has its origin in a parallel movement in painting represented by the early twentieth century works of Kokoschka, Kollwitz, Munch, Kandinsky, and a number of others, mostly German. Something akin to expressionism is found in the novels of Kafka and in the poetry of Paul Stefan George. Possibly influenced by the writings of Sigmund Freud, expressionism in all of the arts is characterized by a preoccupation with the inward realities of the human mind and spirit. The expressionists were intensely interested in the conflicts and torments of the soul, quite different from the impressionist painters' concern with impressions of things outside of the self such as still lifes, the play of light, and form and design in objects perceived. Expressionism was anticipated in the music dramas of Wagner so that, in a sense, it can be characterized as an aftermath of German romanticism, although it was also a reaction to French impressionism.

Gradually during this time, Schoenberg's new harmonic language began to evolve. He began to feel the need of a new unifying concept that could replace the old tonal concept and thus enable him to compose works of greater scope and longer duration. The new technique, which he evolved in the years following World War I, he called "the method of composing with twelve tones."

The system, which is well adapted to contrapuntal thinking, makes use of an established order or series of the twelve chromatic tones, an arbitrary arrangement of notes that is called the "tone row." A particular tone row becomes the unifying idea or basis for a complete movement or for a complete work, each movement or work being thus characterized by its own unique tone row. In the last movement of his *Five Piano Pieces,* Op. 23 (1923), the new technique was fully revealed for the first time. Every note in the movement is derived from the tone row shown in Figure 127.

Figure 127.

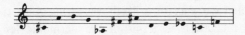

One of the basic principles of the system is that all of the tones must be presented in the established order before any one of them is played again. (Immediate repetition of a tone is allowed as an extension of the original.) There are four possible forms or arrangements of the row: (1) the basic row as presented in Figure 127, (2) the melodic inversion of the basic row, (3) the retrograde (reverse order, last note first, etc.) of the basic row, and (4) the retrograde inversion (melodic inversion of the retrograde form). In addition, each of these four forms may begin on any one of the twelve tones of the chromatic scale—four forms with twelve transpositions each, furnishing the composer with a total of forty-eight different rows to work with. Several of these may be used simultaneously or they may overlap each other, one form of the row beginning before another is completed. In the strictest use of the technique, all melodic and harmonic materials must be derived from the various forms of the tone row with each tone of each row being presented in the established sequence. Because of the use of the notes in series, the system is often called the "serial" technique. In Europe the term "dodecaphonic" is also used.

Tone rows of fewer than twelve tones have been used in more recent years and techniques of serialization have also been applied to rhythm, timbre, texture, and articulation. Indeed, some present-day composers attempt to utilize these techniques to control every aspect of their music. Since the terms "twelve-tone technique" and "dodecaphonic" apply specifically to the harmonic aspects of the twelve tones of the tempered scale (not to the other elements of music), the expression "serial technique" has become the preferred term for the recent developments in the system.

In most of the works of Schoenberg's third period (1923–1933) the twelve-tone system is quite consistently applied. In general, works (such as those of this period) which incorporate the strict application of twelve-tone principles are less accessible to the average listener than works which demonstrate greater freedom in its use. In no instance, however, should the listener attempt to concentrate on the tone row organization of a twelve-tone piece. This is an impossibly tedious task, even for the most experienced of listeners. Much twelve-tone music can be heard in the same way as any piece of serious music—with concentration upon the flux of tension and relaxation, the interplay of lines and colors, and the forward motion of the musical phrase. The principles of form and design are the same for a Schoenberg chamber work as for a Beethoven string quartet; and if one can feel tension and relaxation in terms of the harmonic language of Beethoven, one can, with experience, perceive the same thing in Schoenberg's music. Among the most significant works of Schoenberg's third period are the *Suite for Piano, Op. 25,* the *String Quartet No. 3, Op. 30,* and the *Variations for Orchestra, Op. 31.*

Schoenberg could not remain in Austria under the Nazi regime, and in 1933 he came to live in the United States. The period from that time until his death in 1951 is known as his fourth period. During that time he frequently departed from the strict application of his method, often using the row with great freedom, and occasionally returning to a purely tonal style, even with key signatures. Among the more accessible works of this period are the cantata *A Survivor of Warsaw* (1948), the Piano Concerto (1942), and the *Kol Nidre* (Op. 39) for speaker, chorus, and orchestra. The strict twelve-tone works of this period include the Fourth String Quartet, Op. 37, a String Trio, Op. 45, and the Violin Concerto, Op. 36.

The twelve-tone system has been frequently criticized for being arbitrary and therefore too restrictive to the composer. Perhaps there is an atom of truth in this, but it must be remembered that any system or preconceived plan for the creation of a work of art will be restrictive if the artist lacks the true gift of invention. Without this gift he is dependent upon the system, but with it he can transcend any reasonable restriction. That the twelve-tone technique is not excessively restrictive is proven by the fact that many composers of widely varying styles have subscribed to its tenets and yet maintained their individuality. In any event, Schoenberg's uncompromising conviction in the rightness of his doctrines sustained him through many years when his compositions were grossly misunderstood. Today it is generally acknowledged that the principles he advanced in the twenties pointed to the future and led to other significant developments in the technique of musical composition.

Pierrot Lunaire, Op. 21 (1912)

This work, which can be translated as "Moonstruck Pierrot," is an excellent example of Schoenberg's intense brand of musical expressionism. It is not a twelve-tone work, but its general musical effect is very similar to later works which made strict use of the tone row. Representing the style of his second period, it is freely atonal (without traditional diatonic tonal organization) with melodic intervals unrelated to harmonic considerations, and is rhythmically irregular in a way that emphasizes the departure from traditional techniques.

The work is scored for contralto soloist and five players: flute (alternating with piccolo), clarinet (and bass clarinet), violin (and viola), cello, and piano. The abandonment of the diatonic system is further accentuated by the use of *sprechstimme* (speaking part) in the voice part. That is, the voice intones its part in a speechlike manner with free inflections according to the meaning of the words. Approximate pitches are indicated in the voice part but are not intended to be clearly defined, while the rhythm is strictly notated throughout. The effect is one of mysterious intensity and concentrated emotional impact.

The rather decadent text of the twenty-one short songs is by the French poet Albert Giraud, set by Schoenberg in German translation. Each song is a miniature scored for some combination of the eight instruments and five players, and each deals with a separate adventure in the private reality of an insane Pierrot. As in many vocal works, formal unity is furnished by the text itself, with purely musical structures such as the intricate canons of numbers 17 and 18 also contributing to the overall design of the work.

ALBAN BERG (1885–1935)

In Schoenberg's role as a teacher in the Viennese musical community he attracted many students, some of whom became close friends and disciples of their teacher as well as distinguished composers. The most gifted of these were Alban Berg and Anton Webern who, with Schoenberg, constitute the modern Viennese school of composition. Berg was endowed with a keen dramatic sense and his expressionism finds its most characteristic outlet in his operas *Wozzeck,* completed in 1922, and *Lulu,* not quite completed at the time of his death in 1935.

His use of the twelve-tone system inclined toward greater freedom than did Schoenberg's and he often included conventional triads in his tone rows, which permitted him to use a somewhat more traditional harmonic language and occasional tonal passages. For this reason the music of the modern Viennese school is best approached by listening first to certain of Berg's most accessible works such as the Violin Concerto (1935) and the *Lyric Suite* for string quartet (1926). The tone rows of both of these works contain triads and, because their link with music of the past is very clear, both have achieved a considerable degree of popularity among today's concert audiences.

Wozzeck, an Opera in Three Acts

The source for the libretto of this opera is the nineteenth century play of the same name by George Büchner (1813–1837). Berg himself adapted the libretto and began work on the opera in 1914. The music is continuous and is organized into a series of fifteen scenes, five in each act, plus an orchestral interlude before the final scene of Act III. Each of the scenes has its own self-contained abstract musical form which is not dictated or controlled by the text. The composer has drawn a graphic illustration of the relationship between the music and the dramatic action as shown in the following diagram:

DRAMATIC ACTION	MUSICAL FORMS
ACT I: *Wozzeck related to his everyday surroundings*	*Five Character Pieces*
SCENE 1. Wozzeck and the Captain	SCENE 1. Suite (eleven sections)
2. Wozzeck and Andres	2. Rhapsody (based on three chords)

3. Marie and Wozzeck	3. Military March and Lullaby
4. Wozzeck and the Doctor	4. Passacaglia (twenty-one variations)
5. Marie and the Drum Major	5. Andante Affetuoso: Quasi rondo

ACT II: *Development: Wozzeck gradually becomes convinced that Marie is unfaithful to him.*

Symphony in Five Movements

SCENE 1. Marie and child, later Wozzeck (the first suspicions)	SCENE 1. Sonata movement
2. Captain and Doctor, later Wozzeck (They torment and deride Wozzeck regarding Marie.)	2. Invention and Fugue
3. Marie and Wozzeck (He accuses her.)	3. Largo in free form
4. Beer-Garden (Marie and Drum Major dance.)	4. Scherzo with three trios
5. Wozzeck's Barracks (Wozzeck, Drum Major, and Andres. Drum Major manhandles and threatens Wozzeck.)	5. Rondo with introduction

ACT III: *Catastrophe and Epilogue. Wozzeck murders Marie and then kills himself.*

Six Inventions

SCENE 1. Marie and child	SCENE 1. Invention on a theme
2. Marie and Wozzeck (He kills her at the pond.)	2. Invention on one note

3. The Inn (Wozzeck drinks heavily.)	3. Invention on a rhythm
4. Wozzeck's suicide	4. Invention on a six-tone chord
EPILOGUE: Orchestral Interlude	Invention in the key of D minor
5. Children at play with Marie's child	5. Invention on an eighth note figure

A clue to the manner of listening to this opera is found in Berg's own words in the *Neue Musik-Zeitung* of 1928:

> . . . from the time when the curtain rises until it falls for the last time, no one in the audience ought to notice anything of these fugues and inventions, suite and sonata movements, variations and passacaglias—everyone should be filled only with the idea of the opera, an idea which far transcends the individual fate of Wozzeck.

Presumably the "idea" that Berg is speaking of here is that of the inevitability of fateful violence that grows out of everyday circumstances and situations. Wozzeck, an ordinary barber, typifies the common man, but more importantly, symbolizes commonplace things which always possess a potential for violent consequences.

The opera is unified as a whole by the use of a few leitmotifs, but the drama is so gripping that one is not often aware of them. Schoenberg's influence is apparent in the use of *sprechstimme* and in the freely atonal style, but the opera is not a twelve-tone work. Many passages, however, suggest serial technique even though the opera was completed before Schoenberg had fully formulated the new method. The theme of the passacaglia in Act II, for example, is composed of twelve notes. The work is forbiddingly difficult to perform but, in spite of this, is already recognized as a classic work of great power and compassionate humanity.

ANTON WEBERN (1883–1945)

If Berg represents the more conservative aspects of the modern Viennese school, then the figure of Anton Webern personifies its most radical elements. Both Schoenberg and Berg showed an inclination toward short forms, building larger forms out of concise units. In Webern's music the urge for brevity is carried still further and many movements among his works are shorter than a minute in duration. He applied the principles of the twelve-tone technique more strictly than either of his distinguished colleagues, even extending the idea of serial construction to encompass and control the elements of rhythm and timbre.

Today, in twelve-tone circles, no composer's influence is felt more strongly than that of Webern. Stravinsky has based his most recent style upon Webernian principles, and such celebrated avant-garde composers as Pierre Boulez and Karlheinz Stockhausen have attempted to carry Webern's serial techniques to the extreme of controlling every aspect of musical composition—pitch, rhythm, timbre, density (texture), and dynamics. From this the term total serialism has arisen. An important characteristic of Webern's technique was his use of two-, three-, and four-note melodic fragments in a texture created by passing the fragments from one instrument to another in a constantly fluctuating pastiche of subtle tone colors. Schoenberg had developed a technique known as *Klangfarbenmelodie,* utilizing frequent changes of instrumentation during the course of a single melodic line. Webern carried the technique even further, in some instances assigning each tone of a melodic line to a different instrument. This more than any other aspect of his style has influenced composers of today.

His musical language is extremely subtle. Dynamics are very carefully notated with an abundance of small crescendos and diminuendos, usually at a low level. His textures are light and transparent with the relationship of one instrument to another worked out in careful detail as to counterpoint and instrumental color; and complex canonic devices are handled with great lucidity and skill. His rhythmic organization, intricate as it is, conveys a feeling of great freedom of thought and clarity of design.

He endured considerable hardship during his lifetime, particularly under the Nazi regime in Austria, and did not live to see his artistry fully recognized and appreciated. Tragically, this quiet, retiring man of genius was accidentally killed by a soldier of the American occupation forces in 1945 just after the close of the war. Within the last twenty years his works have been widely performed and he is now recognized as a leading figure among twentieth century composers.

Webern's total output of thirty-one works covers so short a time span that they have been recorded in full on four LP records. No composer in the history of music achieved such remarkable economy of means. Each movement is a tiny gem of perfection—a microcosm of profound expression. During his early pretwelve-tone period he composed a number of songs with accompaniments for piano and for various instrumental combinations. These demonstrate his remarkable lyrical gift, as do several significant instrumental works of this time such as the *Five Pieces for Orchestra,* Op. 10 (1913) and the *Five Movements for String Quartet,* Op. 6 (1909). His first twelve-tone work was the *Three Sacred Folk Songs,* Op-17 (1924) for voice and three instruments, and in the years that followed he continued to refine his style, producing such masterworks as his Symphony, Op. 21 (1928), *Concerto for Nine Instruments,* Op. 24 (1934), the two cantatas, and the *Variations for Orchestra,* Op. 30 (1940).

Earlier in this chapter it was said that Schoenberg's chamber music can be understood in much the same manner as Beethoven's, provided that the listener can think in terms of the new harmonic language. This cannot be said of the works of Webern, for here a totally different state of mind is required. Not only is the harmonic language different, even from that of Schoenberg and Berg, but also the concept of time is completely altered. The listener cannot think in terms of action and events within a significant time span, at least, not the kind of action referred to in the drama analogy discussed earlier. Webern's movements are too short in duration for this to be practical. Because of the extreme brevity, the ear can sometimes apprehend a whole Webern movement as easily as one hears a phrase or period in eighteenth and nineteenth century music. So concise and concentrated is Webern's organization within a short time span, that the listener must accept the idea of total concentration upon every aspect of the texture. It is like quickly passing one's eyes over a beautiful and intricately chiseled piece of sculpture. One can apprehend the spatial aspects of the work in a few moments, but to fully appreciate and *comprehend,* one must examine it in detail. It is not necessary to be constantly aware of the techniques of organization—the canons, retrogrades, and inversions of Webern's music. It is necessary only to hear the interrelationships of the fluctuating rhythms, timbres, and lines and, to this end, repeated hearings will be of great value. The rewards are considerable for those who are willing to enter this unique world of sound.

Cantata No. 1, Op. 29 (1939)

This work is scored for soprano, mixed chorus, and orchestra and shows Webern's unique lyrical gift at the height of its powers. The three movements total about seven minutes in duration and the contrapuntal and harmonic organization is based on the tone row shown in Figure 128. The

German text is by Hildegarde Jone and the small orchestra consists of flute, oboe, clarinet, bass clarinet, French horn, trumpet, trombone, mandolin, timpani, percussion, harp, celesta, and strings without double basses.

Figure 128.

The first movement, for chorus and orchestra, begins with a short orchestral introduction presenting the tones of the row in three soft chords. The shifting meters and fluctuating instrumental colors of the introduction build toward a sudden accented sonority in the percussion and trombone, at which point the chorus enters. The dramatically effective choral writing is predominantly homophonic laced with occasional contrapuntal passages. Contributing much to the emotional impact of the movement is the alternation between the slow solemn pace of the opening and the lively tempo heard later. The movement concludes with the orchestra alone.

The opening of the second movement presents an aspect of Webern's style that led toward total serialization in later composers. The clarinet presents the tone row with both dynamics and rhythm organized according to a serial pattern. The rhythm of the first twelve tones, in fact, reads the same backward as forward. Other examples of rhythmic serialization are found elsewhere in the movement. Scored for soprano solo and orchestra, the movement makes frequent use of text painting devices. The wide unvocal leaps in the voice part are typical of the twelve-tone style, but serve also to emphasize the meaning of the words. This kind of vocal line is extremely difficult to perform, although a surprising number of singers have begun to meet the challenge of dodecaphonic vocal music and have found the musical rewards to be well worth the effort.

The final movement, with solo, chorus, and orchestra, opens with a two-part canon in the chorus. The frequent use of silence as an expressive element is apparent in this opening, representing one of the important stylistic traits of Webern. The transparent contrapuntal texture continues with both orchestra and chorus, the orchestra then taking over in a broad crescendo that leads to the entrance of the soprano solo on the word *"Charis."* This is the most intense moment in the cantata, the climax of the movement as well as of the total work. The chorus and soloist then continue in a contrapuntal exchange and the movement concludes quietly on the word *"Vollendung"* (perfection).

Among the many twentieth century composers who adopted, in whole or part, the principles of the dodecaphonic system are Luigi Dallapiccola, Ernst Krenek, Wallingford Riegger, Rolf Liebermann, and numerous younger composers in Europe and the United States. For many the system has been treated simply as a useful tool to be used with other techniques as the need arises. For others it has been embraced as a religion, dominating every musical thought and, in a few instances, freeing the composer's imagination from an outworn tradition.

SUGGESTED ASSIGNMENTS

1. Under the guidance of the instructor, examine the tone row of the Webern cantata discussed above (Figure 128). Note the natural division of the row into six-note groups. Compare the two hexachords and try to determine their relationship to each other. Carrying this reasoning further, determine the effect of this relationship upon the other forms of the row.
2. Examine examples of expressionism in the visual arts and in literature, and attempt to find expressionistic traits common to all of the arts.
3. In the works discussed in this chapter find specific examples of links with German romanticism.
4. Expand your knowledge of the music of the modern Viennese school by listening to other works mentioned in this chapter, such as Schoenberg's *Transfigured Night,* the Berg Violin Concerto, and Webern's *Five Pieces for Orchestra.*

TWENTY-TWO

BARTÓK AND HINDEMITH

Each of the composers under discussion in this chapter has, in his own way, fused the musical traditions of past centuries with modern musical concepts. Both wrote in a variety of forms and media and neither found it necessary to strongly associate himself with a particular school of twentieth century composition. In their own unique musical languages, Bartók and Hindemith have made distinguished contributions to the literature of twentieth century music.

BÉLA BARTÓK (1881–1945)

Bartók's consuming interest in the folklore of his native Hungary and the surrounding countries exerted a strong influence upon his art. In a sense he represents a continuation of the nationalist tradition into the twentieth century but his use of folklike rhythms and melodies is quite different from that of the romantic era. Unlike Dvořák, for example, Bartók was able to truly *assimilate* the rhythms and inflections of his homeland into abstract instrumental forms without appearing to be mixing styles or casting materials in the wrong mold. He made arrangements of Hungarian and Slovak folk songs, some of which had never been written down before; and through his painstaking research methods he was able to correct much widespread misunderstanding regarding the nature of Hungarian folk music. He was aided in this by his friend and distinguished fellow composer Zoltán Kodály (1882–1967), whose works also manifest the folk influence.

Bartók's scientific approach to folklore dates from 1907, the year of his appointment as a piano teacher at the Royal Hungarian Music Academy in Budapest. Kodály was also a member of the faculty of the Academy and through their studies they began to adopt into their music a concept of dissonance found in Hungarian folk music. Part of this concept involves thinking of the intervals of fourths, fifths, seconds, and sevenths as being consonant and usable for the construction of basic harmonies, a concept that is closely related to quartal harmony. Also, folk music led Bartók to the use of unusual modes or scales which he occasionally used in poly-harmonic or polymodal textures. Such devices, along with a unique treat-ment of triadic structures and the whole tone scale, constitute the impor-tant elements of his harmonic language. His rhythmic style also was influenced by folk music and, indirectly, by the natural cadence of the Hungarian language; for folk song, by its very nature, must always be linked to the inflections of the language in which it is sung.

Bartók was heir to the styles of Liszt, Wagner, and Strauss but his studies of folk music soon freed him from these influences and he found instead a unique idiom that evoked the spirit of the twentieth century at the same time that it reached back to the classical period and the universality of Beethoven. His prodigious developmental skills and contrapuntal tech-niques are particularly apparent in his instrumental music where he seems to be expressing the same human truths experienced in the greatest of Beethoven's instrumental works. Indeed, Bartók's string quartets place him in direct line with the tradition established by Haydn and continued in the works of Mozart, Beethoven, Schubert, and Brahms.

He believed strongly in the power of music to express human emotion and experience, and in this he was at odds with the neoclassicism of the "French Six" and Stravinsky. Yet he was influenced by the music of these composers as he was by the atonalism of Schoenberg and the modern Viennese school. He was able, by the very force of his musical personality, to assimilate these influences and yet maintain his own unique identity. His rhythmic style, for example, has considerable affinity with that of Stravin-sky. Both liked ostinatos, and both had a penchant for irregular meters and terse asymmetrical rhythmic figures. Yet Bartók's rhythms are distinct from Stravinsky's, perhaps because of Bartók's background as a virtuoso pianist; for there is a percussive, driving quality in his rhythmic style that is unique to twentieth century piano writing.

The earliest of his piano works, written between 1908 and 1910, are not unlike the character pieces of the nineteenth century. *Bagatelles* and *Elegies, Burlesques* and *Sketches,* they show his love of the miniature and the influence of folk song. Of greater stature are the Piano Sonata and the *Concerto for Two Pianos and Orchestra* (1938) in addition to the famous *Mikrokosmos,* a collection of graded piano miniatures in five volumes known to every student of the piano. Crowning his achievements as a piano composer is the Third Piano Concerto (1945) composed in the United States during the year of his death at a time when he was beset by every possible deprivation and discomfort. He had come to America in 1940 as a result of the Nazi invasion of Austria and Hungary and, though he received some recognition as an artist, his last years were plagued by economic insecurity and poor health. It was at this time that he was working feverishly upon his famous Viola Concerto, completed after his death by his friend Tibor Serly.

He composed several outstanding works for chamber orchestra, including *Music for Strings, Percussion, and Celesta* and the *Divertimento for Strings*. Among his outstanding works for large orchestra are his *Concerto for Orchestra,* the Violin Concerto, and the ballet *The Miraculous Mandarin*. In addition to his six string quartets, which stand as monuments in this century, his chamber works include two sonatas for violin and piano, and a collection of forty-eight short duos for two violins. His vocal works include the *Cantata Profana* (1930), the opera *Bluebeard's Castle* (1911), and numerous songs, many of which are simple arrangements of folk songs.

String Quartet No. 6 (1939)

Bartók's six string quartets were composed throughout his life, the first in 1910 and the last in 1939. They show the gradual evolution of his style and, as a group, represent his greatest achievement. Within them are found new string techniques such as col legno (bowing or striking the string with the wood of the bow), "snapping" the string against the fingerboard in pizzicato, plucking with the fingernail, glissandi, and new possibilities for harmonics and double stops. So fully do these works explore new string techniques that they constitute a compendium of new string sounds available to twentieth century composers. In the last four quartets the folk element is completely assimilated so that it seems to be an intrinsic and natural part of his musical language. Perhaps the finest among them is the Sixth.

It was commissioned by the New Hungarian Quartet and was Bartók's last work composed in Hungary. Premiered in New York in 1941 by the Kolisch Quartet, to whom it was dedicated, it has since become a staple of the string quartet repertoire. Its tonal center is D, with F as an important secondary tonal area. These centers are established not by the major and minor key feeling of the diatonic system, but by devices such as centering around a given tone or by the use of modes which are oriented to certain pitches. The four movements are linked together by a common theme, marked *Mesto,* which is heard at the beginning of each movement and which becomes the basic thematic material of the brief final movement. The word "mesto" means introspective or melancholy, and the theme, initially presented by the viola, evokes a feeling of deep sadness (see Figure 129).

Figure 129.

Arch form does not appear in this quartet as in other of his instrumental works such as the Second Piano Concerto, the Violin Concerto, and the Third, Fourth, and Fifth string quartets. In fact, the first movement uses a form that almost exactly parallels the classical sonata allegro form. The main theme of the first tonal group, presented after the slow introduction, is shown in Figure 130.

Figure 130.

Its first three notes are derived from the unison passages just preceding it and it soon begins to be developed in a motivic filigree texture characteristic of Bartók's contrapuntal style. The first tonal group concludes with a harmonically static ostinato passage in which all four of the instruments play with different manifestations of the three-note motive.

The main theme of the second tonal group possesses a modal flavor and is centered on F (see Figure 131). Its rhythm is characteristic of Hungarian folk music and, in the course of the movement, it is identifiable more by its peculiar rhythmic qualities than by its pitches. The exposition closes with material that is closely related to the mesto theme with a codetta based on the second tonal group. The final cadence of the exposition on an F major triad emphasizes the tonal structure of the movement with its relationship between the tonal centers D and F, not unlike the typical tonal structure of a classical sonata form in the minor key.

Figure 131.

The development section begins with the three motivic tones presented in unison like the material just preceding the opening of the first tonal group. Then the four instruments begin their intricate dialogues in a polyphonic fabric that demonstrates Bartók's phenomenal technique in thematic development and motivic elaboration. Canons, stretti, ostinati, inversions, and similar techniques are used with great expressive power, never for meaningless technical display.

The recapitulation is preceded by a canonic treatment of the first theme passed in turn from viola to second violin to first violin. This is followed by a section that functions very much like the dominant preparation preceding the recapitulation in many of Beethoven's sonata forms. The active voices in this preparation are the first violin on a trill figure and the cello on an ostinato. The recapitulation then begins like the exposition except that the theme in the first violin is now accompanied by all of the instruments.

The recapitulation is compressed but follows the same order of presentation of ideas as the exposition. Just preceding the coda there is a cadence and fermata on a D major triad firmly establishing the central tonality of the work. Within the coda a drone bass on G in the cello and guitarlike strummings in the viola display the element of folk music in the work. The movement concludes much like the exposition, this time with a D major triad as the final sonority.

The mesto theme introducing the second movement is presented in a sort of dialogue between first violin and cello accompanied by tremolando in the other two parts. Then the *"Marcia"* begins in a vigorous two-part canon in which the first part is borne by the first violin and cello in a two-octave doubling and the second part is assigned to the two inner voices in an octave doubling. The movement is bitonal with the first voice centering on B and the imitating voice on G sharp. The overall form is ABA and the central tonalities of B and G sharp dominate both A sections. The free and rhapsodic middle section begins with the cello alone on accelerating repetitions of an A flat, followed by a glissando to a high A harmonic to introduce an intense melody in the highest register of the cello accompanied by harmonic rustlings in the violins and guitarlike strummings in the viola. At the end of this extended cello passage a quasicadenza in all of the instruments effects a transition to the return of the A section. The final A section is longer than the first and uses variation techniques to modify the earlier presented material. Much of this is a free inversion of the first A section, apparent to the listener in the increased contrast without sacrifice of unity. The movement concludes with the two central tonalities sounding simultaneously.

The introduction of the third movement finds the mesto theme considerably extended and cast in a three-voice texture with the viola entrance adding the fourth voice shortly after the opening. The movement proper is entitled *"Burletta"* and is filled with biting dissonances and assertive rhythms. Its ABA form is similar to that of the second movement and there are thematic references to the opening movement of the quartet. This movement in particular is filled with unique string techniques such as glissando, ricochet bowing, harmonics, etc.

The final movement is a brief but highly concentrated epilogue and résumé of the total work. The mesto theme is heard at the opening and is extended and developed to become the basis of the first part of the movement. Then, in a slightly faster tempo, the main events of the first movement are presented in compressed form. This is more than a cyclical technique; it is a synoptic view of the first movement, furnishing a feeling of consummation in the total work as well as formal unity. After another brief reference to the mesto theme, the work concludes with polytonal references to the two most important tonal centers of the work—D and F, with D predominating.

The six string quartets of Bartók reveal his phenomenal technique, deep imagination, and sincere belief in the power of music to express universal human emotions. Among the composers of this century he is a lonely figure who espoused no particular school or technique of composition but in whose works can be seen many twentieth century musical ideas and techniques fused into a unique and powerful idiom of expression. Frequently misunderstood during his lifetime, his works have now taken a well-deserved place in the standard repertoire where they will surely remain for generations to come.

PAUL HINDEMITH (1895–1963)

As the most distinguished German-born composer of the twentieth century, Hindemith represents a continuation of the best aspects of the German tradition. A most versatile professional musician, he achieved considerable distinction as a violist and conductor during his early career. Author of textbooks in music theory and composition, he was an active teacher—at the Prussian State Academy of Music in Berlin from 1927 to 1935 and subsequently at Yale University. His last years were spent in Switzerland.

Extremely prolific, he has composed successfully in almost every musical medium; and his well-organized musical language bespeaks his belief in the power of music to communicate moral and ethical states of mind. Always highly polished and often austere, in rare instances his music can be warm, humorous, or whimsical, as in *Symphonic Metamorphoses on Themes of Weber* (1944), a work easy to listen to which will serve well as an introduction to his music. He wrote much chamber music, including seven string quartets, several chamber concertos, and many sonatas for various solo instruments with piano accompaniment. Many of these sonatas are outgrowths of his support of the cause of *Gebrauchsmusik* (music for use), an active movement during the third and fourth decades of this century which was guided by the beliefs that music should not be exclusively the domain of professionals, but should be widely performed by amateurs as well, and that music should be composed for a purpose. Hindemith was the strongest supporter of this philosophy and composed numerous pieces for performance by amateurs and students, as well as for now-obsolete mechanical media such as the player-piano.

In his earlier works he showed a free and boldly experimental treatment of form and traditional tonal concepts. These include several operas composed during the twenties, such as *Cardillac* (1926), and *News of the Day* (1929), a bizarre expressionistic work based on news stories. His style of this period is austere and, at times, extremely dissonant with a kind of linear counterpoint characterized by an apparent disregard for the harmonic relationship of the voices. During the next decade, in line with his support of Gebrauchsmusik, he modified his style to make it more meaningful to the large mass of listeners. In the music of this time an almost romantic warmth began to appear, with expressive melodic lines, less dissonant counterpoint, and more clearly defined tonal structures. The important works of this period are the two ballets *Nobilissime Visione*

(1938) and *The Four Temperaments* (1940), the opera *Mathis der Maler* (1934), three piano sonatas, and the *Symphony in E Flat* (1940). Gradually in the works of this period he evolved a style that is akin to neoclassicism but is more appropriately called neobaroque. For in addition to using classical forms in new ways, it utilizes numerous forms and techniques of the German Baroque, such as fugal techniques, passacaglia, and the concerto grosso concept.

Some of the significant works of the period after 1940 are the opera *Die Harmonie der Welt* (The Harmony of the World), the song cycle *Marienleben* (revised in 1948 from an earlier version), *Ludus Tonalis* (a work for solo piano that fully explores the world of Hindemith's contrapuntal mind), and a choral work to the text of Whitman's "When Lilacs Last in the Dooryard Bloom'd" (1946). Since he composed so prolifically, it is understandable that a few of his works are relatively undistinguished. He has nevertheless had a tremendous impact upon the musical thought of this century and his best works are more than sufficient to establish his place in the history of music.

Symphony, *Mathis der Maler*

For this symphony the composer extracted three orchestral movements from the score of the opera *Mathis der Maler* (Matthias the Painter). The opera is based on the life of Matthias Grünewald (1460–1528), a German renaissance painter of distinction. Each of the movements of the symphony deals with one of the painter's religious works but the depiction is not of a literal sort—not in the manner of nineteenth century program music. Hindemith sought rather to use a modern musical language to convey the states of mind evoked by the paintings.

The first movement, "Concert of Angels," opens with an introduction based on a medieval religious folk song entitled *"Es Sungen drei Engel"* ("There Sang Three Angels"). Three trombones intone the song in modal harmonies to establish a mood of archaic serenity. The allegro movement which follows bears many characteristics of the classical sonata pattern. There are two themes in the exposition (shown in Figure 132) and the development presents one against the other in an imitative contrapuntal texture.

The slow movement is entitled "The Entombment." It opens on a note of subdued sorrow achieved by the use of muted strings and flutes. There follows an elegiac oboe melody accompanied by pizzicato strings, characterizing Hindemith's broadly arching melodic style. An imitative dialogue

Figure 132.

between the oboe and flute then leads to an orchestral climax followed by a serene conclusion.

The final movement, "The Temptation of St. Anthony," demonstrates Hindemith's brilliance as an orchestrator. His link with the nineteenth century German orchestral style is apparent in several passages that sound almost Straussian in their lush grandeur. The movement is introduced by a declamatory passage in unison strings. The allegro which follows moves with driving frenzy toward a point of climax in the brass instruments. A prolonged trill high in the violins is then followed by a more relaxed, almost voluptuous section. Then the orchestra drives forward again in syncopated passages that lead to a fugato; and the spirit of renaissance Germany is evoked by the triumphant chorale which follows. The tune upon which the chorale is based, *Lauda Sion Salvatorem* (Praise Zion That Shall Save Us), bespeaks St. Anthony's conquering faith as well as Hindemith's belief in the moral and ethical attributes of music.

Suggested Assignments

1. Listen to recordings of the folk song arrangements of Bartók and Kodály. How do they differ from the popular conception of Hungarian or so-called "Gypsy" folk music?
2. Try to find traces of the folk music influence in the harmonic, rhythmic, and melodic inflections of Bartók's music.
3. Compare the Bartók Sixth String Quartet with the Beethoven Quartet, Op. 59, No. 1. Note differences and similarities.
4. Find examples of baroque and classical techniques in Hindemith's Symphony, *Mathis der Maler*.
5. As a special project read excerpts assigned by the instructor from Hindemith's *A Composer's World* and *The Craft of Musical Composition*.
6. Expand your knowledge of the works of both composers by listening to several of the compositions mentioned in this chapter.

TWENTY-THREE

FOUR AMERICAN COMPOSERS

Until the end of the nineteenth century, American music was dominated by the influence of European composers and performers. The few examples of creative excellence in American music before 1900 appear as tiny oases in a vast wasteland of mediocre imitations of European models. Among the more worthwhile pre-1900 works are the compositions of such remarkable figures as William Billings and Stephen Foster. Dvořák's sojourn in this country at the end of the nineteenth century had stimulated some interest in the establishment of a native musical art, but it developed slowly and often took the wrong directions. Early in this century a few composers, such as Charles Griffes and the New England genius Charles Ives, made genuine contributions to the literature of American music, but the real upsurge did not begin until after World War I. Among the first twentieth century musicians to achieve true distinction as serious American composers are the four discussed in this chapter.

WALTER PISTON (1894–   )

Emphasis upon the classical instrumental forms, technical perfection, and balance of form and expression characterize Walter Piston's work. Like many American composers of the twentieth century, he studied composition in Paris with the famous teacher of music Mlle. Nadia Boulanger, and his polished style and superb craftsmanship can be attributed in large part to her influence. Through a consistent avoidance of programmatic elements and a rejection of conscious Americanism such as the use of American folklore, he developed a neoclassical style that is in the European tradition without being dominated by it. Any American elements in Piston's music appear as natural and intrinsic factors in his musical language, not as outgrowths of nationalism.

In 1926 he joined the musical faculty of Harvard University where he remained in various capacities until his retirement in 1960. As a teacher of music he has written four textbooks which are used throughout the country. The mature elegance of his music, the frequent use of canonic and fugal devices, and the adoption of harmonic principles similar to those of Schoenberg suggest the academician; but other characteristics bespeak a less serious side of his personality. Among these is the assimilation into his style of elements of American popular music and jazz.

He has composed seven symphonies, of which the Third (1947) received the Pulitzer Prize in Music. His other orchestral works include the *Concerto for Orchestra* (1933), the *Concertino* for piano and chamber orchestra (1937), the ballet *The Incredible Flutist* (1938), and the Violin Concerto (1939). His chamber works are frequently performed and include four string quartets, a piano trio, a quintet for piano and strings, a sonata for violin and harpsichord, a nonet for four winds and five strings, and other works for various combinations.

The Incredible Flutist

This delightful ballet, the most popular of Piston's works, is most frequently heard in the composer's arrangement as a concert suite for orchestra. The colorful story takes place at carnival time in a Spanish village and includes an assortment of village characters and all the excitement of the arrival of a circus in town. The star attraction of the circus is the Incredible Flutist whose playing not only charms the animals but captivates the daughter of a local merchant as well. In the evening, when young couples are all around, a rich but prudish widow succumbs to the charged atmosphere and grants a kiss to a rich merchant who has been wooing her for some time. Their prolonged embrace is discovered by onlookers and the widow swoons in embarrassment. The Flutist rushes to the rescue and with a little dancing and playing he soon revives her. The magic spell of the evening is broken, the band strikes up, and the circus, Incredible Flutist and all, is on its way again.

The episodes in Piston's symphonic abridgement of the ballet are as follows: (1) Introduction, a slow melody that establishes the Spanish atmosphere, (2) Dance of the Vendors, brusque and dissonant in quality, (3) Entrance of the Customers, (4) Tango of the Merchant's Daughters, characterized by a smooth stepwise melody in 5/8 meter, (5) Entry of the Circus, with shouts of joy from the crowd, (6) Circus March, (7) Solo of the Flutist, in a slow and languorous mood, (8) Minuet, (9) Spanish Waltz, (10) Eight O'Clock, the magic hour when the young couples appear, (11) Siciliano, a dance in compound meter, and (12) Finale, a rousing polka.

HOWARD HANSON (1896–   )

No American composer has done more for the cause of a native musical culture than Howard Hanson. His considerable achievements as a composer parallel his career as teacher, conductor, and director of the well-known Eastman School of Music of the University of Rochester. He took over this last position at the age of twenty-eight and for nearly forty years devoted much time and labor to the propagation of American music and to the training of promising music students at the Eastman School. Dozens of well-known American works received their first performances at the Festivals of American Music founded by Hanson in Rochester, and many distinguished composers of today received their early training there. Although he retired in 1963, he continues to be a strong force and inspiration in the training of American musicians.

In his teaching he has encouraged freedom of expression and a diversity of styles, but in his own music he is neoromantic in the extreme. Throughout the twentieth century he has courageously clung to his belief in music for a mass audience—universality in the late nineteenth century tradition. His style is strongly linked with that of Sibelius and, like Sibelius, he is at his best in symphonic media. His major works include five symphonies, a single movement for orchestra entitled *Mosaics,* an opera *Merry Mount* (performed by the Metropolitan Opera Company in 1934), a piano concerto, and several tone poems in the tradition of Sibelius, such as *Lux Aeterna* and *Pan and the Priest. A Lament for Beowulf,* and *Cherubic Hymn,* both for chorus and orchestra, have also been frequently performed.

Symphony No. 2 (Romantic)

Although Hanson's Fourth Symphony was awarded the Pulitzer Prize in 1946, the Second is by far the most popular and representative of his five symphonies. Written for Serge Koussevitsky and the Boston Symphony, the work was premiered in 1930. It is in three movements, the first of which is a free sonata form with a slow introduction. The movement utilizes several short motives—"motto themes" they have been called—woven into an attractively lush orchestral fabric. His romantic gift for lyricism is particularly apparent in the second theme of the exposition played by the oboe (see Figure 133).

Figure 133.

The second movement is predominantly monothematic although there are references to motives from the first movement near the middle. Its mood of tender lyricism is heightened by the composer's sensitivity in handling orchestral color.

Cyclical elements appear more prominently in the finale, which is built out of some new thematic material, but which relies heavily upon the return of material from the first movement, extended and developed. Fanfares, long singing melodies, and shattering climaxes characterize this symphony and much of the composer's work.

The melodrama, musical rhetoric, and romantic lyricism of this gifted composer served a definite need during the first half of this century, for these things assured the conservative masses in our audiences that—midst seeming chaos—there were still composers concerned with immediate and direct communication with the average concertgoer. Greater than this, his contribution to the cause of American composers is of historical significance.

ROY HARRIS (1898–   )

Harris has made it his mission to give musical expression to the American spirit—to America's highest aspirations and noblest ideals. Whether or not he has succeeded has been a point of dispute. Certainly he made good use of such Americana as Civil War songs, hymn tunes, and cowboy songs. But the American quality in his work goes deeper than the assimilation of indigenous material into his style. His music, even when it uses no folk material, strives to evoke the spirit of American plains and mountains, to portray indomitable American determination and the idealistic yearnings of the American spirit. This was his message in the thirties at a time when America was ripe for this kind of nationalistic expression. It was then that his career reached its peak.

For a while he was *the* American composer. He had adopted a musical career at a rather late age, and his first works, though technically crude, were filled with promise of later achievement. Howard Hanson's presentation of the Harris *Andante for Orchestra* in 1926 did much to establish his name, and when he subsequently returned from two years of study in Paris with Nadia Boulanger, his career was on its way. His success stemmed from an ability to speak directly to a large portion of the concertgoing public and, unlike Howard Hanson, he avoided excessive use of the musical language of the nineteenth century. The Harris vogue continued into the forties but then it began to be apparent to critical ears that the technical crudities found in his earlier works were still present and that the promise of later achievement was not coming to pass. Today, although his works written during the thirties continue to be frequently performed, they have lost some of their former magnetism.

His style is marked by a unique orchestral sound that bears some semblance to that of Sibelius and Tchaikovsky. His predominantly triadic and diatonic harmonies are colored by polytonality and dissonant added tones along with frequent modal passages. Streams of blocklike chords move in parallel motion with strong dramatic impact, while his textures abound in devices such as canons, fugatos, and passacaglias.

He is at his best in large-scale symphonic forms and has written seven symphonies, of which the Third is the finest and most popular. His *Chorale for String Orchestra* and the overture *When Johnny Comes Marching Home* are typical of his shorter orchestral works. He has also composed a number of excellent chamber works, of which the Third String Quartet and the Quintet for piano and strings are most significant. A number of short piano works and his two major choral works *Song for Occupations* and *Symphony for Voices* complete the list of his best-known compositions.

Symphony No. 3

This one-movement symphony was completed in 1938 and has since become one of the most popular American works in Europe as well as in the United States. It is scored for a large, conventional orchestra and is perhaps the best example of this composer's orchestral mastery. Harris has furnished the following description of the various sections of the work:

Section I: *Tragic*—low string sonorities.
Section II: *Lyric*—strings, horns, woodwinds.
Section III: *Pastoral*—emphasizing woodwind color.
Section IV: *Fugue*—dramatic.
              A. Brass, percussion predominating.
              B. Canonic development of Section II material, constituting background for further development of fugue.

C. Brass climax. Rhythmic motive derived
from fugue subject.

Section V: *Dramatic-Tragic* —restatement of violin
theme of Section I.

The work opens with a spacious melody in the cellos. Instruments are
gradually added but the orchestral color remains dark and brooding until
the entrance of the violins in a unison melody that also appears in the final
section of the work. There is no break between sections. One moves
smoothly to the next with gradual changes of mood. The rhythm is flexible
and the contrapuntal texture is characterized by linear freedom. Triadic
harmonies predominate, contrasted at times with quartal sonorities. The
fugue subject of Section IV (shown in Figure 134) is first presented by the
unison strings and is echoed by the trombones. Its elaborate development,
using fragments of the subject, builds toward the "brass climax." As the
work nears its end, the violin theme from the first section is heard in a
section that functions as a coda to the total work.

Figure 134.

The idea of the one-movement symphony was not totally new. It had
been anticipated in the romantic tone poem, in Sibelius' Seventh Symphony, and in several extended symphonic compositions by American
composers such as Samuel Barber's successful First Symphony. The Harris
Third Symphony, however, has a formal unity that places it among the very
best efforts in this direction, and it continues to rank among the very finest
of American symphonies.

AARON COPLAND (1900–   )

Copland was born in Brooklyn, New York, received early training in
music, and at the age of fifteen had decided to make his career as a
composer. He was the first of the many Americans to study composition
with Nadia Boulanger in Paris. He worked under her guidance from 1921
to 1924 and since then several generations of American composers have
sought the counsel of this remarkable woman and continue to do so, even
today. Boulanger advocated a neoclassical approach and in the Parisian

environment of Stravinsky and the French Six, Copland, in his early works, became frankly experimental.

Among the compositions written during the twenties is the *Symphony for Organ and Orchestra,* revised in 1928 without organ to become his First Symphony. His *Music for the Theatre* (1925) and the *Concerto for Piano and Orchestra* (1927) reflect his consuming interest in composing music that the listener will identify as being clearly American. Both works use jazz elements in combination with neoclassical techniques. Although he found frequent occasion in later works to make use of American folk material and other elements that could be identified as American, he never again returned to the use of jazz.

During the early thirties he inclined toward leaner textures and austerity of expression in works such as the *Piano Variations* (1930) and *Statements for Orchestra* (1935). The late thirties and early forties saw a renewed interest in Americanism and the frequent use of folklore and American literature and poetry. His three major ballets of this period are *Billy the Kid* (1938), *Rodeo* (1942), and *Appalachian Spring* (1944), all of which evoke the American spirit by the use of folklike material. *Appalachian Spring* is perhaps his best-known work and in its concert version has established a lasting place in the orchestral repertoire. During this time he also composed much music that fits into the category of Gebrauchsmusik, including a work for student orchestra entitled *Outdoor Overture* and numerous film scores. One of his most popular orchestral scores, *El Salon México* (1936), is based upon materials collected during the composer's Latin-American travels during the thirties.

In a more serious vein are several distinguished instrumental works such as the Piano Sonata (1941), the Sonata for Violin and Piano (1943), and the Third Symphony (1946). Indicating the direction Copland's art was to take in the fifties is the Quartet for Piano and Strings (1950) which makes use of serial techniques, a practice which he continued in later works such as the *Fantasia for Piano* of 1958. His free use of the twelve-tone technique is typical of many present-day American composers who have found that they need not sacrifice their individuality to the system, and that dodecaphonic techniques can be used with other devices in a variety of styles. The Copland style, like that of Stravinsky, remains unique and recognizable in spite of his use of the twelve-tone system.

Mention should be made of Copland's single opera *The Tender Land* (1954), commissioned by Richard Rodgers and Oscar Hammerstein for the thirtieth anniversary of the League of Composers. The work is gently tuneful and attractive from the musical point of view but lacks the elements necessary for success in lyric drama. In short, it does not work well as theater.

The simplicity and directness of Copland's melodic style bespeaks his interest in American folklore. His harmonies are fresh and original but not particularly daring. He is essentially diatonic or modal with triadic and quartal sonorities predominating. Clear contrapuntal textures and occasional polytonal passages appear in his music, all welded together by a masterful grasp of musical architecture.

Concerto for Piano and Orchestra

This work represents a trend that was much in vogue during the twenties and thirties: the assimilation of American jazz and popular music into serious concert music. George Gershwin, of course, stemmed from the Tin Pan Alley tradition, but many other composers, such as Stravinsky, Milhaud, Poulenc, Honegger, Krenek, and Hindemith found American popular music to be a refreshing new sound that was useful in breaking ties with the outworn traditions of the nineteenth century. Many of these jazz-symphonic hybrids remain popular today and have a certain nostalgic appeal of the time when jazz was new and fresh.

The work is scored for a large standard orchestra with an expanded percussion section plus saxophone. It is in two movements, the first a slow movement depicting the blues, and the second representing "up tempo" aspects of jazz. The saxophone and other solo wind instruments are used effectively in the first movement, coloring the melodic lines with typical blues inflections. Rhythmically the movement is characterized by slow, swaying syncopations in a square rhythmic framework.

The second movement begins with the piano alone with the percussive use of major and minor seconds for dissonant effect in an angular rhythmic pattern. Syncopations dominate the movement in an antiphonal exchange between piano and orchestra. An extended cadenza appears near the end, lightly accompanied at certain points by the solo trumpet. The piano continues with the orchestra in ragtime effects set off at one point with a passage that sounds very much like Dixieland. The coda utilizes the piano solo with the full ensemble in a climactic conclusion.

Appalachian Spring

This ballet was completed in 1944 on a commission from the Elizabeth Sprague Coolidge Foundation, and was premiered by Martha Graham. The work, which earned a Pulitzer Prize for the composer, represents Copland at his best in the use of folk elements. It is recorded in an arrangement by the composer as a concert suite.

The action of the ballet centers in a pioneer settlement in Pennsylvania in the early nineteenth century. In general the folk nature of the work is achieved by the use of material that sounds like folk music without actually quoting existing melodies. The one exception is the use of the famous Shaker tune "Simple Gifts" (Figure 135). The composer has

Figure 135.

Copyright 1945 by Aaron Copland. Reprinted by permission of Aaron Copland, copyright owner, and Boosey and Hawkes, Inc., sole publishers and licensees.

furnished the following description of the action in the concert version of the ballet:

1. *Very Slowly*. Introduction of the characters, one by one, in a suffused light.
2. *Fast*. A sudden burst of unison strings in A major arpeggios starts the action. A sentiment both elated and religious gives the keynote to this scene.
3. Duo for the bride and her intended—scene of tenderness and passion.
4. *Quite Fast*. The revivalist and his flock. Folksy feeling—suggestions of square dances and country fiddlers.
5. *Still Faster*. Solo dance of the bride—presentiment of motherhood. Extremes of joy and fear and wonder.
6. *Very Slowly* (as at first). Transition scene to music reminiscent of the introduction.
7. *Calm and Flowing*. Scenes of daily activity for the bride and her farmer husband. There are five variations on a Shaker theme.

Copland continues to be an active force in American music. Unlike many of the composers of his generation, he has continued to expand his musical resources and remains actively in touch with contemporary musical thought. His compositions represent an ideal fusion of classical and romantic elements in American music.

Suggested Assignments

1. Several rather different approaches to the art of music are represented in the four American composers discussed in this chapter. Try to define these approaches and, as a special research project, try to determine which younger American composers have adopted one or another of the approaches practiced by these composers.
2. Listen to the works of other American composers mentioned in this chapter such as William Billings and Charles Ives.
3. As a special project investigate the role of the serious composer in contemporary American life—his economic and social status, how he is viewed by society, what he conceives to be his role in society, etc.
4. Compare your findings in the preceding assignment with composers of earlier periods.
5. Listen to some of the other works mentioned in this chapter such as Piston's string quartets, Hanson's Fourth Symphony, Harris' overture *When Johnny Comes Marching Home*, Copland's Third Symphony, etc.

TWENTY-FOUR

CONCLUSION
AND NEW PATHWAYS

In this book we have surveyed some of the outstanding examples of music literature from the Renaissance to the present. We have discussed, in varying degrees of depth, the elements of music theory and composition, the esthetics of music, music history, and musical performance. Advice has been offered to increase the listener's perception of the sounds of music and to stimulate his imagination. Above all, the listener has been furnished with a broad view of music literature in the hope that he will set out confidently in whatever directions his inclinations may lead him.

Obviously, there is much excellent music that we have not discussed, for it is impossible within a single volume to comprehensively survey the literature of music. Within this century alone there are dozens of widely varying approaches to musical composition and in recent years many striking innovations in style and technique have been developed. Webern is the progenitor of much recent experimentation, which in some cases leads toward stricter control of the elements of music by means of electronics or new notational devices, and in other instances reaches toward greater freedom of interpretation in performance.

One of the major influences in contemporary European music, along with that of Webern, has been the work of Oliver Messiaen (1909) who has attempted to apply the rhythmic subtleties of Far Eastern music, particularly that of Hindu music, to his own musical language. He has used contrapuntal devices applied purely to rhythms, with the result that percussion instruments of all kinds abound in his scores. His rhythmic canons, augmentations, and diminutions (notated in durations with complex ratios) eliminate conventional rhythmic symmetry and create in his music a feeling of freedom in a highly organized rhythmic structure. He is something of a mystic in his musical philosophy, having adopted a view of

318

oneness with nature that is related to deeply felt religious feelings. The Hindu influence is particularly apparent in his *Turangalîla Symphony* (1948), a work for large orchestra.

Karlheinz Stockhausen (1928) and Pierre Boulez (1925) both studied with Messiaen shortly after World War II, and his influence along with that of Webern has led them into further rhythmic explorations. Stockhausen is the foremost figure in the new music of Germany, while Boulez is of prime importance among the new generation of French avant-garde composers. Through expansion of Webern's principles of serialization they have striven for a musical expression in which the composer has total control over every aspect and dimension of musical sound.

For Stockhausen, one of the means to total control has been the medium of electronic music. Today the term electronic music denotes the stereophonic recording of purely electronic sounds from signal generators— electronic sound sources capable of producing any pitch or dynamic level that can be heard by the human ear. Overtone structures can be adjusted by various means (filters, condensors, etc.) to furnish an infinite variety of possible timbres; and articulation can be manipulated in many ways, even to include many different percussive sounds. Harmonic effects are produced by using signal generators in combinations as well as by splicing and re-recording. The tapes are painstakingly prepared, often with technical assistance from an electronic engineer, and are then played back for the listener. Some excellent pieces have been composed for recorded electronic sounds in combination with conventional instruments. But attempts actually to imitate the sounds of conventional instruments by electronic means have been less successful, for electronic music is a unique and separate medium that is at its best when it deals with abstract sounds impossible to produce with conventional musical media.

Stockhausen has also experimented with new techniques of composition for conventional instruments. Of particular interest is his *Piano Piece XI* (1956), a work for solo piano that allows a variety of interpretations on the part of the performer. The pianist may play the nineteen fragments of the piece in any order that he likes and with any of six different tempos, dynamics, and articulations. Obviously, the element of chance is introduced into such a composition, for no two performances can be even similar in their total musical effect. This is quite the opposite of the total control practiced by Stockhausen in other works and reflects an increasing contemporary interest in the use of random "happenings" in art. The adjective *aleatory* (from *alea*, Greek for dice) is frequently applied to music that utilizes the element of chance. In his more recent compositions for instruments he has followed the path indicated in his *Time Densities* (1956) for woodwinds, the notation of which utilizes new techniques peculiarly suited to his unique style. He has also experimented with methods of notating electronic music.

Boulez has approached the problem of total control primarily by carrying serialism to every aspect of his art. Added to the tone rows are the duration rows, articulation rows, and dynamics rows, all of which are used in series and are retrograded, mutated, and combined to produce a musical texture that is always logical in terms of the system. (Some contemporary musicians have questioned such extreme use of this kind of structural logic on the grounds that it does not necessarily contribute proportionately to the musical value of a composition.) *Le Marteau sans maître* (The Hammer Without a Master) (1954) for contralto and six instruments will serve well as an introduction to his music. His Third Piano Sonata is also worthy of notice.

Boulez also has been vitally interested in electronic music as well as in another type of electronically produced music known as *musique concrète,* which differs from electronic music in that it uses as its raw material the real sounds that are heard in the world around us. Sounds such as the purr of a motor, the roar of a jet engine, a slamming door, a few tones from a musical instrument, and endless other possibilities are recorded on tape and then manipulated in various ways to produce the end product. They can be combined by splicing and re-recording, raised or lowered in pitch by varying the speed of the tape, reversed by running the tape backward, distorted with reverberations and echoes, and so on as the composer may choose. The final composition is then recorded on a final tape to be replayed for the listener. The effect is quite different from pure electronic music which uses only electronic sound sources. An eerie, almost mystical effect is sometimes produced because many of the sounds are recognizable or *almost* recognizable in their altered form, and may evoke strangely distorted images of present day phenomena.

Luciano Berio (1925), a significant and forward-looking composer of Italy, has composed a work that is of particular interest as an example of musique concrète entitled *Hommages à Joyce* (1959). To compose this work a fragment from *Ulysses* read by a female voice was recorded and then expanded by numerous re-recordings with electronic alterations to produce an extremely attractive composition based completely upon spoken sounds. Another significant Italian composer is Bruno Maderna

(1920), who has been strongly influenced by the Viennese twelve-tone composers and, like Stockhausen and Boulez, has moved in the direction of total serialization. He has composed electronic music as well as music for groups of conventional instruments.

In the United States the best known composers of music for electronic media are Milton Babbitt (1916), Vladimir Ussachevsky (1911), and Otto Luening (1900). Luening is the pioneer of electronic music in America and works with his two younger colleagues at the Electronic Music Center, operated under the joint auspices of Columbia and Princeton Universities. Electronic music centers are springing up at a number of American universities and many of our younger composers have been attracted to this new and fascinating medium.

Chance or aleatory music has also received much attention in recent years in this country, championed, among others, by John Cage (1912). He has experimented with such devices as allowing the order or sequence of musical fragments to be determined by dropping the separately notated fragments on the floor and playing them in the order in which they are picked up, by simply throwing dice to determine certain aspects of a performance, and other even more surprising techniques. Obviously such devices have been viewed with considerable consternation in certain musical circles; but the fact that similar devices have been used by serious practitioners of the graphic arts and drama suggests that there may be more validity to chance art than at first meets the eye.

Cage has also gained considerable notoriety by his experimental tamperings with the insides of the piano. His "prepared piano" consists of an ordinary grand piano that has been fixed up for the performance of a specific piece of music by placing various assorted pieces of hardware or paper (or anything) inside of the piano in such a way as to drastically alter the tone on certain pitches. The performer may also be called upon to reach inside of the piano to pluck or thump the strings or soundboard during the course of the composition. In spite of the unconventionality of Cage's methods, there are those who think that his work has significantly influenced the course of music. For the serious listener this is difficult to believe, but there is no doubt that he has stimulated a great deal of interest in an extreme kind of experimentation.

Among the many outstanding American composers of the younger generation are Lucas Foss (1922), Gunther Schuller (1925), and Easley Blackwood (1933). Foss has had a surprisingly long and distinguished career in spite of his youth and is now recognized as one of the foremost

American composers. His *Time Cycle* (1960) for soprano and orchestra based on texts of Auden, Housman, Kafka, and Nietzsche is a most attractive and moving work. Schuller has been very active in experimental jazz as well as in compositions for more conventional media; while Blackwood has shown promise of becoming a contemporary symphonist of stature.

A number of American composers of an older generation such as Elliott Carter (1908) and Vincent Persichetti (1915) are well in touch with the latest developments in contemporary music and retain their stature among present-day composers in spite of the more sensational innovations of the younger generation. Carter is particularly distinguished for his rhythmic daring and has been eminently successful as a composer of chamber music. Of special interest is his *String Quartet No. 2* which is a work in the tradition of Beethoven and Bartók at the same time that it is strikingly innovative from both the rhythmic and harmonic standpoints.

So numerous are the outstanding composers of this century that there are many whom we have been unable to discuss. England's greatest present-day composer Benjamin Britten (1913) has written a number of choral works and operas of lasting worth, while in this country the operas of Gian Carlo Menotti (1911) have enjoyed tremendous popularity. Roger Sessions (1896) and Samuel Barber (1910) also rank as distinguished American composers, and in Germany Carl Orff (1895) has contributed significantly to the literature of vocal music. (His *Carmina Burana* [1936] for chorus, orchestra, and soloists is a work of tremendous beauty and impact.) Nor have we been able to discuss the music of Serge Prokoviev (1891–1953) and Dmitri Shostakovich (1906), both of whom have contributed much of great value to the orchestral repertoire, as have also the three most active members of the "French Six," Milhaud, Poulenc, and Honegger.

The literature of music is being constantly enriched by the many new talents that continue to appear; and later generations may say that ours was one of the great periods in the history of music. For the wonder and excitement of music lies not only in the great works of the past, but also in the strikingly original music of our own time. Finally, it should be remembered that whatever musical path we may take, it is not the dry stuff of history and biography that lends fascination to the world of music, but the live tones of music itself—the interplay of lines and colors, the logic of musical architecture, the contrast of musical textures, and the fluctuating motion of the melodic phrase.

APPENDIX I

MUSICAL NOTATION

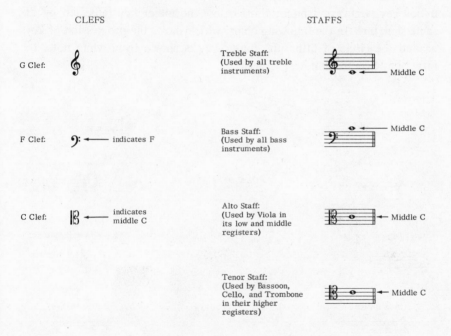

CLEFS

G Clef:

F Clef: — indicates F

C Clef: — indicates middle C

STAFFS

Treble Staff:
(Used by all treble instruments)
— Middle C

Bass Staff:
(Used by all bass instruments)
Middle C —

Alto Staff:
(Used by Viola in its low and middle registers)
— Middle C

Tenor Staff:
(Used by Bassoon, Cello, and Trombone in their higher registers)
— Middle C

METER SIGNATURES

The upper number of a meter signature indicates the number of notes in each measure of the type indicated by the lower number. For example, the signature 6/8 means that there are six eighth notes in a measure; 4/4 means that there are four quarter notes in a measure. Notes and rests in each measure must be equivalent to the indication in the meter signature. The following examples show various ways of notating correct equivalent measures in several common meters.

323

KEY SIGNATURES

Each diatonic signature indicates a major key or a minor key depending upon which tonal center (major or minor) is established by the music. The minor key is always a minor third below the major key indicated by the same signature. In the following chart, which shows the progression of keys around the circle of fifths, the major key is shown by a white note, the minor key by a black note.

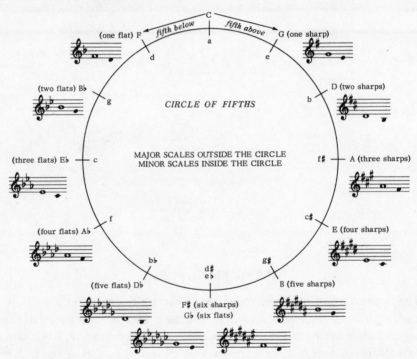

APPENDIX II

RANGES OF THE INSTRUMENTS OF THE ORCHESTRA

The extreme limitations are shown in white notes, the practical range in black notes.

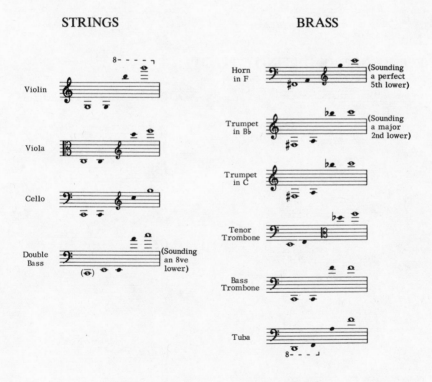

STRINGS

BRASS

WOODWINDS

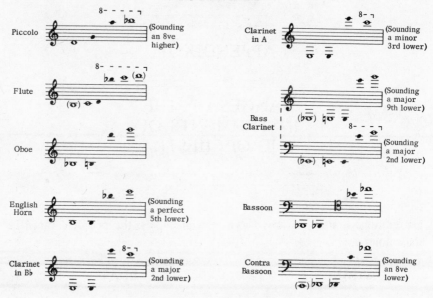

PERCUSSION OF DEFINITE PITCH

ADDITIONAL INSTRUMENTS

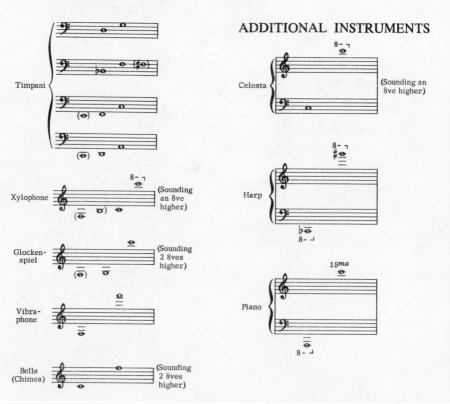

APPENDIX III

TRANSPOSITION

Transposing instruments are those instruments for which the notated pitches are not the same as the actual pitch sounded. For example, when the English horn plays a *written* C it will actually *sound* the F one fifth lower than the notated pitch. There are various reasons for the different transpositions found among the wind instruments, usually having to do with the history and technique of the instrument. The transposition for the English horn enables the player to alternate between oboe and English horn without learning a completely new set of fingerings. In the woodwind section the English horn and the clarinets are the only transposing instruments. (The piccolo sounds an octave higher than written but the pitch name remains the same.) Among the brass instruments the French horn and trumpet are both transposing instruments. There are no transposing instruments among the strings. (The double bass sounds an octave lower than written but the pitch name remains the same.)

Chart of transposing instruments

(Note that the letter name of the transposition is the pitch produced by playing a *written* C.)

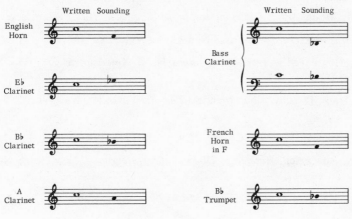

SUGGESTIONS FOR FURTHER READING

Abraham, Gerald. *This Modern Music,* New York: Norton, 1952.

Apel, Willi. *Harvard Dictionary of Music.* Cambridge: Harvard, 1944.

Barzun, Jacques. *Berlioz and the Romantic Century.* Boston: Little, Brown, 1950.

Bauer, Marion. *Twentieth Century Music.* New York: Putnam, 1947.

Berger, Arthur. *Copland.* New York: Oxford, 1953.

Berlioz, Hector. *Memoirs.* New York: Knopf, 1948.

Blom, Eric (ed.) *Grove's Dictionary of Music and Musicians,* 5th ed. New York: St. Martin's, 1954, 1961.

Blom, Eric. *Mozart.* London: Dent, 1935; New York: Farrar, Straus, 1949.

Blom, Eric (ed.) *Mozart's Letters.* Bristol: Western Printing Services, 1956.

Brown, Maurice J. E. *Schubert.* New York: St. Martin's, 1958.

Bukofzer, Manfred F. *Music in the Baroque Era.* New York: Norton, 1947.

Chase, Gilbert. *America's Music.* New York: McGraw-Hill, 1955.

Coates, Henry. *Palestrina.* London: Dent, 1938.

Cohen, Albert and John White. *Anthology of Music for Analysis.* New York: Appleton-Century-Crofts, 1965.

Copland, Aaron. *What to Listen for in Music.* New York: Whittlesey, 1939.

Copland, Aaron. *Our New Music.* New York: Whittlesey, 1941.

Cowell, Henry (ed.) *American Composers on American Music.* New York: Ungar, 1962.

David, Hans T. and Arthur Mendel. *The Bach Reader.* New York: Norton, 1945.

Debussy, Claude. *Monsieur Croche.* New York: Lear, 1948.

Deutsch, Otto Erich. *Handel: A Documentary Biography.* New York: Norton, 1955.

Einstein, Alfred. *A Short History of Music.* New York: Knopf, 1947.

328

Einstein, Alfred. *Mozart: His Character, His Work*. New York: Oxford, 1945.

Einstein, Alfred. *Music in the Romantic Era*. New York: Norton, 1947.

Ewen, David. *The Book of Modern Composers*. New York: Knopf, 1942.

Fellowes, Edmund H. *William Byrd*. 2nd ed. London: Oxford, 1948.

Ferguson, Donald N. *Masterworks of the Orchestral Repertoire*. Minneapolis: University of Minnesota Press, 1954.

Geiringer, Karl. *Brahms: His Life and Work*. New York: Oxford, 1947.

Geiringer, Karl. *Haydn*. New York: Norton, 1946.

Grout, Donald Jay. *A History of Western Music*. New York: Norton, 1960.

Grove, George. *Beethoven, Schubert, Mendelssohn*. New York: Macmillan, 1951.

Hamburger, Michael (tr. & ed.) *Beethoven—Letters, Journals and Conversations*. Garden City, New York: Doubleday, 1960.

Hardy, Gordon and Arnold Fish. *Music Literature: A Workbook for Analysis*. New York: Dodd, Mead. *Volume I: Homophony*, 1964. *Volume II: Polyphony*, 1966.

Hindemith, Paul. *A Composer's World*. Cambridge: Harvard, 1952.

Kobbé, Gustav. *Complete Opera Book*. London: Putnam, 1954.

Lang, Paul Henry. *Music in Western Civilization*. New York: Norton, 1941.

Lang, Paul Henry (ed.) *Stravinsky, A New Appraisal of His Work*. New York: Norton, 1963.

Leyda, Jay and S. Bertensson. *The Mussorgsky Reader*. New York: Norton, 1947.

Lockspeiser, Edward. *Debussy*. London: Dent, 1951.

Machlis, Joseph. *Introduction to Contemporary Music*. New York: Norton, 1961.

Morgenstern, Sam (ed.) *Composers on Music—From Palestrina to Copland*. New York: Pantheon, 1956.

Newman, Ernest. *The Life of Richard Wagner*. New York: Knopf, 1933–1946.

Parmet, Simon. *The Symphonies of Sibelius*. London: Cassell, 1959.

Pincherle, Marc. *Corelli: His Life, His Music*. New York: Norton, 1956.

Pincherle, Marc. *Vivaldi*. New York: Norton, 1957.

Redlich, H. F. *Alban Berg*. New York: Abelard-Schuman.

Reese, Gustave. *Music in the Middle Ages*. New York: Norton, 1940.

Roland-Manuel. *Maurice Ravel*. London: Dobson, 1947.

Sachs, Curt. *The Commonwealth of Art*. New York: Norton, 1946.

Sachs, Curt. *Our Musical Heritage: A Short History of Music*. 2nd ed. New York: Prentice Hall, 1955.

Schoenberg, Arnold. *Style and Idea*. New York: Philosophical, 1950.

Schrade, Leo. *Monteverdi: Creator of Modern Music*. New York: Norton, 1950.

Schumann, Robert. *On Music and Musicians*. New York: Pantheon, 1946.

Schweitzer, Albert. *J. S. Bach*. New York: Macmillan, 1935.

Sitwell, Sacheverell. *Liszt*. Boston: Houghton Mifflin, 1934.

Slonimsky, Nicolas (ed.) *Baker's Biographical Dictionary of Musicians*. 5th ed. New York: Schirmer, 1958.

Slonimsky, Nicolas. *Music Since 1900*. New York: Coleman-Ross, 1949.

Šourek, Otakar. *Antonín Dvořák*. New York: Philosophical, 1954.

Spitta, Philipp. *Johann Sebastian Bach*. New York: Dover, 1951.

Stevens, Halsey. *The Life and Music of Béla Bartók*. New York: Oxford, 1953.

Stravinsky, Igor. *An Autobiography*. New York: Norton, 1962.

Stravinsky, Igor. *Poetics of Music*. New York: Vintage, 1956.

Sullivan, J. W. N. *Beethoven: His Spiritual Development*. New York: Knopf, 1947.

Thayer, A. W. *The Life of Ludwig van Beethoven*. ed. H. E. Krehbiel, New York: Beethoven Association, 1921.

Thompson, Oscar and Nicolas Slonimsky. *International Encyclopedia of Music and Musicians*. New York: Dodd, Mead, 1953.

Thompson, Oscar. *Debussy: Man and Artist*. New York: Dodd, Mead, 1937.

Tovey, Donald Francis. *The Forms of Music*. Cleveland: World Publishing, 1956.

Toye, Francis. *Giuseppe Verdi*. New York: Knopf, 1931.

Ulrich, Homer and Paul Pisk. *A History of Music and Musical Style*. New York: Harcourt, Brace, and World, 1963.

Wagner, Richard. *Prose Works*. London: Kegan Paul, 1892–1899.

Watson, Jack M. and Corinne. *A Concise Dictionary of Music.* New York: Dodd, Mead, 1965.

Weinstock, Herbert. *Chopin: The Man and His Music.* New York: Knopf, 1949.

Weinstock, Herbert. *Tchaikovsky.* New York: Knopf, 1943.

Westrup, J. A. *Purcell.* New York: Dutton, 1937.

GLOSSARY OF TERMS

A cappella. Designation that choral music is to be performed without instrumental accompaniment. In the strictest sense it should be applied only to sacred music of the Renaissance.

A tempo. Marking used in musical notation indicating that the performer is to return to the normal or previous tempo.

Accidentals. Collective term for sharps, flats, naturals, double sharps, and double flats.

Adagio. Very slow.

Allegretto. Moderately fast.

Allegro. Fast. Though the term literally means "cheerful," it does not necessarily have this connotation when used as a tempo indication.

Andante. Moderate speed. A rather variable indication which frequently means a bit slower than *allegretto*.

Antiphonal. Term describing music which utilizes two or more self-contained groups of voices and/or instruments, sounding in contrast to each other either in alternation or simultaneously.

Arpeggio. An arrangement of the tones of a chord in such a way that they are played one after another rather than simultaneously.

Bar line. Vertical line through the musical staff used to indicate the beginnings and ends of measures.

Cadence. The point of repose or resting-place at the end of a phrase. Cadences which conclude on the dominant are said to be half-cadences since they do not have the feeling of finality evoked by a cadence which ends on the tonic.

Canon. A piece or portion of a piece which utilizes the technique of canonic imitation, i.e. the various voices entering at different times but with the same thematic, material. Often the voices enter at different tonal levels.

Chromatic. An adjective applied to music which frequently utilizes tones other than those found in the diatonic scale. The chromatic scale is a scale made up completely of half steps, spanning all twelve tones.

Counterpoint. Music in which two or more distinct voice lines are utilized in such a way that they will make musical sense when sounded together. Frequently the various voices in a contrapuntal texture will have different rhythms, producing an interesting rhythmic contrast among the voices.

Crescendo. Gradually increasing in volume. Indicated by the abbreviation *cresc.*
or the symbol ◁ .

Da capo. Italian term indicating that the performer should return to the beginning of the piece in the musical notation. *Da capo al fine* means to go to the beginning and play to the point where the word *fine* appears. *Da capo* forms are ABA forms in which the final repetition of A is effected by means of the *da capo* device.

Decrescendo. Gradually decreasing in volume. Indicated in musical notation by the abbreviation *decresc.* or by the notational symbol ⟩ .

Diatonic scale. Eight-note scale spanning an octave. The intervals between the third and fourth scale degrees (in ascending order) and between the seventh and eighth scale degrees are half-steps. All other intervals in the scale are whole steps. It is the scale which has served as the basis for conventional harmony for the past 350 years.

Diminuendo. Synonym for *decrescendo.*

Divisi. Indication that a group of instruments or voices of the same kind (i.e.: all violins or all sopranos) are to divide into two or more separate parts.

Double period. A formal unit in music composed of two periods, a period being two phrases which are strongly linked to each other. In folk songs or other short forms, a double period can form the complete piece.

Enharmonic. A term used to describe the relationship between two tones or sonorities which sound the same pitch but are notated differently, as D sharp and E flat.

Entry. The appearance of a fresh statement of the subject in an imitative texture.

Forte. Loud.

Fortissimo. Very loud.

Glissando. Sliding. Used when an instrument or voice is to move from one pitch to another pitch, sliding through without clearly defining the intervening pitches.

Grave. Slow, with an implication of solemnity.

Homophonic. Musical texture in which all of the voice parts play the same rhythm at the same time to give the impression of block chords, as in a conventional hymn or chorale.

Imitation. Repeating a melody in close sequence but in another voice part, while the initial presentation of the theme continues. An imitative texture may have several entries of the thematic material each in a different voice.

Intonation. Refers to playing in tune. "Good intonation" implies playing very well in tune, while "bad intonation" means playing out of tune.

Key signature. The pattern of sharps or flats found at the left end of the musical staff just to the right of the clef. It indicates the diatonic key center of the music, and the sharps or flats indicate the accidentals which have to be applied in order to arrive at a diatonic scale on that key center. See Appendix I.

Larghetto. Moderately slow, but not as slow as *largo.*

Largo. Very slow, with an implication of broadness.

Legato. A term indicating that the tones of a melody are to be very closely connected one to another.

Marcato. Well marked or emphasized. Frequently implies separation of tones as well as accents.

Measure. Rhythmic or metrical unit enclosed by bar lines. The meter signature indicates the number of beats to be found in a measure. See Appendix I.

Meter. Measurement of the flow of music. Meter is indicated by the meter signature found at the left end of the musical staff just to the right of the key signature. A meter signature found at the beginning of a piece of music prevails until a different one is indicated. See Appendix I.

Mezzo forte. Medium loud.

Mode. The raw material of pitches upon which a particular musical composition is based. All scales can be thought of as modes, but the term is most frequently applied to the ancient Greek modes or the Ecclesiastical (church) modes (Phrygian, Dorian, etc.).

Modulation. The process of moving from one key center to another during the course of a piece of music.

Motive. A thematic fragment (usually 2 to 6 tones) with a clear rhythmic and melodic identity. It serves as a building block for larger formal units.

Moderato. Moderately fast.

Mute. Mechanical device used to lower the volume of a musical instrument, frequently changing the tone quality as well.

Nuance. Subtle shades of expression, particularly applied to melodic inflection (fine gradations of dynamics and tempo).

Opus. Literally "work." Any major composition of a composer may be designated with an opus number. The numbers are usually assigned by the composer and are often in chronological order, spanning his total output. (Abbreviated: Op.)

Ornaments. Embellishing tones used to "decorate" a melody, particularly in the area of the cadence. They are frequently indicated in the notation by symbols rather than being written in notes. In other instances they were improvised by the performer without indications in the notation according to the practices of the time. Among the common ornaments are the trill (rapid alternation between the two notes of a major or minor second, indicated by *tr⌣⌣*); mordent (indicated by ⌄⌄); and turn (indicated by ∾).

Pentatonic. Term describing music based on the pentatonic scale, a scale of five notes commonly used in folk music.

Phrase. A complete musical thought, longer than a motive and which ends in a cadence.

Piano. Soft.

Pianissimo. Very soft.

Polyphonic. Term describing music in two or more voice parts in which the separate voices have independent rhythmic and melodic inflections. Opposite of homophonic.

Presto. Very fast.

Primary triads. The tonic (I), dominant (V), and subdominant (IV) triads as used in the conventional diatonic tonal system.

Rallentando. Gradual slowing down. Synonym of *ritardando.*

Resolution. Consonant tone or sonority following a dissonant tone or sonority. The consonance is said to be the resolution of the dissonance.

Ritardando. Gradual slowing down. Synonym of *rallentando.*

Rubato. Term used to indicate a certain freedom in the performance of tempos and rhythms. Certain kinds of music are conventionally performed with stylized rhythmic liberties.

Seventh chord. A chord which includes a fourth note above a triad, continuing the vertical projection of thirds so that the interval from the root of the triad to the fourth note is a seventh.

Sforzando. A forceful accent.

Slur. A notational symbol placed above or below a passage to indicate phrasing, breathing, or bowing in performance.

Sostenuto. Sustained.

Staccato. Term indicating that notes are to be shortened or separated. Indicated by a dot above or below the note.

Tempered tuning. System of keyboard tuning which divides the octave into twelve equal half steps. In common use since the late baroque period.

Tempo. Speed or frequency of the beat in musical performance.

Tonal center. The tone which functions as the focal point in the harmonic system in a given piece of music. In the diatonic system the tonal center is usually the "key" of the music.

Triad. A vertical projection of three notes, all separated by thirds.

Tutti. Term indicating that all or nearly all of the instruments in a large ensemble are to play at the same time.

Vivace. Fast and lively.

INDEX

337